THE FOREST OF DEAN BRANCH

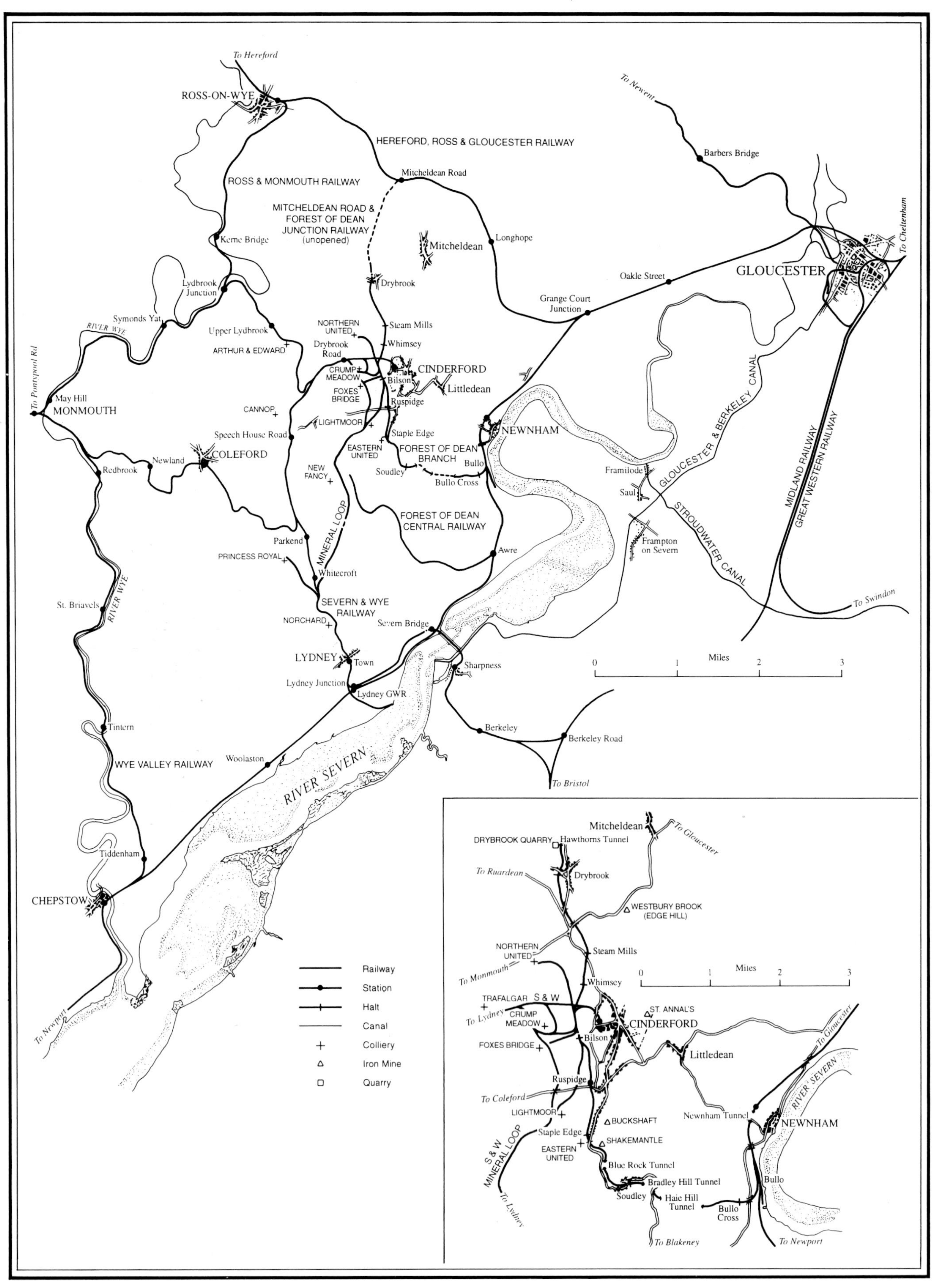
To Hereford
ROSS-ON-WYE
HEREFORD, ROSS & GLOUCESTER RAILWAY
ROSS & MONMOUTH RAILWAY
Mitcheldean Road
MITCHELDEAN ROAD & FOREST OF DEAN JUNCTION RAILWAY (unopened)
Mitcheldean
Longhope
Kerne Bridge
Drybrook
Lydbrook Junction
Symonds Yat
RIVER WYE
Upper Lydbrook
ARTHUR & EDWARD
NORTHERN UNITED
Steam Mills
Whimsey
Drybrook Road
CRUMP MEADOW
CINDERFORD
Bilson
Littledean
FOXES BRIDGE
Ruspidge
To Pontypool Rd
May Hill
MONMOUTH
CANNOP
LIGHTMOOR
Staple Edge
Speech House Road
EASTERN UNITED
FOREST OF DEAN BRANCH
Bullo
NEWNHAM
Newland
COLEFORD
Redbrook
NEW FANCY
Soudley
Bullo Cross
FOREST OF DEAN CENTRAL RAILWAY
Parkend
MINERAL LOOP
Awre
PRINCESS ROYAL
Whitecroft
SEVERN & WYE RAILWAY
St. Briavels
RIVER WYE
NORCHARD
Severn Bridge
LYDNEY
Town
Lydney Junction
Lydney GWR
Sharpness
Tintern
WYE VALLEY RAILWAY
Woolaston
RIVER SEVERN
Tiddenham
CHEPSTOW
To Newport
To Newent
Barbers Bridge
To Cheltenham
GLOUCESTER
Oakle Street
Grange Court Junction
GLOUCESTER & BERKELEY CANAL
Framilode
Saul
Frampton on Severn
STROUDWATER CANAL
MIDLAND RAILWAY
GREAT WESTERN RAILWAY
To Swindon
Miles
0
1
2
3
Berkeley
Berkeley Road
To Bristol
Railway
Station
Halt
Canal
Colliery
Iron Mine
Quarry
Mitcheldean
To Gloucester
DRYBROOK QUARRY
Hawthorns Tunnel
To Ruardean
Drybrook
WESTBURY BROOK (EDGE HILL)
NORTHERN UNITED
Steam Mills
To Monmouth
Whimsey
Miles
0
1
2
3
TRAFALGAR
S & W
To Lydney
CRUMP MEADOW
ST. ANNAL'S
CINDERFORD
Bilson
FOXES BRIDGE
Littledean
To Gloucester
RIVER SEVERN
Ruspidge
To Coleford
LIGHTMOOR
BUCKSHAFT
Newnham Tunnel
NEWNHAM
Staple Edge
SHAKEMANTLE
EASTERN UNITED
S & W MINERAL LOOP
Blue Rock Tunnel
Bradley Hill Tunnel
Bullo
Soudley
Haie Hill Tunnel
Bullo Cross
To Lydney
To Blakeney
To Newport

THE FOREST OF DEAN BRANCH

by
IAN POPE & PAUL KARAU

Volume Two
THE CHURCHWAY AND WHIMSEY BRANCHES

WILD SWAN PUBLICATIONS

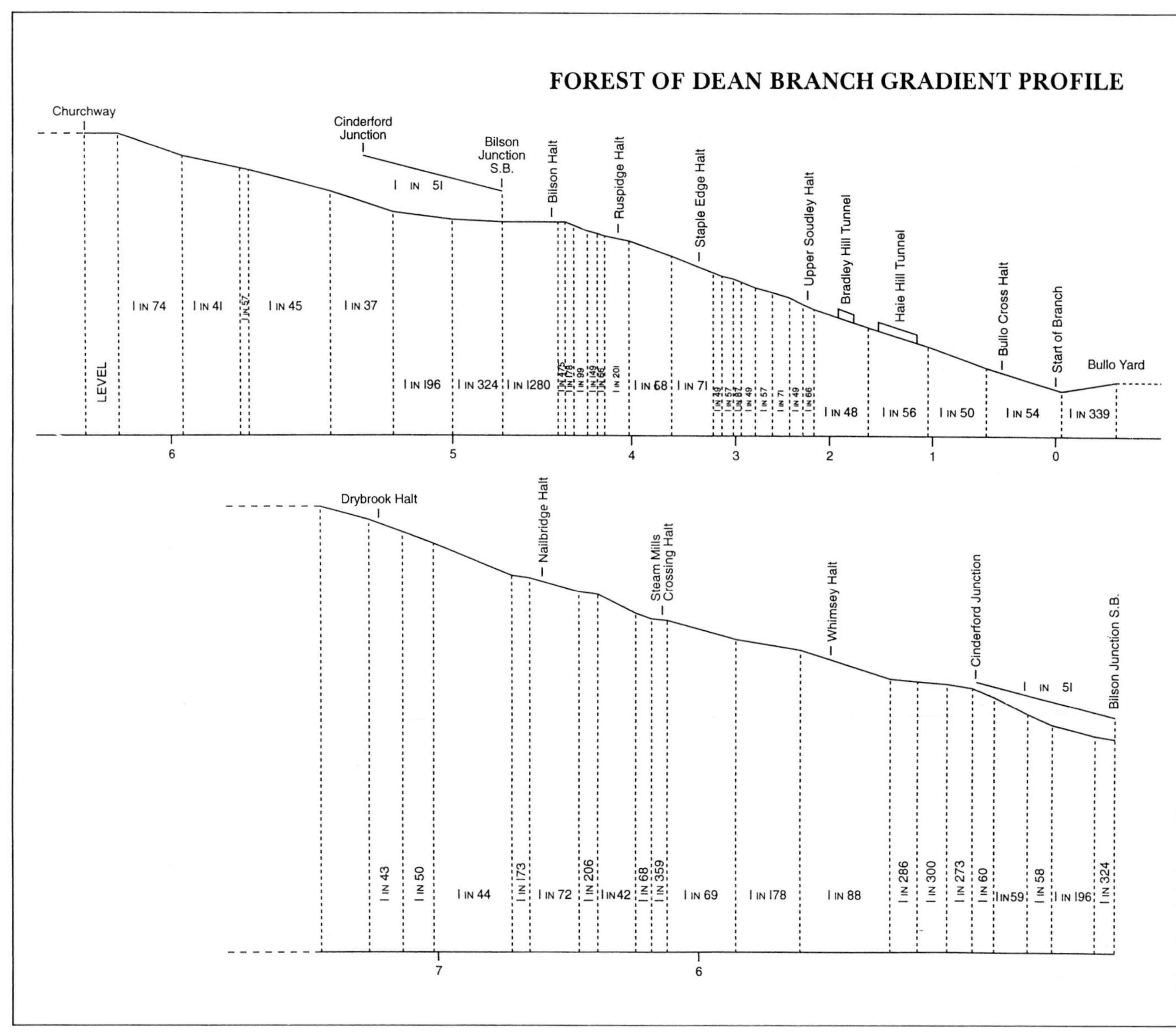

ISBN 1 874103 36 4

Designed by Paul Karau
Printed by Amadeus Press, Huddersfield

Published by
WILD SWAN PUBLICATIONS LTD.
1-3 Hagbourne Road, Didcot, Oxon, OX11 8DP

Title page: The fireman's view from the cab of a 57XX 0–6–0PT propelling a train of empties to Northern United Colliery in December 1965. *R. H. Marrows*

CONTENTS

Looking south from the S & W embankment on 28th September 1947, once again with Northern United Colliery empties stabled on all available roads including the southern end of the Lightmoor empties road and even the running line. The clear road was the top end of the 'run-round'. The concrete block and tiebars were a wartime measure to get around the timber shortage, but here they have been used in interlaced fashion to replace rotting point timbers.

L. E. Copeland

THE CHURCHWAY BRANCH

The Churchway branch began at the northern end of Bilson Yard and ran north-north-west past Laymoor Quag. To the west was Birch Wood enclosure, whilst to the east lay the marshy open expanse of Broadmoor. The Winning Colliery was sited immediately alongside the line on the east, whilst a little further, on the same side of the line, came the Bowson Colliery where one of the earliest attempts to work the Coleford High Delf in the deep was begun in 1863.

Bilson S&W Junction ground frame with the south junction to the triangle of Cinderford Old station beyond the bridge carrying the Cinderford Extension. The water tank on the right was the only supply on the branch and was fed from local streams. July 1948.
C. A. Townley

A closer view of Bilson S & W Junction ground frame which features in the foreground of the previous view. This picture was taken on 18th June 1933.
L. E. Copeland

Looking north over the triangular junction with the S & W at Bilson, this view was taken on 6th October 1946 from the embankment carrying the Cinderford Extension. Cinderford Old station (described in *The Severn & Wye Railway Vol. 2*) was situated just off the left of this view on the northern side of the triangle and closed when the new Cinderford station opened in July 1900. The gateposts in the foreground marked the boundary between the S & W and the GWR, the two lines connecting off the right of the picture at Bilson S & W South Junction.

The sidings at Cinderford Old station were used for the interchange of traffic with the Severn & Wye line. During the Second World War they were used for storage purposes, especially prior to the D-Day invasion. It is recorded that on 8th May 1944 twenty-five American bogie tank wagons were stored at Bilson Junction. These had been imported in kit form, probably through Newport Docks.

In the far distance the line to Churchway can be seen climbing towards Winning Colliery engine house on successive gradients of 1 in 45, 41 and 74, and levelling out near the colliery.

The gated crossing, which features in the middle distance, had given the good folk of Cinderford access to the Severn & Wye station and was also very convenient for inhabitants of Brierley, the Pludds and Lydbrook who walked through the woods to reach Cinderford and its shops. The crossing was also used by colliers going to and from work. After the closure of Cinderford Old station, the large gates were padlocked as vehicular access was no longer required and the V-stiles for pedestrians were replaced by swing gates. However, in October 1909, to the great consternation of local people, the GWR removed the gates and replaced them with palings, thereby cutting off the route. This action prompted a flurry of letters to the local press on the subject.

By November it transpired that workmen were crossing the line further up the Churchway branch instead, after being issued with notices warning them that if they continued to go the original way they risked a penalty of 40 shillings. The following letter appeared in the *Mercury* during December: 'Sir, Hoo his tha Tareiff Reform mon? His im tha un us stopdd how gwayn drow tha geates by Laymore, hand put a board by Mobly's brickyard to zay a

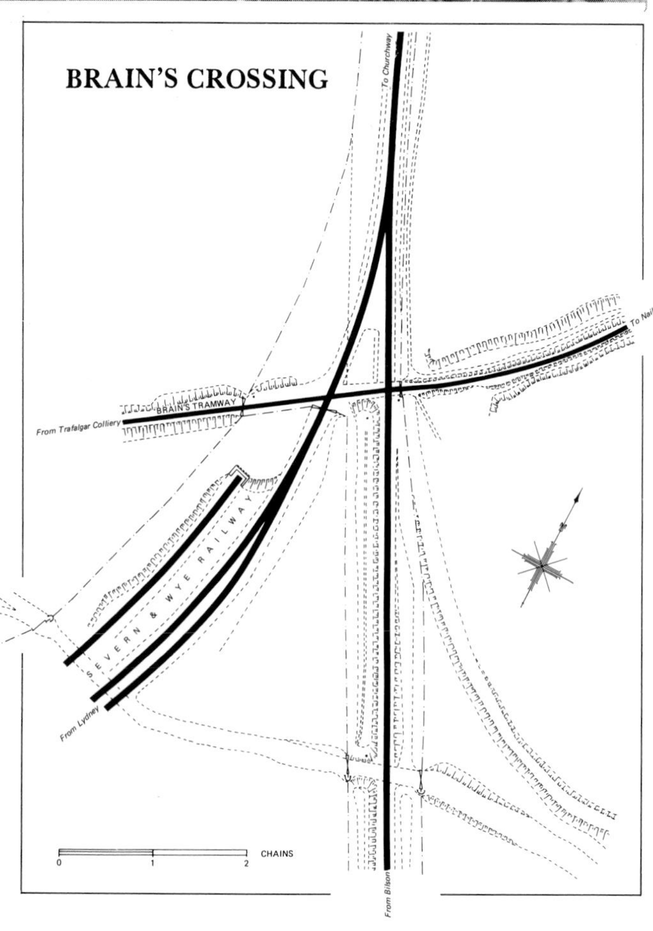

penalty or two pounds va gwayn thick rock – doo hit mean we shall have two pounds var getting over?'

It wasn't long before the new palings were ripped off the posts, one of the panels later turning up in a brook and the other in an empty wagon at Trafalgar Colliery. However, the crossing itself was often obstructed by lines of wagons stored on the old S&W sidings (perhaps the reason for closing the crossing?). Consequently, both men and women were scrambling under the trucks to reach the path on the other side of the line or further trespassing by walking all the way round them in the dark. Incidentally, around this time the GWR had also locked the crossing gates on well established pathways at Soudley claiming that it was for safety purposes with the newly introduced passenger services but this excuse couldn't be applied to the mineral-only Churchway branch.

The gates question was eventually resolved in favour of pedestrians, thus restoring the route from Cinderford to Brierley, although, unfortunately, one morning in February 1910 an aged woman was knocked down and killed by the engine of the early goods from Whimsey as she crossed the Whimsey branch just before 9.00 a.m. on her way from Brierley to Cinderford. *L. E. Copeland*

A 1930 picture of the disc and crossbar signal protecting Brain's Tramway Crossing (see *The Severn & Wye Railway Vol. 2* page 316). The post was a length of Barlow rail. The level crossing of the tramway over the Churchway branch dated from 1869 when Brain's Tramway was extended to the Golden Valley Iron Mine at Drybrook. The agreement with the GWR was signed by Thomas Bennett Brain and William Blanch Brain on 19th November 1872. A GW minute of 3rd April 1878 notes that a signal was erected to protect Brain's Crossing at a cost of £17. The provision of a disc and crossbar at this late time and the low cost involved, suggests that the signal was probably a redundant piece of equipment but nevertheless adequate for the purpose at this backwater. Although the tramway closed in 1925, the signal remained in situ until around the time of the Second World War. *L. E. Copeland*

This picture of 0–6–0PT No. 7723 propelling a train of empties to Northern United Colliery during the final years provides a good view of the north side of the bridge carrying the S & W Cinderford Extension over the Churchway Branch at Bilson S & W Junction. All trains from the direction of Churchway had to be brought to a stand at the Bilson Junction Severn & Wye ground frame home signal. The porter/signalman would then lower the signal and the train would draw forward to the junction with the Whimsey branch where it had to be brought to a stand clear of the junction and await a hand signal from the man in charge of Bilson Yard. *J. Norris*

0–6–0PT No. 3675 propelling another train of empties for Northern United on 11th October 1965. The conspicuous pump house in the foreground was built in connection with 'improvements of locomotive water supply £795' authorised on 1st October 1943. Note the notice board marking the commencement of the single line; trains passing beyond this had to be in possession of the train staff. *W. Potter*

Another train of empties near the old Winning Colliery engine house. Apart from the first vehicle, the train was entirely made up of steel mineral wagons, referred to as 'tin uns' by many of the Forest railwaymen. *J. Marshall*

BOWSON COLLIERY

The derelict New Bowson Colliery alongside the Churchway branch with what looks like Hawkwell Tinplate Works in the background, to the left of the chimney. The taller engine house contained an 85 inch Cornish engine rebuilt into a double-acting engine to pump water. The smaller building housed the winding engine. *Courtesy John Hodges*

The Bowson Gale was granted in June 1843 to Cornelius Walding of Ruardean Hill who was to get the coal from the Coleford High Delf vein and all the unallotted veins between it and the Churchway High Delf by means of a pit situated at a place near Churchway. The work was to be known as the New Bowson Colliery. The gale formed one of the 'deep gales' of the Forest and as such remained untouched until sufficient capital could be found to sink the shafts to the required depth. Within the Forest a single Free Miner was unlikely to be able to provide such a sum and so it was not until 1863 that a company was formed to commence development. Even so, the area provided by the Bowson Gale, about 128 acres, was insufficient for economic development and so a further 172 acres of coal were obtained by purchasing the northern part of the East Dean Deep Gale which had been granted in December 1852 to Richard Cook of Drybrook, but, like Bowson, had not been worked as the development costs, estimated at between £60,000 and £70,000, could not be found.

The development of the gales was begun by the Great Western Deep Coal Company Ltd., founded in January 1863 with a capital of £50,000 in the form of 5,000 £10 shares. The promoters of the company were mainly from London and included Henry Whitworth who took 50 shares, Richard Ridley with 200 shares and a John Watson of Whitby, 50 shares. Interestingly, the majority of the shareholders came from the Pontefract area of Yorkshire and included members of the Holden family who came to have far more of an interest. The first registered office of the company was at Whitworth's address of Abchurch Chambers, Abchurch Lane, London, but by December 1863 it was Carlton Buildings, Cooper Street, Manchester, which again shows the North Country interest in the concern.

In February 1864 the sinking of two shafts had begun close to the Winning Pits belonging to Messrs. Goold & Heyworth, the owners of the Bilson and Crump Meadow collieries. A dispute soon arose between the two parties for, in order to reach their allotted coal, the Great Western Deep Coal Co. had to sink their shafts through ground already granted to Goold and Heyworth. The coal in the Churchway High Delf seam which had been worked from the Winning Pits was by this time exhausted and so the area had no real commercial value, but local legend has it that when the shaft sinkings broke into some of the old Winner workings they were met by Goold's men and a fight developed underground. Whether or not there was any truth behind the story is unknown, but, according to the report on the ensuing litigation, when the Great Western Deep Coal Co. commenced sinking, Goolds immediately applied for a petition to restrain them. Goolds also drove a level from one of their old workings in such a manner as to obstruct the Great Western Deep Coal Co. pit, thus the tale could be true. In February 1864 a notice was issued to stop the Great Western Deep Coal working, so they filed a cross petition against Goolds. On reaching court in June 1864, the judge found in favour of the Great Western Deep Coal Co. It was stated that water from their workings would pose no threat to Goolds as the Great Western Deep Coal Co. already had an engine at work capable of winding 5,400 gallons per hour whilst a new engine was being erected with a capacity of 30,000 gallons.

The sinking works were bedevilled with problems and accidents. In October 1866, after reaching a depth of

200 yds, a labourer was killed by falling debris. The subsequent inquest, held at the Bell Inn, Ruardean, gives some detail of the operations. The sinking was in the hands of one John Standring who had been engaged in the job since August and informed the coroner that he had never seen any rules for working and that none were displayed on the premises. In overall charge of the works was a Mr. Eggleston. The problem with the shaft appeared to lie where it passed through the Rocky seam of coal; here the brick shaft lining had been replaced with stone and although the work had 'been made substantial', the lining was still being forced out. It was from here that a piece of stone fell, thus causing the fatal accident. To avoid a repetition, workmen were soon engaged to place deal boards over the offending area as the Mines Inspector had pronounced the works unsafe. At the coroner's request, a mining engineer, Mr. Trafford, had visited the works and, on examining the shaft, found it to be in a very unsatisfactory state. The courses of bricks were irregular and crushed in some parts as well as being 'quite out of the perpendicular'! The Mines Inspector's report gives some details of the operation and of the plant in use. The only means of communication between the bottom of the shaft and the surface was the human voice, although as they were now getting deeper, they were preparing to instal a mechanical signalling device. The winding engine in use had a single 12 inch cylinder with a stroke of 2½ feet and a working pressure of 40 lbs per square inch, giving about 12 horse power. He considered this to be of insufficient power to work a large winding drum and pointed out that only a small one of 5ft diameter was fitted, which was not large enough for round wire ropes. The rope in use was barely seven-eighths of an inch thick, which he considered far too thin for such a deep pit. To make matters worse, when he returned to the surface after inspecting the shaft, he noticed a broken cog in the pinion and made it quite clear that if he had noticed this prior to his descent, he would not have gone down!

The pit was 11ft in diameter and down to a depth of 228 yards. The top 8 or 10 yards were faced in dressed stone, the thickness of which could not be ascertained. Below this was standard 4½ inch brickwork which was totally inadequate. Then came another 6 yards of stonework at the depth of the Rocky vein, beneath which came 50 yards of common brickwork, then 9 or 10 yards of iron tubing, then another 32 yards of brickwork followed by a dozen or 15 yards of as yet unlined rock. Trafford thought that the shaft could have been located in a better position as it was well known that sinking a new shaft through old workings brought about many problems.

The bad construction of the shaft was not the only problem for when the shaft for the deep pit had been sunk to a depth of about 240 yards, a feeder of water was met which came through the stone 'like so many gas jets or springs'. Furthermore, when a depth of about 280 yards was reached in the pit, the sinkers tapped a rock and water came flooding in so quickly that the men were lucky to escape. At this time the only method of removing the water was by hauling it up the shaft in wooden containers, for which purpose 'two large engines' were being used. In early September 1867, whilst this task was being performed, the chain used for winding snapped when the load was within a few yards of the top, and the heavy container full of water fell back to the bottom of the shaft with a resounding crash, narrowly missing the workmen at the bottom.

The management and the engineer, John Watson, finally realised that they could not possibly de-water their shaft by this means and so it was decided to purchase a Cornish beam pumping engine from the recently closed St. Day United, or Poldice, copper mine in Cornwall.

This engine had been erected in 1821 to the design of William Sims with parts supplied by the Neath Abbey Ironworks in South Wales. Originally it had a 90in cylinder but it was rebuilt with an 85in one in 1845, and between 1830 and 1850 it was reputed to be the hardest worked engine in Cornwall. It was sold to the Great Western Deep Coal Co. for the sum of £700 and was dismantled at Poldice and taken to the nearby Perran Foundry for rebuilding. Curiously, Watson had it rebuilt as a double-acting engine which entailed the scrapping of most of the original and obviously successful machine; indeed it is likely that only the cylinder was re-used which at £700 made it very costly indeed!

The demolition of the engine house showing the extended beam of the Cornish engine c.1925. *Collection Marjory Oakey*

Another accident report in the *Gloucester Journal*, dated 18th January 1868, reveals that a second shaft, which was to be the Land Pit, was down to a depth of about 168 yards. Three men were employed here at a depth of about 30 yards and on the occasion concerned one of them, Edward Hooper, was returning to the surface to collect some equipment. They had called to be drawn up and the banksman relayed the message to the engine driver, William Jordan, who started the engine. Despite shouts to stop once the tub containing Hooper had reached the surface, winding continued taking the tub up over the winding wheel and through the opening into the winding engine house, in the course of which Hooper was thrown out to his death. The engineman, Jordan, was arrested and charged with manslaughter but found not guilty as the witnesses did not attend the court at the proper time!

A further accident occurred in July 1868 when three of the sinkers charged a hole with gunpowder. One of them unwisely looked into the hole using a candle for illumination. The resulting explosion injured two of them.

With all of the problems involved in the sinking and with the expense of removing the water from the workings as the Cornish pump had yet to be delivered, the Great Western Deep Coal Company Ltd. gave up the unequal struggle and went into voluntary liquidation on 19th March 1868.

A new company, the New Bowson Deep Coal Company Ltd., was formed in June 1868 with a capital of £25,000 in 250 £100 shares to purchase or lease New Bowson and a portion of East Dean Deep gales. Once again the majority of the shareholders were from the North Country, including one Isaac Holden. The company secretary was Henry Rowbotham who had performed the same task for the Great Western Deep Coal Co.

With a fresh injection of capital, work recommenced at Bowson and a licence for a siding was taken out with the Crown. Although no details of the full extent of the siding are known, its stub remained in 1878 to be recorded by the Ordnance Survey's surveyor.

The work on the secondhand Cornish engine had continued at the Perran Foundry and now work was put in hand to receive the engine at Bowson. By July the sinking of a staple pit to receive pumps was begun and by July was, according to the *Mining Journal*, down to a depth of 60 yards. The same journal, on 2nd January 1869, reported that the house for the pumping engine was 'up and covered in'. The engine itself was installed and in working condition by 17th July. As mentioned above, the engine was rebuilt as a double-acting engine, hence the need to sink a staple pit. The use of a double-acting engine closely followed North Country practice where the engine would draw up water from the bottom to a mid-point in the main shaft from where it would flow to the staple pit. Here it would be drawn to the surface. With the Bowson engine the staple pit was actually inside the engine house, and because the engine's beam had been extended at the cylinder end, the pumping strokes were uneven. At the outdoor end, over the main shaft, the pump stroke was 10ft, as was the stroke in the cylinder, but because the pump rod in the staple pit was attached beyond the cylinder, the stroke here was 13ft.

To make the engine double-acting, a new set of valve gear had to be fitted as steam had to be admitted to the cylinder on either side of the piston. When starting, the driver had to guard against overstroking in both directions and so provision was made to cut off the steam prematurely.

It is reputed locally that the engine house cracked on the first stroke of the engine, but whether the crack was in the bob wall or internally is not recorded. It is possible that the Perran Foundry who, in the tradition of erecting Cornish engines, might have overseen the building of the engine house, may have made an error in calculating the stresses that a double-acting engine would impart.

Messrs. Insole and Bunning, writing in the *British Society of Mining Students Journal* in December 1881, list all of the pumping plants in the Forest of Dean. Under Bowson they quote that in the main shaft was one 60 yard bucket lift and one 100 yard forcing lift, whilst in the Staple pit were two 65 yard forcing lifts. The nominal horsepower was given as 296. The engine was supplied with steam from four egg-ended boilers, three of which were in use at any one time.

It would appear that the engine was unsuccessful in dealing with the water problem, perhaps having to work at a reduced number of strokes per minute if there was a problem with the engine house, and a report in the *Mining Journal* for 2nd April 1870 reveals the sad plight of the undertaking.

> 'Report from the Forest of Dean, March 30th . . . The Bowson Company . . . is considered . . . to be a partial failure . . . depth of their shafts is about 284 yards . . . porous strata from which the water filled the shafts . . . The company decided to erect an engine and pumps . . . too small for the purpose . . . although their manager asserted that they had the 'Largest engine in the Forest' . . . they could not keep it [the water] out, the engine going about 8 strokes, (i.e. a little over 1,000 gallons per minute.)'

The water problem finally overcame the company which was wound up voluntarily on 17th December 1870 and

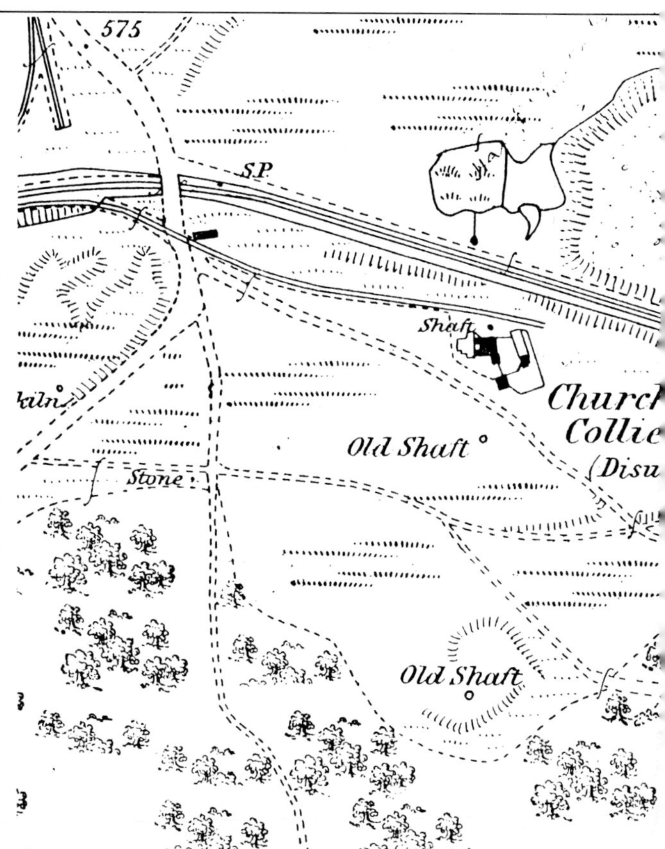

work was abandoned in 1871 after about £80,000 had been lost. To protect nearby gales, a dam was put in the shaft in 1874. It is likely that the gales then passed into the hands of the New Bowson Coal Company which was started by members of the Holden and Illingworth families who had been connected with both of the previous undertakings. They were working the adjoining East Slade Colliery and held other adjacent gales. Indeed a private siding agreement was taken out on 19th February 1875 by the New Bowson Coal Co. when the siding appears to have been known as 'Pumping Station Siding'.

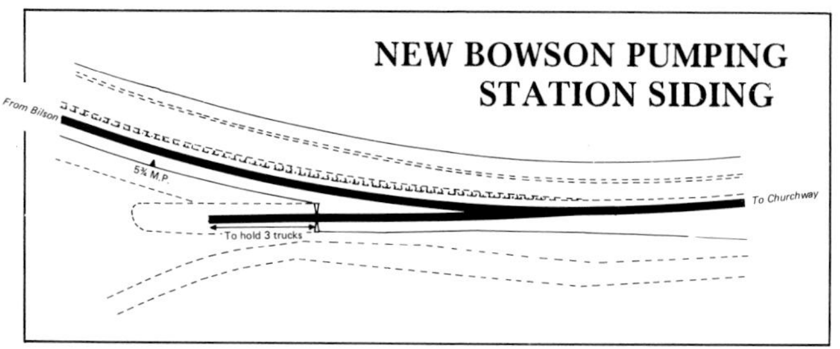

In 1877 they were attempting to sell off the plant at New Bowson. An advertisement was placed in early July and the plant was listed as:

> 'One Double Powered PUMPING ENGINE, with 85 inch cylinder and 10 ft stroke; two lifts of pumps 18 inch diameter, and one lift 20 inch diameter; pump rods, rod plates, plungers, buckets, clacks and all complete.
> One powerful CRAB ENGINE, with a pair of 12 inch cylinders and 2 ft stroke.
> One WINDING ENGINE, with a pair of 26 inch diameter cylinders and four ft stroke.

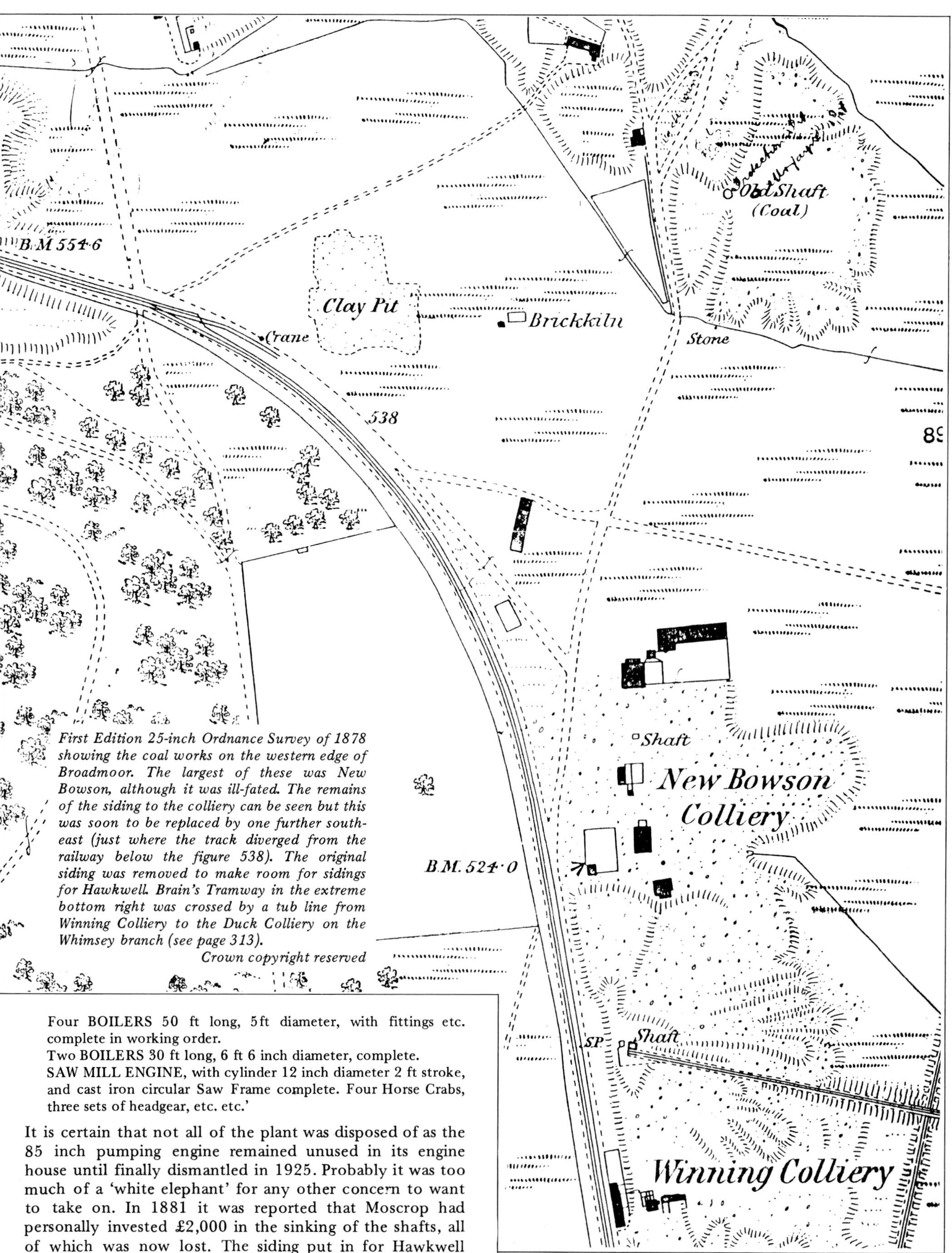

First Edition 25-inch Ordnance Survey of 1878 showing the coal works on the western edge of Broadmoor. The largest of these was New Bowson, although it was ill-fated. The remains of the siding to the colliery can be seen but this was soon to be replaced by one further south-east (just where the track diverged from the railway below the figure 538). The original siding was removed to make room for sidings for Hawkwell. Brain's Tramway in the extreme bottom right was crossed by a tub line from Winning Colliery to the Duck Colliery on the Whimsey branch (see page 313).

Crown copyright reserved

Four BOILERS 50 ft long, 5ft diameter, with fittings etc. complete in working order.
Two BOILERS 30 ft long, 6 ft 6 inch diameter, complete.
SAW MILL ENGINE, with cylinder 12 inch diameter 2 ft stroke, and cast iron circular Saw Frame complete. Four Horse Crabs, three sets of headgear, etc. etc.'

It is certain that not all of the plant was disposed of as the 85 inch pumping engine remained unused in its engine house until finally dismantled in 1925. Probably it was too much of a 'white elephant' for any other concern to want to take on. In 1881 it was reported that Moscrop had personally invested £2,000 in the sinking of the shafts, all of which was now lost. The siding put in for Hawkwell

Sunday morning, 13th September 1931, with Ralph Addis of Eastern United Colliery inspecting the headframe at Bowson before its removal to Northern United.
Cty. Marjory Oakey

Colliery in 1877 (see page 248) was immediately north of the one serving New Bowson. The following year a siding was also provided for the Hawkwell tinplate works which came off the southern end of the Hawkwell Colliery siding (which by now was in the form of two loop sidings). This ran over the site of the Bowson siding which had since been relocated further south (see track plan on page 244).

The hopes of working the deep coal at New Bowson were revived with the passing of the 1904 Dean Forest (Mines) Act. The New Bowson and East Dean Deep gales were to be amalgamated with Holly Hill United and Richard Whites under the ownership of the New Bowson Coal Co. Ltd. The Crown would permit the amalgamation providing several conditions could be met. The New Bowson Coal Co. had to be prepared to acquire the Holly Hill gale after which the Crown would carry out the amalgamation. The grant was to extend for seven years but if after that time new applicants came forward who were prepared to develop the Coleford High Delf seam, then the New Bowson Coal Co. would be given first option on sinking further down. If they were not prepared to do this then all the seams below the Brazilly were to be surrendered subject to the newcomers paying the New Bowson Coal Co. £5,000 for the New Bowson Pits and machinery. If fourteen years elapsed without any work being done then the Crown had the right to forfeit the seams below the Brazilly without any sum being paid.

In November 1906 it was reported that the Lydney & Crump Meadow Collieries Co. Ltd. were interested in acquiring the interests of the New Bowson Coal Co. By this date the New Bowson Co. was largely in the hands of the Illingworth family. Indeed the registered owners of New Bowson were given as Sir Angus Holden, Edward Holden, Alfred Illingworth, Henry Illingworth, May Illingworth, Percy Holden Illingworth and Albert Holden Illingworth. The latter two suggest that the Holden and Illingworth families were probably united by marriage. Both Alfred and Henry Illingworth senior were involved in the textile industry in Bradford and Alfred was also a Yorkshire MP. Henry Illingworth died in 1895 leaving his interest to his son Henry Holden Illingworth, whilst Alfred died in 1907 leaving his estate to his wife and six sons, the eldest of whom was Frederick. The largest shareholder was Henry Holden Illingworth and the terms of amalgamation suggested that he should receive £4,500 in shares and debentures in the Lydney & Crump Meadow Collieries Co. Ltd., although he was to provide £1,000 in cash for development purposes. In February 1907 it was reported that Illingworth had spent a total of £94,000 at Bowson and in the rest of the Forest since 1863. (Another interest held by the family was the ill-fated Arthur & Edward Colliery at Lydbrook [see *The Severn & Wye Railway Vol. 3*, Pope & Karau, Wild Swan Publications 1988] which in 1907 was also sold to the Lydney & Crump Meadow Collieries Co. Ltd. who then made a go of it.)

It is recorded that between 1906 and 1908, 10,016 tons of coal were raised from the East Dean Deep gale. This was undoubtedly raised through another gale, possibly Crump Meadow or the Duck Pit.

As allowed for in the agreement with the Crown, the Holly Hill gale was transferred to the Lydney & Crump Meadow Collieries Co. Ltd. via the Free Miners in November 1907. The entire amalgamated area came to be known as the Northern United gale. Although it was reported that work on riming out one of the Crump Meadow shafts was to begin before the end of March 1909, no work seems to have been done until 1912/13. The Brazilly seam had been proved by a staple pit sunk at Crump Meadow and the coal was being brought to the surface through the Crump Meadow shaft and the Duck Colliery, also owned by the Lydney & Crump Meadow Collieries Co. Ltd.

Around the period 1912/13 a Lancashire boiler was installed on the New Bowson site and it was intended to fill the middle pit. The First World War, however, interrupted this work and it was not until 1918 that any further work appears to have taken place. On 15th January a private siding agreement was signed allowing the Lydney & Crump Meadow Collieries Co. Ltd. the use of the New Bowson pumping station siding for a period of six months from 31st December 1917 in order to take coal and materials to Bowson. In 1921 a new steel headframe was erected, but by 1925 all hopes of winning coal from this site were abandoned and the engine house, together with the 85 inch pumping engine, were demolished.

The Northern United gale itself was not given up and in 1932 it was sold to Henry Crawshay & Co. who began work on a new site further to the north-west and gained the Coleford High Delf seam by sinking a new shaft. On 19th May 1932 it was recorded that the New Bowson pumping station siding had been removed.

The story of the highly successful Northern United is told on page 271.

A guard's view of his train of coal from Northern United. *R. Dagley Morris*

Another train of coal from Northern United, seen from the opposite side of the line. In August 1962 a meeting was held to consider an application from Messrs. Beaver Transport Ltd for a private siding connection to serve a coal washing plant which they had recently installed next to the Churchway branch. The plant was to wash material recovered from coal tips in the Forest and it was intended to load the recovered small coal into railway wagons over a loading bank. A siding for 20 wagons was considered and it was expected two clearances would be required per day. However, once the costs were known, the siding idea seems to have been dropped and the material was taken by road instead. The washery was located just south of the Bowson Colliery site. *R. H. Marrows*

HAWKWELL COLLIERY

Hawkwell Row, built by Jacob Chivers for his workmen at Hawkwell Colliery. *Collection Neil Parkhouse*

Hawkwell Colliery, probably named after the nearby Hawkes Well, worked the Small Profit gale. This was awarded in 1841 in equal shares to Thomas Winnall and George Jaynes. The colliery was to work the coal in the Coleford High Delf and all other veins above and below it. In September 1844 the Reverend George Jaynes conveyed his half of the concern to William Stallard who, in May 1846, obtained the other half from Winnall. Unfortunately, the colliery was abandoned about this time due to an influx of water which could not be contained when the shaft had reached a depth of about 100 yards.

On 1st January 1874 William and John Stallard and Sarah Winnall conveyed the colliery to Jacob Chivers, who was born in the Forest in 1815 and at some point in his career worked for the Cambrian Iron & Spelter Co. at Maesteg before moving to Spain in the 1840s where he operated a lead mine. In 1860 Chivers returned to this country and purchased a tinplate works at Kidwelly. These were extended and other sites acquired in the district during the 1870s by which time Jacob was in partnership with his son Thomas. This arrangement was not destined to last and in 1877 the partnership was dissolved. Jacob must have retained an interest in the Forest of Dean area as under the agreement reached on the split with his son he was to retain properties at Bishop's Wood near Lydbrook and Woodville in Ross-on-Wye.

Chivers expended capital upon the colliery and erected a secondhand Cornish pump with a 50in cylinder and 10ft stroke. This enabled him to de-water the colliery and sink the shaft deeper, until in September 1876 it was reported in the *Gloucester Journal* that he had succeeded in reaching the Coleford High Delf. This was quite an achievement as it was the first time that the seam had been worked in the deep in the Forest. The coal proved to be 3ft 6in thick with a second measure 1ft thick, the two being separated by a band of clod. The manager of the colliery at this time was Alfred Ridler and the concern was worked under the title of the Hawkwell Colliery Co. Having struck the most valuable seam of coal in the Forest coalfield, development work at the colliery began in earnest. In September 1877 Chivers was applying to the Crown for land on which to build a manager's house, offices and cottages. In January 1878 a licence was granted by the Crown for the construction of a 12ft wide formation for a 'railroad' in connection with the colliery, and the following month an agreement was taken out with the GWR for a siding off the Churchway branch. It was to this siding that the 'railroad' (probably a narrow gauge railway on which it is believed a locomotive was used for a period) was laid. The siding took the form of two loops and a short siding.

In 1878 Chivers began to develop a tinplate works at Hawkwell, details of which are given below. In 1881 he took the works manager Alfred Charles Bright into partnership and in 1883, following the death of Chivers, Bright took over both the colliery and the tinplate works.

In August 1884 Ernest Williams, William Davis and A. C. Bright were wanting extra tip space at the colliery. The manager at this time may have been Marcus Letcher who in November 1884 was applying to burn coke close to the Hawkwell Tinplate works. In June 1885 Williams and Davis mortgaged four-fifths of the colliery to the Gloucester Banking Co., suggesting that they may have leased the colliery from Bright. It was about this period that the New Bridge Engine gale was acquired (see page 349) and in June 1885 it was said that preparations were being made to work it through Small Profit and take the coal up the shaft at Hawkwell.

At the end of February 1887 an accident occurred at the colliery when the flywheel spindle on the winding engine cracked. The men underground at the time were got out by

The disused engine house at Hawkwell prior to rebuilding for use by Northern United Colliery.
Cty. Marjory Oakey

a 'small engine' a few at a time. The breakage necessitated a suspension of the work until repairs were completed.

In September 1887 Bright raised a mortgage on both the colliery and the tinplate works from the Capital & Counties Bank, the full story of which is related below.

In August 1890, when it was reported that the waste tip was on fire, the colliery manager was given as Mr. Arblaster. In February 1892 A. C. Bright was taking Messrs. Illingworth & Co. to the High Court over a problem with water coming into Small Profit. Illingworth & Co. were working several adjoining gales such as New Bowson. By this time other gales were being worked by Hawkwell including New Bridge Engine and New Roberts Folly.

In October 1893 A. C. Bright & Co. Ltd. was formed but the company went into liquidation in December 1895. The colliery probably ceased work at around this time and in March 1899 the Small Profit and the New Roberts Folly gales were forfeited back to the Crown.

HAWKWELL TINPLATE WORKS

As already mentioned, Chivers had had an interest in a tinplate works at Kidwelly and, having successfully developed Hawkwell Colliery, his thoughts returned to tinplate manufacture. An interest had been shown in purchasing the moribund Parkend works from the Crawshays but this fell through and Chivers then decided to set up a new works close to his Hawkwell Colliery and alongside the siding off the Churchway branch. These works were on land belonging to the New Roberts Folly Colliery gale for which a lease from the Crown was taken out in October 1878.

The works are reported to have opened in February 1879 and four mills were installed. Some power at the works was provided by gas supplied by the Bilson Gas Light & Coke Co. who in November laid a main from the gasworks at Bilson to Hawkwell alongside the tramroad and the Churchway branch to avoid paying a wayleave to the Crown. The manager of the works at this time was said to be E. M. Letcher but this may only have been a temporary measure until Alfred Bright arrived from Kidwelly where he had also been a manager under Chivers. In 1881 Bright was taken into partnership with Chivers and, following the latter's death in 1883, Bright acquired the whole of the business. It is likely that due to Chivers' ill health towards the end of his life Bright had in fact been in overall charge since 1881. Bright now carried on the business by himself, trading as A. C. Bright & Co. The works were profitable throughout the 1880s but in the early '90s things began to go wrong. Whilst for the year ending June 1891 the net profit was £2,679 7s 2d, by the following year it was down to £34 4s 3d. The year ending 1893 brought a loss of £4,172 11s 2d, probably due to the decline of the Forest's ironworks. With most of them having closed, it meant that he had to look further afield for his raw material and thus increased his costs.

Bright realised that this declining state of affairs could not continue. He was deeply in debt to the Capital and Counties Bank as a consequence of the original purchase of the business from Chivers. When ordered to pay off the overdraft, which at the time stood at around £7,600, Bright decided that the way out was to form a limited company.

On 6th October 1893 A. C. Bright & Co. Ltd. was incorporated with a capital of £25,000 in 25,000 £1 shares. The subscribers were listed as A. C. Bright himself, Jasper Foster and John Hughes, both of London, together with Maria Bright, wife of Alfred, and Alfred William Mostyn Bright, John Meek Bright and Edwin Marcus Letcher, all of whom were related. £18,000 was to be the purchase price, of which £12,000 was for land, gales, collieries, buildings, goodwill and fixed plant, and £6,000 for the stock in trade. This sum was to be made up of £10,000 in fully paid up shares to Bright plus a cash sum of £8,000, the latter being sufficient to pay off the overdraft.

PROPOSED NEW SIDING FOR HAWKWELL COLLIERY 1878

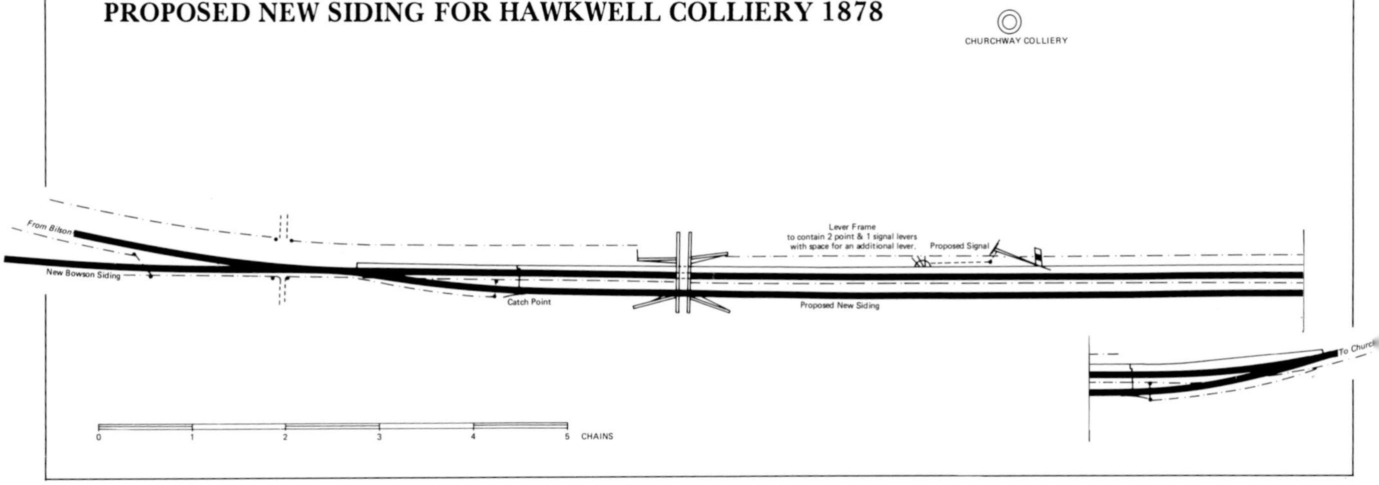

It would appear that Bright's sole reason for forming the limited company was to raise capital to pay off the overdraft. At the second meeting of the directors, held on 26th October, Bright's 10,000 shares were allotted amongst the above listed subscribers as gifts; 9,246 went to Bright, 250 each to Hughes and Foster, 250 to a Mr. Lawrence, and one each to the members of Bright's family. None of these shares were paid for and thus no money was raised. In order to obtain the £8,000 cash that was needed to pay off the bank, it was resolved that 80 debenture shares should be issued at £100 each.

Whilst these financial manoeuveres dealt with the immediate needs, they left no working capital for the company and this was to be its downfall. In the past Bright had survived on the overdraft from the bank which was secured by the deeds to the property. Now with the deeds in the hands of the debenture holders, the bank would advance no monies.

The company also took on Bright's own liabilities which in September 1894 stood at £2,262 13s 2d. Thus it had a considerable deficit to contend with as well as no working capital. For the year ended September 1894, the loss on the business was £2,447 18s 5d and in the following year £3,054 1s 8d. In March 1895 Bright had reported to the directors that he was unable to meet his liabilities and by October 1895 the business was practically closed. In December 1895 the Blaenavon Iron Co. applied to the Court for settlement of debt and A. C. Bright & Co. Ltd. went into liquidation.

It was hoped that the business could be sold as a going concern and the property and stock were valued. The buildings, etc. were put at £9,000, or two-thirds what the company had paid for them and the stock in hand was put at half that shown on the company's books. Virtually no hope was held out for unsecured creditors unless they could obtain their dues from Bright himself.

The machinery and equipment at the works was sold off with some of the mills going to Richard Thomas's works at Lydney. The buildings were bought by the Lydney & Crump Meadow Colliery Co. to secure them against any claims for surface damage caused by their underground workings. They removed the chimney stack together with the majority of the other buildings. The tin house itself was left and early in 1900 it was leased to Messrs. Hughes of King Street, Bristol. In March the *Dean Forest Mercury* reported on the establishment of a new industry with the setting up of a factory for the production of 'patent knife polish, emery wheels, and a composition for cleaning and polishing metals, brass, etc., and also in grinding purposes for brass finishers'. The patent for this had been acquired from Mr. P. H. Wilks, who had been engineer at Crump Meadow Colliery, who was to receive a royalty on all manufactured goods sold. Apparently a great number of alterations had been made at the tinworks and a considerable sum expended on the necessary plant. The works offered the prospect of employment for a good number of men, boys and girls if the goods were packed on the premises. It is possible that material for the works, and possibly some output, came and went over the old tinworks siding although no change in the private siding agreement was made. It may have been discussions over the use of the siding which led to another unauthorised user of the siding saying in June 1901 that the siding had been removed following a squabble 'with the persons who are using the old tin house for a factory for making polish'. The date at which polish manufacture ceased is at present unknown but it was certainly before 1904.

As with the iron-working industries along the valley between Ruspidge and Bilson, the tinplate works left their legacy in the form of heaps of ash and cinders. At the same time as applying to work the cinders around the Forest Vale site (see Vol. 1, p. 193). A. W. Latham also applied to work the heaps at Hawkwell. He offered the Crown a royalty of 2/6d per ton which was accepted, as at Forest Vale, in March 1899. Under the terms of his Hawkwell lease, Latham had to remove the Hawkwell cinders by May 1900 but, due to a depression in the iron trade, only part had been removed by that date.

Another problem with the Hawkwell site was that Latham had obviously been using the old tinplate works siding for loading and dispatching the cinders but in June 1901 he wrote to the Crown asking for a reduction in the royalty charge as the GWR had taken the siding up and he had to haul cinders to Whimsey, the nearest loading point. The royalty was reduced to 2/- and in October 1902 he again wrote to the Crown pointing out that the market price for cinders like those at Hawkwell was 3/6d per ton loaded in railway trucks, and as it was costing him 2/- to clean the cinders and haul them to Whimsey, after taking his profit, the most he could offer the Crown in royalty was 9d. In January 1903 it was recorded that Latham still had not removed the Hawkwell cinders due to the depressed state of the market but by April 1904 he had taken 233 tons 15 cwt and a further 327 tons 19 cwt 2 quarters by October. It would seem that he stopped soon afterwards.

HAWKWELL BRICKWORKS

Hawkwell Brickworks with its six circular kilns pictured here c.1900 with the Churchway branch on the right of the picture. The siding gate for Bowson Colliery's pumping station is just discernible on the original print. *A. J. Pope*

In about 1902 Mr. E. A. Trapnell of Cheltenham, 'a publican who has turned speculator and promoter of schemes', acquired the New Mount Pleasant Colliery gale. Whether he had local knowledge or not is unknown but his interest in the gale appears to have been more in the beds of clay contained therein. These were described as consisting of three distinct varieties and valuable. The topmost clay was a rich yellow colour suited for best quality terracotta ware, next came a clay of remarkably fine texture suitable for glazed ware, art pottery, sanitary ware, best blue bricks and tiles, railway arch bricks, quarry tiles, etc., and the bed was said to be 'practically inexhaustible'. The final layer was a good bed of fireclay.

To take advantage of this raw material, which was effectively a waste product from the winning of coal, Trapnell decided to set up a brickworks and to that effect wrote to the Crown in January 1904 seeking permission to put down brickmaking machinery. In May it was stated that he was to lease the old Hawkwell tinplate works site from the Lydney & Crump Meadow Collieries Co. Ltd. As already seen, it is likely that virtually all of the old tinplate works buildings had been removed, apart from the old offices which had been converted into a cottage, and possibly the old tin house which had been used as a polish factory.

Trapnell formed the Cinderford Coal, Brick, Tile & Fireclay Co. Ltd. and in August 1904 the *Dean Forest Mercury* reported that work had begun 'to establish a comprehensive brick, tile and pottery works' with a group of Staffordshire workmen being employed to erect the kilns and other plant. It was hoped that the works would be ready for output in about two months using the most up-to-date machinery. However, problems were encountered as witnessed by a further *Mercury* report in April 1905. By this date four kilns had been erected, each of which had a capacity of 20,000 bricks. Once the first kiln had been completed, it was used to produce the bricks for the others. It was then found that the boiler used to provide steam to a Tangye 50 hp engine was inadequate to meet the demand and so a Lancashire boiler, measuring 28ft by 7ft, was installed by Messrs. Teague, Chew and Morman of the Haywood Engine Works, Cinderford.

The brickmaking plant, said to be erected and 'ready for production', consisted of two complete machines capable of turning out 7,000 bricks per day each. Provision had also been made for two more once the demand justified them. The first stage in the production process was to crush the shale or clay in two pans, each of which contained crushers weighing fifty hundredweights each. From these, elevators took the clay up and then shot it into another pan, known

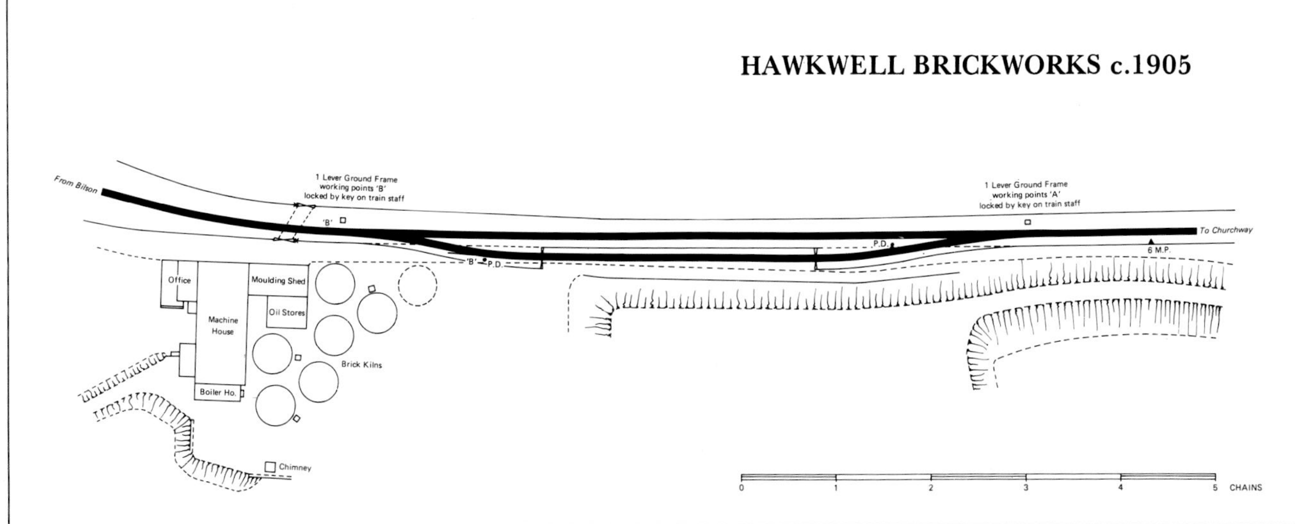

as the 'perforating pan', through which it was crushed. Again elevators took the clay up and passed it through a refiner, or sieve, and then deposited it upon an upper floor. From here it was taken down to the brick pressing machines. The whole of the machinery worked automatically. The speciality of the works was to be the 'granite' engineering and building brick.

In April 1905 the company was said to be desirous of putting in a railway siding and to this end a siding agreement was taken out with the GWR in October. The siding was a simple loop, part of which was to be constructed by the brick company and gated at both ends.

Prior to the completion of the siding, the works were opened amidst great celebrations. In May 1905 a luncheon was held there, probably in the old tin house, for fifty invited guests. Here it was stated that Trapnell had bought the coal property for £3,000 and had started the Cinderford Coal, Brick, Tile & Fireclay Co. with a capital of £18,000. The works now had a capacity to produce 75,000 bricks per week. The employees were not forgotten in the feasting and were given a dinner on the following Saturday.

However, orders for the bricks were not forthcoming. In the period up to 30th September 1905, 196,821 were made and the following year saw only 441,716 completed bricks from a potential capacity of 3,900,000. The clay at this time was brought to the works from the New Mount Pleasant Colliery by means of a tramway on a low embankment.

It may have been the lack of business for the brickworks which led to Trapnell becoming interested in the ash and cinder heaps once more. When he had been managing the New Mount Pleasant Colliery he had applied to the Crown for a heap of iron ore which stood close to the old tinplate works. At the time he was deterred from doing anything about it due to the high cost of rail carriage. In May 1905 Auguste Trapnell & Co. applied to the Crown for permission to remove cinders from Hawkwell, New Bowson Colliery, Bilson Green and Parkend Colliery as they intended to tender for the supply of up to 50,000 tons of ashes for the Cheltenham filter beds. However, it is not known if Trapnell removed any of the cinders from Hawkwell.

In November 1907 the brickworks were said to be doing better and a new kiln was being erected. The upsurge in fortune can only have been shortlived as in February 1910 a very gloomy picture emerged. It would seem that the company had never paid a dividend or the interest on debentures and that it had only kept going through loans found by the directors. If they had not done this then the works would have closed as early as 1906, only one year after commencing operations. The point had now been reached when the situation could no longer continue, and it was intended to put a receiver in possession until either the works could be sold as a going concern or the existing company could be restructured. The reasons given for the company's problems were that they could not get enough local sales, and many collieries, who would be the biggest users, made their own. Some bricks were supplied to both the Cannop and Eastern United Collieries, but difficulty was experienced in selling bricks further afield due to the cost of transportation. A brickworks at the end of a branch could not compete with those alongside main lines and closer to the centres of brick usage.

By November 1910 the company was in the hands of the debenture holders who proposed to sub-let to Mr. Healey, the works manager, who would now work the machinery for his own profit. Healey's inside knowledge of the firm's difficulties does not seem to have deterred him and in November 1913 the siding agreement was transferred to Messrs. Healey & Company.

Healey's attempts at turning it into a going concern were hindered by the First World War and in May 1918 he was seeking to lease off part of the works, the greater part of which had already stood idle for nearly two years, to allow for the manufacture of leather substitute. The working of coal from the New Mount Pleasant Colliery had also stopped in 1917.

In July 1919 it was reported locally that a W. E. Rhodes, a mining and mineral agent of Cinderford, was attempting to form a new company to purchase the Hawkwell brickworks and restart work. The value of the structure was put at £355 and the land on which it stood at £155. In July 1920 Healey was still in possession and in September 1921 it was stated that he was to buy the works for £500. The partners in Healey & Co. were Joseph Calvert Healey, of Belle View Road, Cinderford, and Kate Healey, his wife. During the early 1920s Healey was developing a rubber works at Bullo Pill (see Vol. 1, p. 73) and by July 1923 he found it necessary to give up the works at Hawkwell which were sold to Mr. George Henry Milsom of Pontypool who intended carrying on brick-making.

Milsom's tenure at the works was shortlived and obviously unprofitable. He attempted to sell out in 1925 but the would-be purchaser was unable to complete the transaction. The report of a theft in September 1927 revealed that the buildings were all open and that there was no caretaker, so the works were evidently disused. A Mr. F. J. Milsom was the assistant manager and in June 1928 it was reported that Milsom was no longer in a position to carry on the works. The agreement of 21st October 1905 was terminated on 31st December 1929.

What happened to the property after this is unclear; the buildings presumably fell into disrepair and were later removed. The siding was transferred to a Simeon Harris in 1929 who probably used it for loading coal from the New Mount Pleasant Colliery which he had taken over following its re-grant in 1926. The brickworks siding may have been removed in 1932 and it had certainly gone by 1935 when the Northern United Colliery sidings were built. The southern connection to these joined the Churchway branch at the same position as the southern connection to the brickworks.

THE COLEFORD BRICK & TILE CO. LTD.

A late 1930s view of Coleford Brick & Tile Company's siding on the site of the former northern connection to Hawkwell brickworks siding. The line to Churchway can be seen climbing away in the distance past the gated 'loaded road' from Northern United, the ground frame for which was at 5 miles 69 chains. Because there were no passenger services over the line, it was not necessary to provide facing point locks, so the two sidings were controlled with single-lever ground frames, 'Brickworks Ground Frame' and 'Northern United South Ground Frame' both featuring in this picture. *L. E. Copeland*

In September 1936 the Coleford Brick & Tile Co. Ltd. were applying to the Crown to build a new brickworks on the old Hawkwell brickworks site. The Coleford Brick & Tile Co. Ltd. had been incorporated in October 1925 to acquire the Marions brickworks near Coleford from the O & C Syndicate Ltd. Within a year, a Colonel L. Frewen had come to have a controlling interest in the company. On 26th November 1936 he met the GWR's Divisional Superintendent, Divisional Engineer and District Goods Manager on site to discuss the 'exact requirements in connection with the Coleford Brick & Tile Company's application for a private siding'. Colonel Frewen said that the old disused building on this land near the entrance to Northern United Company's siding entrance would be demolished and that they intended to erect a fairly large brickworks on the site. He thought their inwards traffic would consist of about 240 tons of coal per month, drawn from Northern United, and sand 'a few trucks at a time'. Outwards traffic would vary from 5 to 10 truckloads of bricks and tiles per day 'at the commencement'.

In February 1937 a letter about the new plant was sent out to the company's shareholders advising them that the new works were to have a 3.5 million brick capacity per annum, the site had been bought freehold and the adjoining clay area was held on a rent merging with royalty basis from the Forestry Commision. A suitable rail rate had been negotiated with the GWR for traffic to London, and as coal to feed the works boilers was available close at hand, the haulage was a fraction of the cost compared to getting coal to Marions works.

An early 1960s view of the same scene showing some of the kilns and Northern United's dirt mound. *R. Dagley Morris*

The erection of the buildings, plant, etc., was in the hands of Mr. T. Linstrum of Leeds who was laying them out with all possible labour-saving devices, although the production of hand-made bricks did not easily lend itself to labour-saving from the moulding stage onwards.

It was also stated that the market for Coleford facing bricks had grown to such an extent that even with the works running to full capacity, they would be hard pressed to meet the demand. However, if demand dropped and price-cutting started, then the company would be in a worse position than many in being so far away from the London market.

An overdraft of £8,000 was arranged to erect the Hawkwell works.

Soon after commencing work, a siding connection was brought into use on 24th June 1937, a one-lever ground frame (Brick Works Ground Frame) being installed at 5miles 67 chains. The estimated cost of the siding and connection was £380, and a siding agreement was signed with the GWR in May 1938.

The Second World War affected the works, much as the First had in Healey's day, and caused the company a few problems. At first the Ministry of Works and Buildings wanted all the bricks the works could produce, but, when a huge stockpile had been accumulated, the Ministry did not use them and the works had to close down in January 1942 until the situation improved. For a while afterwards the buildings were used for storage by the Ministry of Supply.

After the war, brick-making was resumed by the Coleford Brick & Tile Co. Ltd. In June 1946 a meeting was held at Marions works to discuss the future of the company. It would appear that Marions had also closed down during the war but, unlike Hawkwell, it was not to be restarted. One option examined was to restructure the company, with Hawkwell works being sold to a new company, or alternatively finance could be arranged with outside parties. A Mr. H. T. Lavender, of Messrs. Proctor & Lavender Ltd. of Birmingham, was looking into this second option with his associates in Birmingham on the basis that Proctor & Lavender would be given the sole rights for all sales outside the London area and that Mr. Lavender would be made a director. It would appear that this latter course was taken as in October 1946 Mr. Harold Lavender became a director.

Despite restarting work at Hawkwell and despite the obvious demand for brick for war-damaged buildings, things were not easy at the works. In October a shortage of labour led to a bottleneck at the kilns, two of which overburnt, rendering the bricks useless for the contract they had been made for. A new excavator for the clay pit was also needed and it was decided to place an order for one even though delivery could not be effected until the end of 1948. The following extract from a letter to the shareholders at this time gives some idea of the situation:

> 'It is realised and regretted by the Directors of the Company that no interest on existing debentures has been possible through the war years, but circumstances were such that we could not carry on production during those years; our works were requisitioned for Ministry of Supply storage purposes at a very inadequate rental which did not begin to cover commitments, and only for the past 12 months has the Company been able to resume

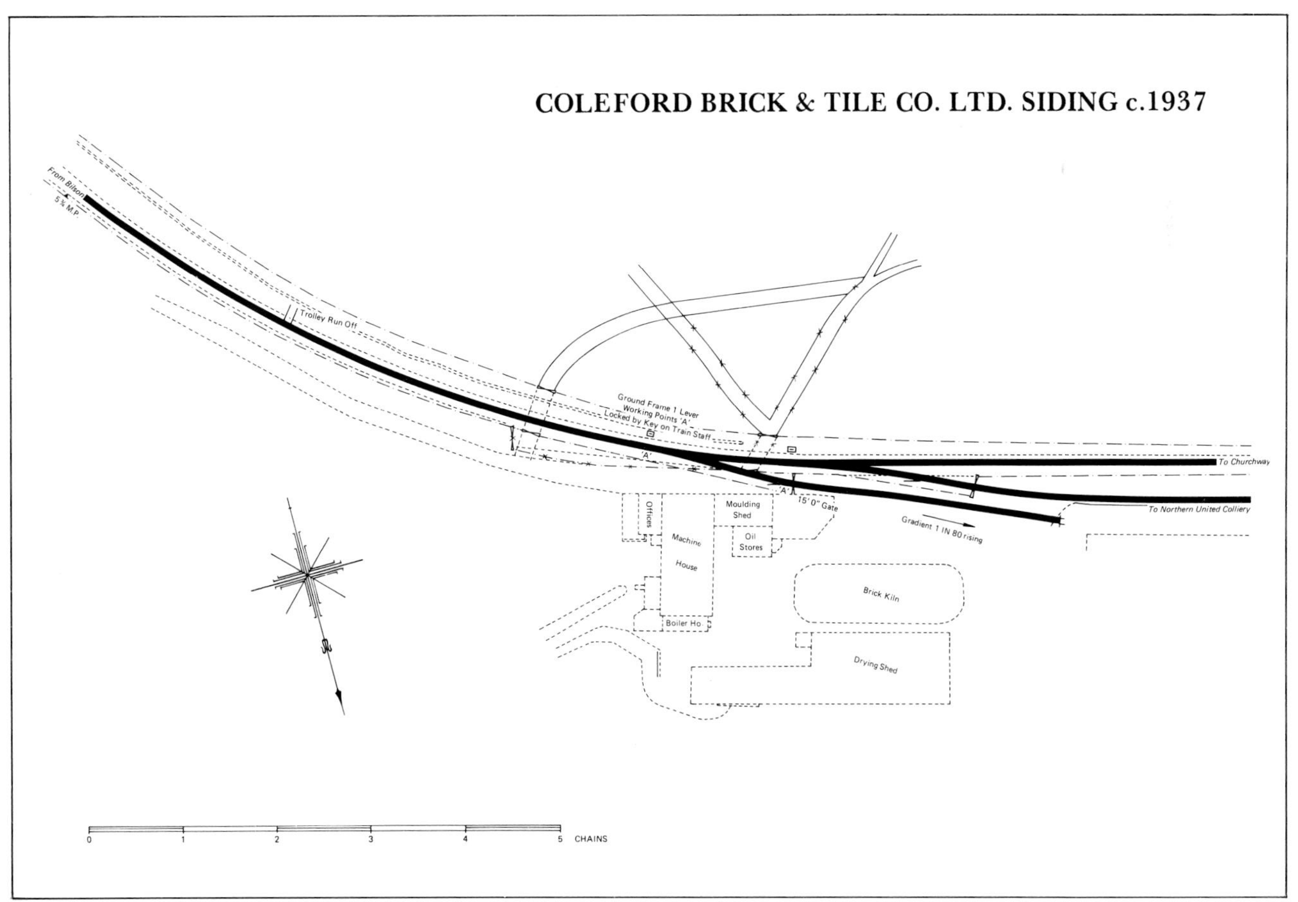

COLEFORD BRICK & TILE CO. LTD. SIDING c.1937

operations. Starting up post-war has been full of difficulties; indifferent labour, frequent changing of hands to try and get better results, war weariness and lack of food and general amenities, and on top of all this the wettest summer known in a generation, followed by the worst winter for many years, so much so in fact that February was a complete blank as regards either production or sales, and March with its heavy blizzard nearly as bad. April began to pick up but then followed the drastic cutting of fuel, so that the amount of fuel allotted only alowed the Company to manufacture 50% of normal output for that month and a slight increase of fuel for May brings the percentage up to 65%. It is understood that we shall be allotted full fuel from June on through the summer, in which case we can pick up to full output, and can only hope the fuel situation will allow us to carry on in the same way throughout the coming winter.

'Debenture interest will be resumed for the year starting May 1st 1947, and it is hoped to pay off the accrued interest gradually over the next few years.'

In January 1947 the Muir Hill dumper in use in the clay pit was struggling due to adverse weather conditions and so a new road was put in to the pit to allow the clay to be got by hand. This was not a good move as the dumper's tyres burst, probably from wear, and even with a high priority rating there was a full month's delay on the delivery of new tyres. The company was still struggling financially, the money coming in not meeting the outgoings. To help resolve the problem, it was decided to take orders over and above the output of the works and then keep deliveries short so that any firm not paying its account would have its deliveries stopped.

Having been messed about during the war by the Ministry of Works, the company now applied to the MOW Scheme for financial assistance to brickworks, under which up to £5,000 could be borrowed for particular works as a short-term loan. However, their application for a £4,000 loan was eventually refused by the MOW. Added to their financial difficulties, the national shortage of fuel made it difficult to get coal for the works and led to a 10% increase in the price of bricks on all contracts except for 'the Atomic Research Station at Abingdon' (Harwell). The company did not want to increase the prices on this contract for fear of losing it and the high priority status it gave them.

The perilous financial position and the shortage of fuel continued throughout 1947 and it was not until the end of 1948 that the position began to improve. It was helped by the appointment in May 1948 of a Mr. Gibbon as a director and sales manager.

In December 1948 it was decided to move the company's head office from Marions works to Hawkwell where a 20ft x 10ft prefabricated building was provided for the purpose. Any possibility of reopening Marions came to an end when in May 1950 it was decided to sell off the plant or move it to Hawkwell.

In November 1950 it was thought desirable to erect a third rectangular kiln of 40,000 brick capacity. Work on this was almost complete in January 1951.

Brick production at Hawkwell continued to increase over the years and new plant was installed. The method of heating the kilns was changed from coal to oil and then natural gas and recently with the provision of new carbon fibre kilns the production of hand-made bricks continues to a high standard.

All Contract offers subject to Strike and Accident Clause and to circumstances over which we have no control

TELEGRAMS: "MARION, COLEFORD

TELEPHONE NO. 3145 COLEFORD

COLEFORD BRICK & TILE CO., Ltd.

MARION WORKS, COLEFORD, GLOS.

WORKS: MARION, COLEFORD
HAWKWELL, CINDERFORD

MULTI-COLOURED
HAND-MADE SAND-FACED BRICKS
SILVER-GREY FACINGS
OLD-WORLD FIREPLACE BRICKS

DIRECTORS:
R. H. STOREY, ESQ. J. P. (CHAIRMAN)
G. W. ROWLAND-OWEN, ESQ.
COL. F. A. MACARTNEY, O.B.E. M.C., D.L.
H. T. LAVENDER, ESQ.
LT. COL. L. FREWEN, D.S.O. (MANAGING)

NOTICE OF EXTRAORDINARY GENERAL MEETING.

Notice is hereby given that an Extraordinary General Meeting of the Members of the above-named Company will be held at Marion Works, Coleford in the County of Gloucestershire on the 22nd day of September I948 at 2.30 p.m. for the purpose of considering and if thought fit of passing the following Extraordinary Resolutions:-

I. That the Directors be empowered to increase the Capital of the Company to £20,000 by the creation of £IO,000 Cumulative Preference Shares of £I each and to issue so many of such shares and to offer them to such persons as they may think fit.

2. That new Articles of Association as approved by the Directors be adopted in place of the existing Articles of Association.

CHURCHWAY

The end of the Churchway branch was the point at which the physical connection between the Bullo Pill tramroad and the Severn & Wye tramroad was formerly made. With the conversion to the broad gauge, several private sidings were connected at Churchway. After passing the Churchway Colliery and crossing a tramroad branch to the pit-head on the level, the railway swung round to the west. After straightening up, a siding trailed in on the up side for the use of the Woodside Colliery.

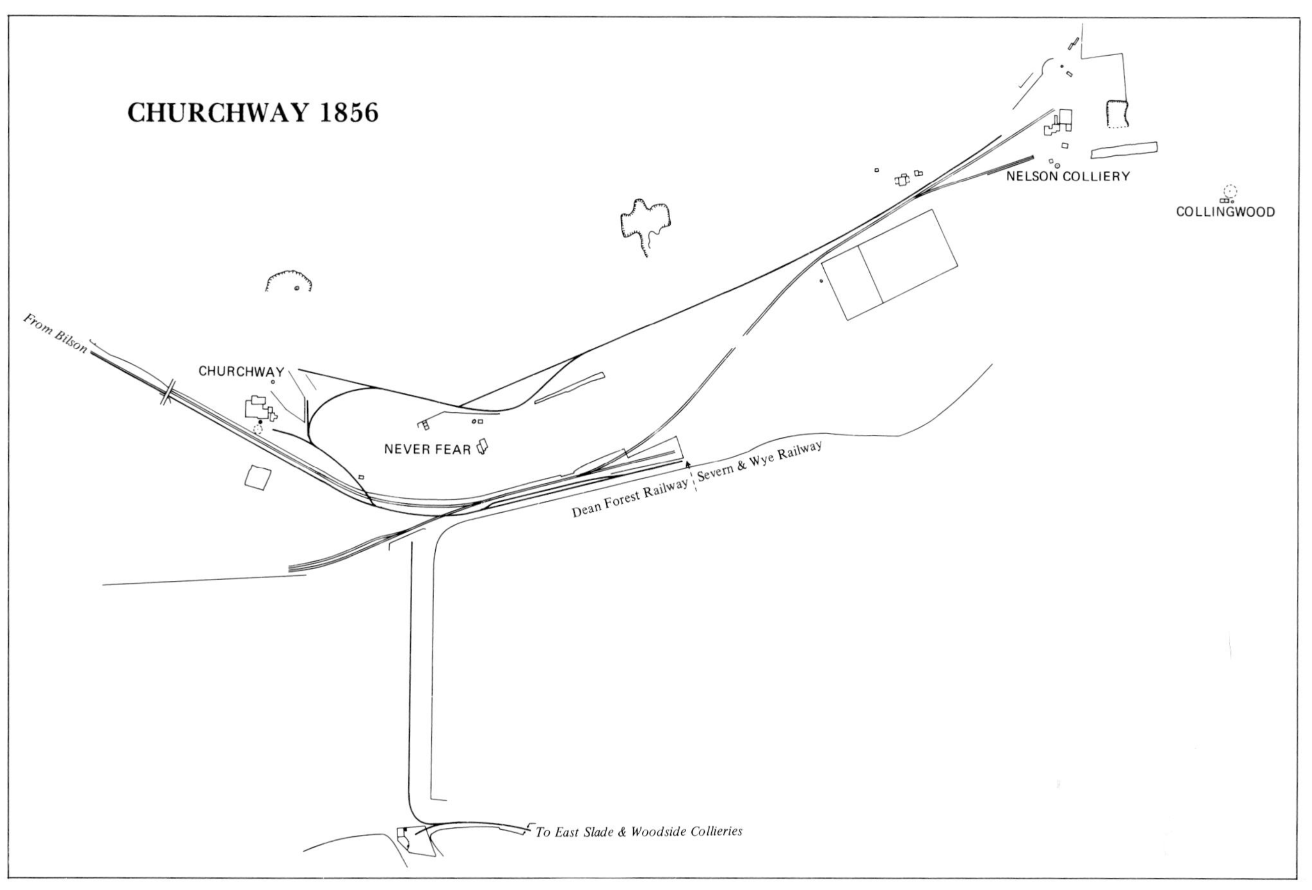

WOODSIDE COLLIERY

Permission for this siding was given to the Woodside Colliery Co. on 30th June 1854 following a letter to the South Wales Board from the colliery company's secretary, a Mr. Pope. It was agreed that the siding should be provided at the expense of the South Wales Railway and it may have been ready for use upon the opening of the line. An 1856 survey shows a siding crossing the Churchway tramroad and then passing a loading wharf before splitting into two storage sidings. A tramroad from the colliery, which was situated at Ruardean Woodside, about 1½ miles distant to the north-west, ran onto the loading wharf. This tramroad was in use by 1850, although a Crown lease for it was not granted until 1854, its existence probably coming to the Crown's notice with the application for the siding! The tramroad originally took the form of a branch from Churchway and served East Slade Colliery en route.

The gales forming Woodside Colliery were applied for after 9th April 1832 (before the passing of the Dean Forest Mines Act in 1838) by Giles Griffiths, a Free Miner. As such they were not granted but this did not deter James Court, a glazier from Coleford, Isaac Jones, an innkeeper from Cinderford, and Giles Griffiths from beginning work. By 1841 the gale was being worked in conjunction with the adjoining East Slade gale under the ownership of the Cheltenham and Forest of Dean Coal Company. The works were described as having a high pressure engine on two pits which had a depth of 60 yards. The colliery, however, was not at work and the gale may have been sold off soon afterwards. Whether the next owners were the Woodside Colliery Co. or not is unknown but they were working it by 1852. It is also possible that they were working the adjoining East Slade Colliery but this is unconfirmed. The colliery was another of those which closed soon after the opening of the broad gauge line and was certainly not at work in 1869. The sidings may have been removed as early as 1863. By 4th February 1876 the gale had been surrendered to the Crown. The gale was re-granted on that date to James Grindell of Milkwall but he did not hold it for long. On 15th October 1888 it was granted to George Stephens and came to form part of East Slade Colliery as detailed below.

EAST SLADE COLLIERY

The pit-head at East Slade, showing the headframe over the down-cast shaft in which was hung two cages. It was here in 1895 that the cages jammed in the shaft, imprisoning the men below ground for 32 hours. *Collection Daphne Booth*

The East Slade Colliery, also situated at Ruardean Woodside, was another of those works applied for after April 1832 for which permission was not given. In this case the gale was applied for by George and James Meek who were both Free Miners and assigned their rights to a company called The Cheltenham and Forest of Dean Coal Mining Company. In 1841 when the works were offered for sale they were 'not at work' and described as extensive. At East Slade pit, which was 70 yards deep, there was a high pressure engine, and there was also the pit at Ruardean Woodside.

The colliery was evidently not sold as in 1842 the output was recorded as 1,845 tons but the following year saw this drop to 587 tons, after which no returns are given. The Cheltenham Co. were still listed as the registered owners in 1847 but by November 1849 the gale had been surrendered. In that month it was re-galed to Isaiah Stephens of Shortstanding, near Coleford. There then followed an uncertain period for the colliery. On 30th April 1850 an advert appeared in the *Gloucester Journal*:

> 'To be sold by private contract (by order of the Official Managers appointed to wind up the Cheltenham & Gloucestershire Bank). A valuable Gale or Coal Field, in the Forest of Dean known as the East Slade & Newham Bottom Collieries, containing about 140 acres of unwrought coal and having 4 shafts sunk the required depth. The collieries are contiguous to railways communicating with Hereford, Gloucester, Cheltenham and the Metropolis. A Tramway extends from the mouth of the principal pit to a branch of the South Wales Railway. The coal is the celebrated High Delf Vein, varies in thickness from 5 to 6 feet, & yields about a ton & a half of superior coal in every square yard. The facilities for conveyance are great. The reserved royalty is 2s. per ton. The title is indisputable . . . '

The foregoing shows that a tramroad from the colliery to Churchway was in existence by 1850 and that it was undoubtedly to the same gauge as the Forest of Dean tramroad, although the communication with 'the Metropolis' was tenuous!

In August 1859 the same paper carried another sale notice which suggests that the colliery had remained unsold over the previous years:

> 'East Slade & Newham Bottom Collieries, being offered for sale at Auction at the Kings Head, Gloucester, 3rd September 1859 without reserve – had been previously offered on two previous occasions but had not reached reserve. Late owners had expended upon the works in excess of £16,000 for sinking four pits and erecting buildings etc.'

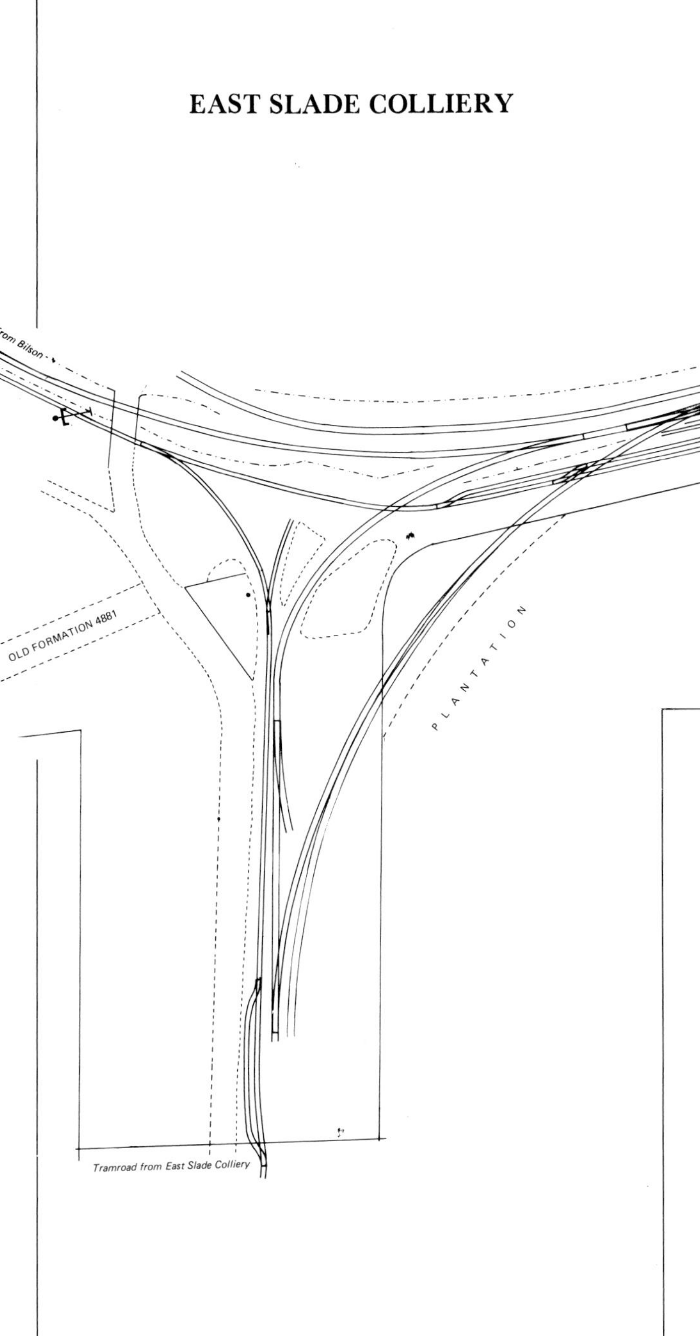

In October the colliery was once again at work as the *Journal* carried an advertisement for the 'Ruardean Collieries':

> 'Ruardean Collieries. The Public are respectifully informed that the above (or True Blue & Newham Collieries) are now being worked, and the COAL, admitted to be the BEST NESH COAL in the Forest can be obtained at the following Ready Money Prices
> AT THE PITS 7s. 0d. per ton BEST BLOCK
> AT CHURCHWAY 7s. 6d. per ton BEST BLOCK
> October 19th 1859'

The new owners may have been the New Bowson Coal Co. who by 1871 were in receivership until bought by Messrs. Holden & Illingworth. In June 1872 the company approached the GWR Engineer's Office in Gloucester to find out what the cheapest mode of junction practicable for a locomotive would be. They claimed that when the company's works were complete, three or four lines would extend from a loading stage to the GWR. On the 17th the New Bowson Co. wrote again explaining that they had laid in a siding 'from the old points and crossings at the Churchway Siding of the Great Western Rly. up to the Wooden House but we find the locomotives cannot go round the curve. Mr. Owen, the GW Rly. Engineer, proposes for us to make a separate or additional branch according to the given radius for the Engine to travel round with the empty trucks. We have decided to do so.' From a study of the plan as supplied by the GWR and reproduced here, it can be seen that the direct tramroad connection has been restored. This may have been done in 1863 when a further Crown licence was granted in respect of East Slade. It would also appear that the point to the old Woodside Colliery siding had probably remained in situ and the New Bowson Co. were attempting to re-use it, hence the very tightly curved siding which locomotives were unable to traverse. The new sidings were to lie between two Crown enclosures and at their far end a screening and loading facility was provided. It was this which was known as the Wooden House. The full extent of the sidings can be seen on the 1878 25-inch Ordnance Survey; the gentler curve which was laid in taking a corner off one of the plantations was probably that used by locomotives to put empty wagons into the sidings whilst the tightly curved siding was probably used for the loaded wagons. Beyond the screens the sidings curved round to the east to form a shunting neck. The screens were connected to the colliery about three-quarters of a mile away by a tramway which at its southern end was on a different alignment to the line dating from the 1850s as detailed above. This new tramway was worked by an endless rope with a haulage engine situated at the pit-head.

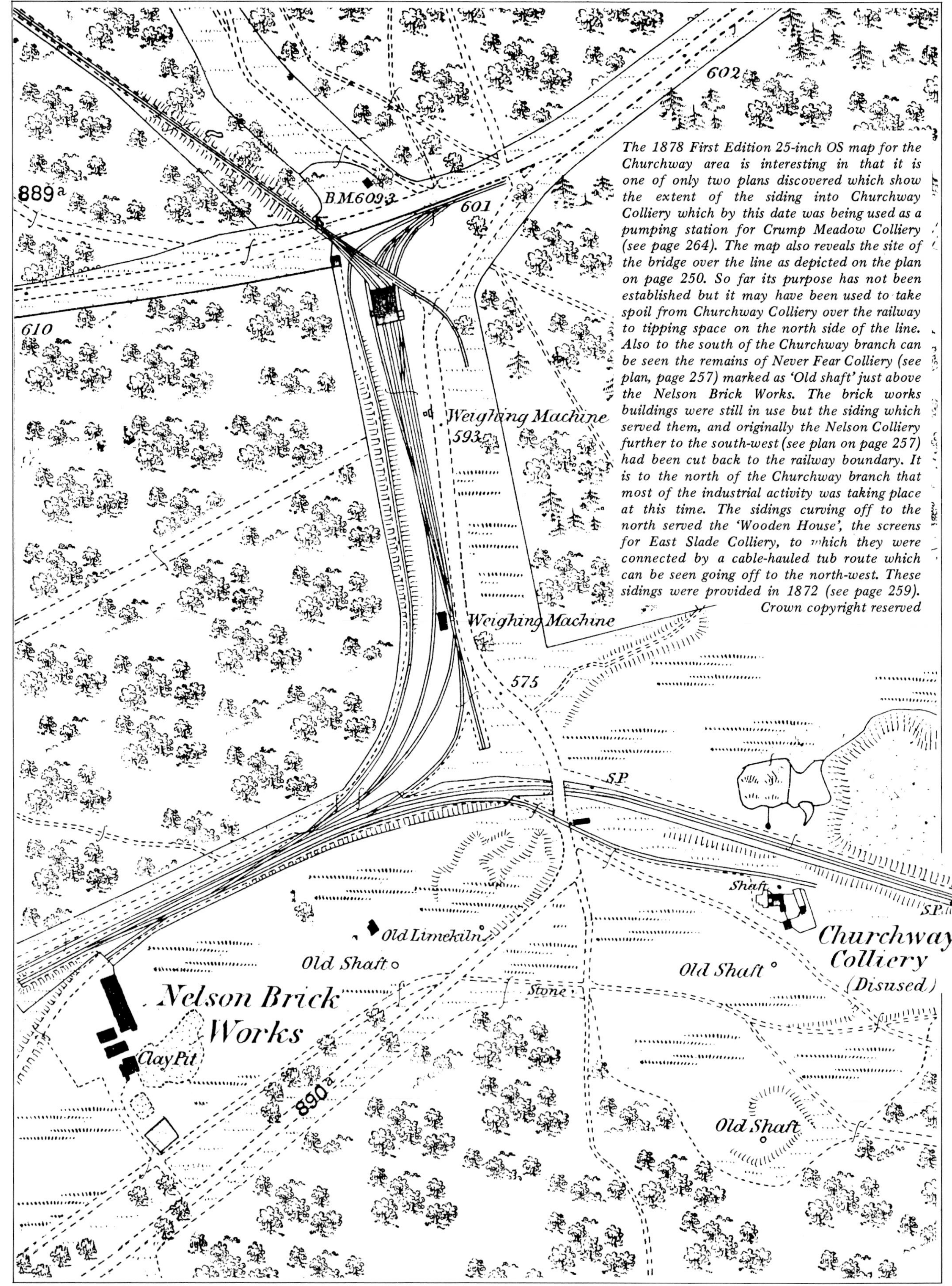

The 1878 First Edition 25-inch OS map for the Churchway area is interesting in that it is one of only two plans discovered which show the extent of the siding into Churchway Colliery which by this date was being used as a pumping station for Crump Meadow Colliery (see page 264). The map also reveals the site of the bridge over the line as depicted on the plan on page 250. So far its purpose has not been established but it may have been used to take spoil from Churchway Colliery over the railway to tipping space on the north side of the line. Also to the south of the Churchway branch can be seen the remains of Never Fear Colliery (see plan, page 257) marked as 'Old shaft' just above the Nelson Brick Works. The brick works buildings were still in use but the siding which served them, and originally the Nelson Colliery further to the south-west (see plan on page 257) had been cut back to the railway boundary. It is to the north of the Churchway branch that most of the industrial activity was taking place at this time. The sidings curving off to the north served the 'Wooden House', the screens for East Slade Colliery, to which they were connected by a cable-hauled tub route which can be seen going off to the north-west. These sidings were provided in 1872 (see page 259).

East Slade Colliery c.1900. The winding drums in front of the headframe let carts down the incline to the 'Wooden House' at Hawkwell. *Collection A. K. Pope*

By September the colliery was being worked under the management of William Burdess. At that time, in order to get sufficient water to the colliery, a water-wheel and small engine had been erected at Brierley, to the south-west of the colliery, to pump water up from the stream there. By October 1874 the company was also working the Brittania and Favourite gales in conjunction with East Slade as they had found that they could not make the latter gale pay. Coal from the other two gales was brought to the surface through the pits at East Slade.

The early 1880s saw several accidents at the colliery; on 2nd October 1880 the *Gloucester Journal* reported on a fatal boiler accident which had occurred:

> 'On Thursday, an accident occurred at the East Slade Colliery, Cinderford Valley, belonging to Mr. Illingworth MP and others. There are two boilers in the pit, one of which was under repair by R. Cooper of Cinderford, William Hurst, and Cornelius Mason. A pipe had been connected with the employed boiler and this burst, killing Cooper and severely injuring the other men.'

Four months later, on 18th February, the *Dean Forest Mercury* reported:

> 'Accident on Friday night. A serious accident befell a man named Arkell, engine driver at the East Slade Colliery whereby he sustained serious injuries, whilst attending to his duties. He stepped into a hole and fell, coming into contact with the fly-wheel which threw him against the wall, injuring his head and hip, and breaking two of his ribs. Dr. Fletcher of Lydbrook, was promptly in attendance, and under his care Arkell is, we believe, progressing favourably.'

A further incident occurred in February 1895 when on the first Wednesday in the month, 58 men and boys were imprisoned for 32 hours at the colliery, said to be in 'one of the most out-of-the-way places in the Forest'. On the morning in question the two cages in the down-cast shaft got jammed some considerable distance down the shaft. The intense cold began to freeze the dripping water in the shaft, and every minute the block became worse. When the 58 men working down the colliery came to the bottom of the shaft to be drawn up, they realised something was wrong and, being unable to communicate with the top, quickly retired to the engine room at the up-cast shaft hoping to find another way out. Unfortunately, as the furnaces were being used, there was no means of escape. As the cages could not be moved, the engine which hauled the tubs from the tips was requisitioned and after rigging up a small 'cowl', this was attached to a special rope and pulley and let down the up-cast shaft to draw the men up. This was a very slow process as only three persons at a time could be brought up and great care was needed. The New Bowson Colliery manager, Mr. J. Burdess, remained at his post until the work was accomplished at 3 o'clock on Thursday afternoon. Every man and boy was brought up without a scratch although they had gone without food for the 32 hours. When the matter had become known in the district, wives and relatives made for the pit and welcomed the men with open arms.

By April 1899 the East Slade and Woodside gales were nearly worked out and the surrender of them was considered.

With the East Slade gale proving unremunerative, a portion at the eastern end was sold in April 1902 to Messrs. A. C. Bright & Co. for them to work through New Bridge

Engine Colliery or Small Profit Colliery; then in May the closure of the colliery was announced and 150 men had their contracts terminated as from the 31st. Between 1872 and closure the colliery had produced some 497,199 tons, most of which undoubtedly travelled down the tramway to Churchway.

In October 1904 and June 1905 the Woodside and East Slade gales were surrendered respectively. The plant at the colliery was bought by the Lydney & Crump Meadow Collieries Co. Ltd. who also bought the East Dean Deep and Bowson gales from the New Bowson Co. (see page 246). Members of the Holden and Illingworth families had remained connected with the company to the end and some now joined the Board of the Lydney & Crump Meadow Co. It is uncertain whether the New Bowson Coal Co. continued trading, but in later years a company of that name operated as coal factors in the Forest and continued in existence until the late 1960s or early 70s under the ownership of the Burdess family who had been connected with the management of the colliery back in 1872.

When the sidings to the Wooden House were removed is unknown, but in 1908 a private siding agreement dated 18th February was taken out by A. Schofield who was working the Addis Hill Colliery.

ADDIS HILL COLLIERY

The gale was confirmed upon James Cowmeadow, a Free Miner from Cinderford, by the 1841 Awards although he had been working it before it had been granted to him. Although there would appear to have been no production between 1841 and 45, an output figure for 1846 is listed against James Cowmeadow of 2,074 tons. The history of the gale before 1873 is not recorded but as James Cowmeadow had died by April 1848, it can be assumed that there was a change in the registered owner. The gale probably passed into the hands of his widow, Elizabeth, as with another of his gales, Cinderford Bridge Pit.

The date at which Elizabeth Cowmeadow disposed of the gale is unknown, but after 1873 it formed part of the Haywood Colliery being worked by the Littledean Woodside Coal Co. (see page 306). In 1885 the Haywood Colliery Co. Ltd. took over following the liquidation of the Littledean Woodside Co. in 1882.

The coal from Addis Hill was being worked through the upper part of Richard White's gale which was leased from Edward Foxall, and was brought to the surface through Haywood Pit.

Work appears to have stopped by 1893 when it was reported that Addis Hill was liable for forfeiture. In April 1890 the colliery was sold to Richard Hadingham for the sum of £200. The gale was said to contain a large area of unworked coal and when it was put up for auction again in March 1900 the registered owners were given as Richard Hadingham and Fred Morgan.

The purchaser appears to have been Albert Schofield who in 1906 wanted to drive a roadway to Inkerman Pit, which was part of Prosper Colliery, in order to provide a second outlet. In July 1907 he was applying for a licence to maintain a short length of siding at Churchway which had previously been used by the New Bowson Co. Schofield appears to have been working Addis Hill from the Haywood Level although he had rigged up winding gear over a shaft which had formerly been used as a ventilation shaft on the Fairplay Iron Mine drainage adit. *Potts Mining Register* for 1908 records that Schofield was employing twenty-two below ground and four on the surface.

It would seem that Schofield had ceased work around 1910 and sold the gale in 1915. In February 1917 the *Dean Forest Mercury* reported that John H. Walby, the proprietor of Addis Hill Colliery, had been fined for failing to provide two exits and also for not employing a competent person

over the age of twenty-two to work the winding machinery. The report said that he had worked the mine for two years and that it had been idle for about five years before this.

In December 1920 the private siding agreement referring to the siding at Churchway was transferred to the Addis Hill Colliery Co. whose proprietor was Walby.

In 1931 Mr. Ivo Baldwin, a coal factor of Ruardean, began working the gale but discontinued work in May 1935 and the gale reverted to the Crown. Addis Hill was working the eastern crop of the Coleford High Delf, which at this point was between 1ft 6in and 6ft 6in thick, from the No. 4 airshaft on the Fairplay Level (890 yards long) and the Brazilly seam from the No. 1 airshaft.

Baldwin may also have been using the siding at Churchway as the agreement was not terminated until 1935 when the sidings for Northern United Colliery were built over the site.

The siding was also used by the Crown for loading timber and other produce, for which permission was given in May 1921. The 25-inch Ordnance Survey of 1921 shows the area to the east of the siding as a timber yard (see page 264). A handwritten note in the Bilson Junction journal referred to on page 221 states the connection to New Bowson siding was taken up in September 1931.

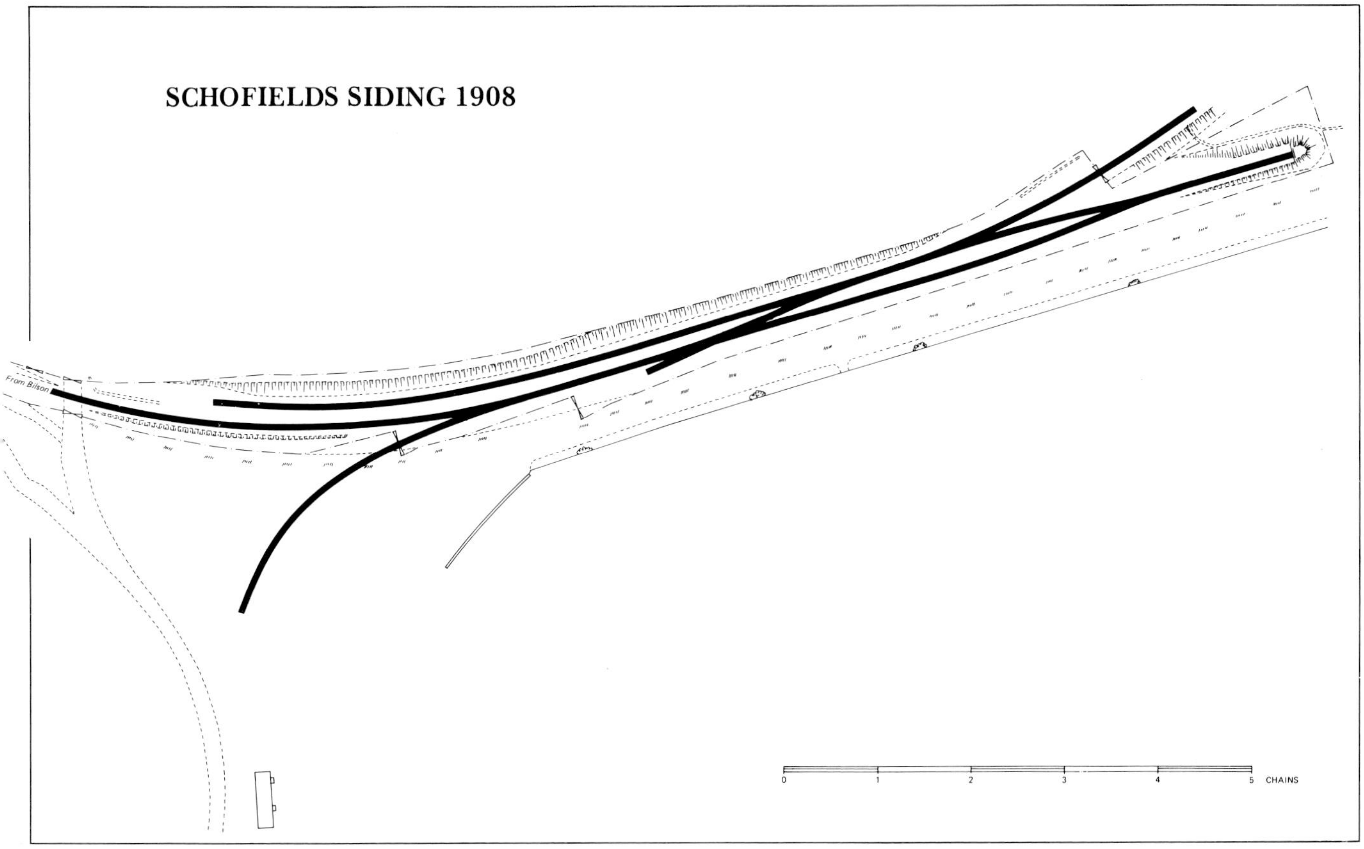

SCHOFIELDS SIDING 1908

From Bilson

0 1 2 3 4 5 CHAINS

A view taken in September 1931 of the proposed site for Northern United Colliery. It shows the site of the East Slade Colliery sidings, the 'wooden house', and, on the left below the trees, the embankment on which the tramway from the colliery ran. The overgrown 'Schofields Siding' can be seen in the foreground. *Collection Marjory Oakey*

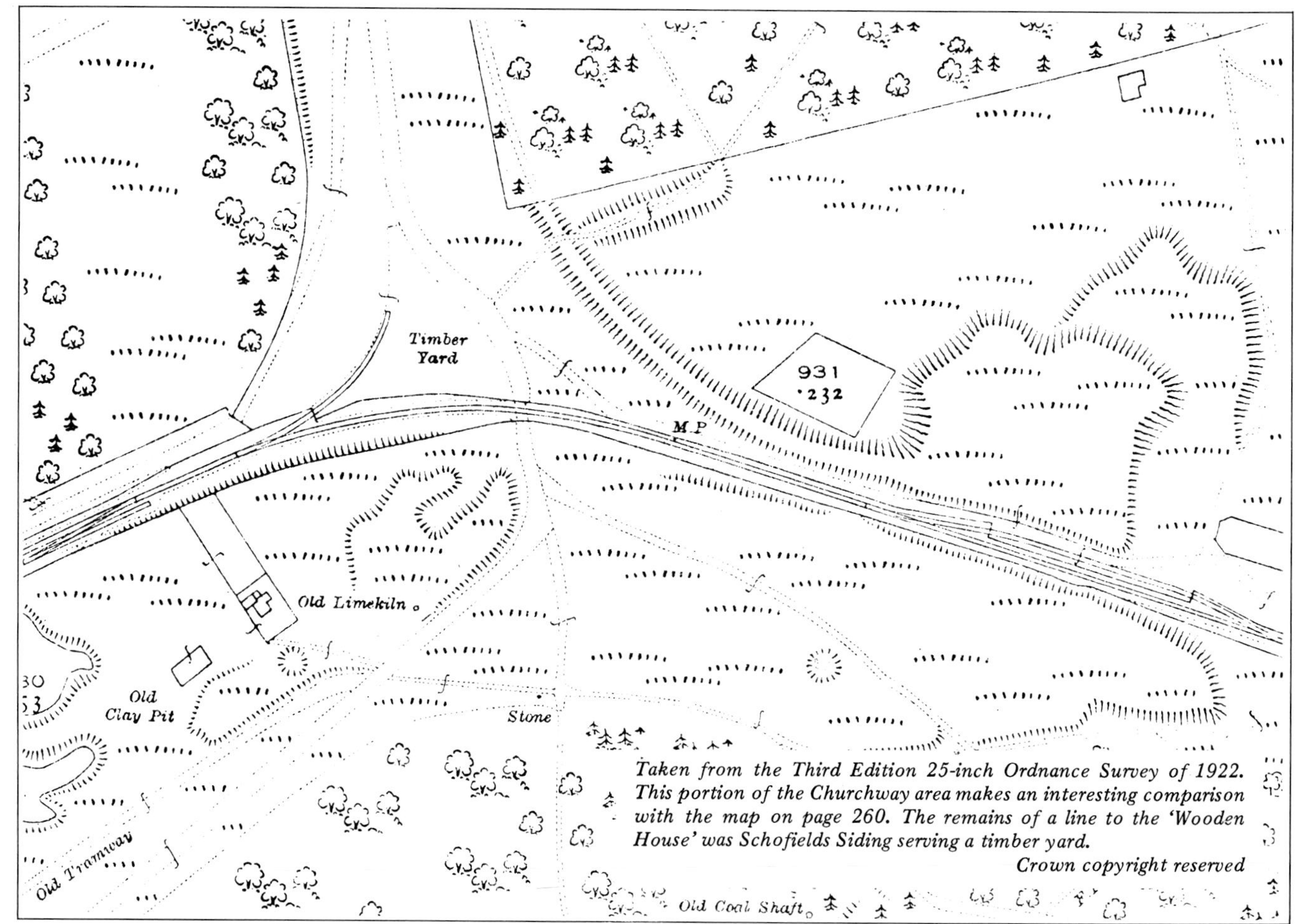

Taken from the Third Edition 25-inch Ordnance Survey of 1922. This portion of the Churchway area makes an interesting comparison with the map on page 260. The remains of a line to the 'Wooden House' was Schofields Siding serving a timber yard.

Crown copyright reserved

CHURCHWAY COLLIERY

Churchway Colliery was begun in 1740 and c.1833 was being worked by Messrs. Bennett and partners under the title of the Churchway Company. It was described at that time as being drained by a steam engine to the Churchway High Delf vein which was met at a depth of 112 yards where 4½ feet of coal was encountered. The Rocky seam was also worked with a thickness of 2 feet. The coal produced was said to be sent on the railway to Bishop's Wood, i.e. via the Severn & Wye tramroad to the wharves on the River Wye, to be sold locally. No mention is made of coal being sent down the Bullo Pill tramroad.

In 1841 the gale was confirmed in the possession of Thomas and James Bennett who held thirteen-twentieths; Thomas Gardiner held an equal share in three-twentieths with John and Letitia Bennett; William Dew, as assignee of John Court held two-twentieths; Giles Griffiths and Thomas Court held one-twentieth each. Soon afterwards Thomas and James Bennett bought out the other shares to become sole owners. The colliery also included the Nofold Land and Deep Pits and the Protection gales further to the east on Nofold Green. In 1841, 2,299 tons were won and the output continued to climb until in 1845 the total was 12,756 tons; the following year, however, saw a slump back to 7,878 tons.

Like other coalfields in the country, young children were employed in the collieries although in the Forest they were more confined to the surface. At Churchway in January 1850 a ten-year-old boy, employed to feed the boiler for the winding engine, lost his life when he became entangled in the engine's flywheel.

A siding was not provided at the colliery upon the opening of the broad gauge and the 1856 plan shows tramroad connections both to the general siding at Churchway and to the siding of the Nelson Colliery also owned by the Bennetts. Coal could therefore have been loaded at either point onto the railway. Churchway Colliery was another of those which ceased production soon after the coming of the railway and certainly prior to 1869.

A siding was laid directly to the colliery at some time between 1856 and 1872 but it may only have been provided to bring coal in to the pumping engine which remained in use after the colliery closed. Both the Churchway and the Nelson gales passed into the hands of the Bilson & Crump Meadow Collieries Co. Ltd. who used them as pumping stations to keep their main collieries free of water. Churchway was kept until 1896 when, in August, it was reported that the engine and boilers were being removed, the pumping engine being a 40 inch cylinder Cornish beam pump with a 7ft stroke working at 8 strokes per minute and lifting 392 gallons in that period. In October they wanted to remove the chimney stack and turn the engine house into rooms, but it is not known whether the later proposal was carried out. The siding appears to have remained in position (although cut back to within the railway boundary by 1908) until at least 1921.

NELSON COLLIERY

Just when the Nelson gale was first granted is not clear but in 1825 James Bennett and Thomas Meek were granted a Crown licence to erect a steam engine. It would appear that little was done as in March 1841 it was reported that the colliery was in the process of sinking and that the shaft was down to a depth of 56 yards. The only name given in connection with the colliery at this time was James Bennett, although it is likely that he was the working partner as the 1841 Awards give the gale to Thomas Bennett and James Bennett, with Thomas having the larger eleven-twentieths share. Soon afterwards, however, Thomas Bennett became the sole owner.

Some coal was being produced in the process of sinking and during 1841 a total of 1,290 tons were brought to the surface. Between 1842 and 1846 the annual output figures were 1,819 tons, 2,568 tons, 2750 tons, 6388 tons and 5,418 tons respectively.

In 1846 Crown licences were granted for tramroad connections to both the Forest of Dean Railway and to the Severn & Wye. In 1856 a licence was granted for a quarter-mile long broad gauge siding to the colliery and the output for the same year was 24,539 tons, the fifth highest in the Forest. An account of working the Forest of Dean branch in 1857 records that three empty trucks were taken daily to the colliery and three loadeds were taken away.

It is not known when the colliery closed; it may have been in 1865, although a *Gloucester Journal* report of 14th August 1869 states that a workman had been killed at the Nelson Colliery while engaged in greasing some trucks which were ready to be dispatched and to which an engine was attached. Apparently he continued greasing the wagons even after the engine was in motion whereupon he was knocked down and fatally injured. A local directory for 1876 lists 'John Brain, Nelson Colliery', so it is possible that some work was being carried out, although Brain was also connected with the Nelson Green brickworks as detailed below.

By January 1881 the gale was in the hands of the Bilson & Crump Meadow Collieries Co. Ltd. who stated that it was of practically no value except as a pumping station. They and their successors, the Lydney & Crump Meadow Collieries Co. Ltd., held the gale to protect their Crump Meadow Colliery until its closure in 1929, at which time the Nelson gale was surrendered.

NELSON GREEN BRICKWORKS

The brickworks on Nelson Green were set up by Messrs. Meek & Brain at some time after the closure of the Nelson Colliery. The 1878 25-inch Ordnance Survey shows the layout of the buildings and the adjacent clay pit. By this date the siding to Nelson Colliery had been cut back beyond the railway boundary fence, so if any traffic was generated by the brickworks it was probably loaded on the short stub remaining.

In April 1882 John Brain was trying to sell the brickworks which were to be 'sold very cheap by Private Contract'. The works were described as situated at 'Churchway Junction' and being sold with all the tools for making bricks, draining pipes, tiles. They were in good condition and ready to be started at once, and the clay was abundant and of the best quality.

Whether the works were sold is unclear, but in May 1898 J. H. Mobberley wrote to the Crown in connection with re-opening works once held by Messrs. Meek & Brain. The works were refurbished and by 1900 S. Mobberley was brick-making at Nelson Green. The establishment of the brickworks at Hawkwell (page 251) hit Mobberley's trade and in March 1910 it was said that the Cinderford Brick & Coal Co. lease made it impossible for him to continue as their works were closer to any sales. Work must have stopped soon afterwards as in May 1912 the site of the works was marked by a broken-down kiln and shed.

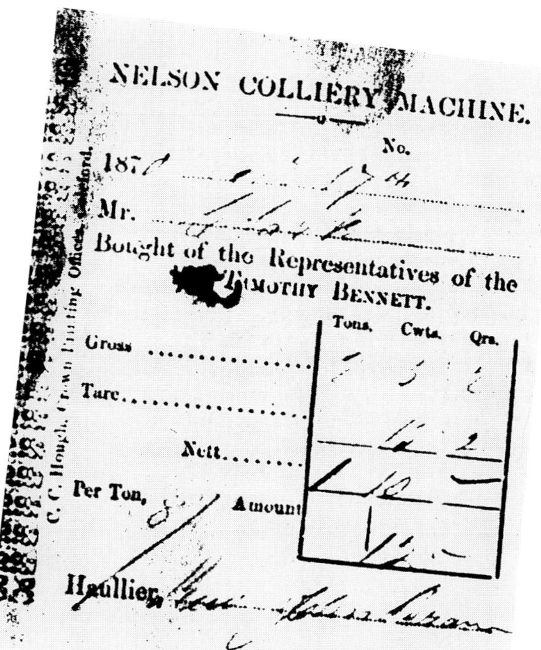
NELSON COLLIERY MACHINE.
No.
187
Mr.
Bought of the Representatives of the
TIMOTHY BENNETT.

	Tons.	Cwts.	Qrs.
Gross			
Tare			
Nett			

Per Ton, Amount

Haullier

C. C. Hough, Crown Printing Offices, ...ford.

A haulier's ticket dated 1870 for coal bought from the Nelson Colliery.
Collection A. K. Pope

MEADOW CLIFF COLLIERY

Roberts Folly gale was first granted on 7th February 1843 to Henry Roberts of the Morse to get the coal from the Twenty Inch seam. Later it was said that any coal of worth in the area had already been awarded to an adjoining gale, probably Nelson, but Roberts still applied for the area which, it would appear, had already been well worked over. The Deputy Gaveller considered it folly on the part of Roberts to take the grant, so it seems likely that the name of the gale stemmed from this! The Deputy Gaveller was probably correct as the gale was surrendered in August 1848. It was re-granted afterwards and by midsummer 1861 arrears of rent stood against Thomas and Cornelius Brain. The gale was still held by the Brain family when in August 1882 it was forfeited back to the Crown for non-working.

The gale was then re-granted as New Roberts Folly in April 1889 to Richard Hale, who immediately conveyed it to William Wilce who, in July 1890 were applying to the Crown for permission to load coal on the Nelson siding in connection with the Roberts Folly gale. They were also working one or two other pits in the area and in February 1891 it was said that they had made arrangements with the GWR for loading coal at another point.

In October 1893 Wilce conveyed the gale to A. C. Bright of the Hawkwell tinplate works and in March 1899 it was once again surrendered by A. C. Bright & Co. Ltd following the collapse of the company.

In February 1904 Timothy Trigg of Newent applied for a re-grant but nothing was done until in September 1907 the gale was granted to a committee of Free Miners. They only held it for two years, or until the dead rent was liable to be paid, and then surrendered it in September 1909, despite the fact that Trigg had offered to work the colliery for them on a royalty basis. The gale was granted again to a committee of Free Miners in September 1910 and in January 1913 it was conveyed from Milson Hamblin to Geoffrey Terry who in July 1915 conveyed it to Moses Howard Teague Cowmeadow.

In August 1915 the Meadow Cliff Colliery Co. Ltd. was incorporated with a capital of £1,000 in 1,000 shares of £1 as a private company. There were two nominee subscribers and the company entered into an agreement with the vendors, Cowmeadow and a Gilbert Ractliffe. Cowmeadow was described as an engineer and Ractliffe as a commercial traveller. They were paid the purchase price of £600 in shares, 350 to Cowmeadow and 250 to Ractliffe, and the two of them, plus James Hooper, a mining engineer from Lydney, became the first directors. Cowmeadow and Ractliffe soon disposed of their interests and in March 1917 were replaced as directors by James Stone, a coal factor, and Arthur Sharp, both of Bournemouth.

At some stage a siding was provided which utilised the old Nelson Colliery connection, coming directly off the end of the siding at the railway boundary. At this point, however, the new siding took a different formation, swinging further round to the south to a loop siding and loading shoot (see map on page 268). The siding was certainly in position by 1921 and may have been there since 1915. In September of that year the company purchased six 12-ton secondhand wagons on seven years deferred purchase from the Gloucester Railway Carriage & Wagon Co. Ltd.

The main headframe at Meadow Cliff being erected by members of the Marfell family who put up many such structures in the Forest. *Cty. Daphne Booth*

In April 1917 the company sought permission to drive a roadway into the Nelson gale in the hope of finding workable coal and to this end the Lydney & Crump Meadow Collieries Co. were prepared to sublet a portion of the Twenty Inch seam in the Nelson gale.

In July 1918 Frederick and Charles Baker, both coal merchants of Southampton, were appointed directors and probably brought with their board-room positions an influx of much-needed capital. In May 1919 the authorised capital of the company was increased by £1,000 but by 1922 the company and the colliery were getting further and further into trouble.

Between them, Godfrey Meek of Lydney and Lloyds Bank held mortgages of £1,300 on the property and in November 1922, following a meeting of unsecured creditors, Meek was appointed managing director. The directors believed that the company could earn £600 per year but stated that they had been seriously affected by the 1921 coal strike. It was said that the directors had from time to time advanced personal money to the amount of £4,908 to keep the concern going. It was probably hoped that the appointment of Meek, who had previously handled all of the colliery's output in his capacity as a coal factor, would turn the company's fortunes around.

An inventory of March 1922 provides some idea of the set-up at Meadow Cliff. The buildings consisted of a wood and corrugated iron office, an examiner's office, a corrugated iron power house, an engine house and boiler shed, a haulage engine house, two weighbridge offices, a magazine and a woodman's shed. The plant included a pair of vertical winding engines, a pair of horizontal haulage engines, two Cornish boilers, a dynamo, one headframe, one small headframe, 220 yards of siding, two points and six railway wagons.

By February 1923 the colliery had reached an output of 120 tons per week but in June all movable plant and buildings were seized by H.M. Collector of Taxes. In July it was reported that the company had recently been sued by about twenty of their workmen for wages due. The following month the colliery was closed due to lack of funds. In November it was said that land sales of coal had amounted to 222 tons whilst 1,480 tons had been dispatched over the siding, although railway returns gave the latter figure as 1,681 tons. These totals probably refer to the preceding year's output. The plant was now sold off and in July 1924 the siding, for which no agreement appears to have been taken out with the Crown, was sold to Captain Pringle of the Wigpool Coal & Iron Co. Ltd. for the sum of £60 to be re-used at Harrow Hill Colliery (page 355). In March 1925 the remaining plant was sold for the sum of £30 which offset some of the money still owing to the Crown. After this date there were no further returns and the company was dissolved in January 1927.

The gale, having been forfeited in 1924, was available for re-grant and, despite its past history, a committee of Free Miners took it in May 1927. They sold it to Messrs. Dennis & Leslie Morgan who in turn conveyed it to Ernest Tremain of Tetbury, Gloucestershire, in April 1928. By July he was busy opening a new slope to give the colliery a second exit, but unfortunately he had done this without seeking Crown permission. In October 1930 the Crown were trying to assist Tremain by granting him the Twenty Inch seam in the surrendered Nelson gale. He had already lost £2,000 in purchasing and trying to work a practically exhausted gale, and it is unlikely that Tremain remained working the colliery for long.

In 1936 Mr. Tremain leased the four gales he held to a Mr. H. Grindle who was working the Nelson gale.

Development work at the colliery, with a Cornish boiler being installed prior to the 'engine house and boiler shed' being erected over it. Note the 'small headframe' and metal chimney in the background. *Cty. Daphne Booth*

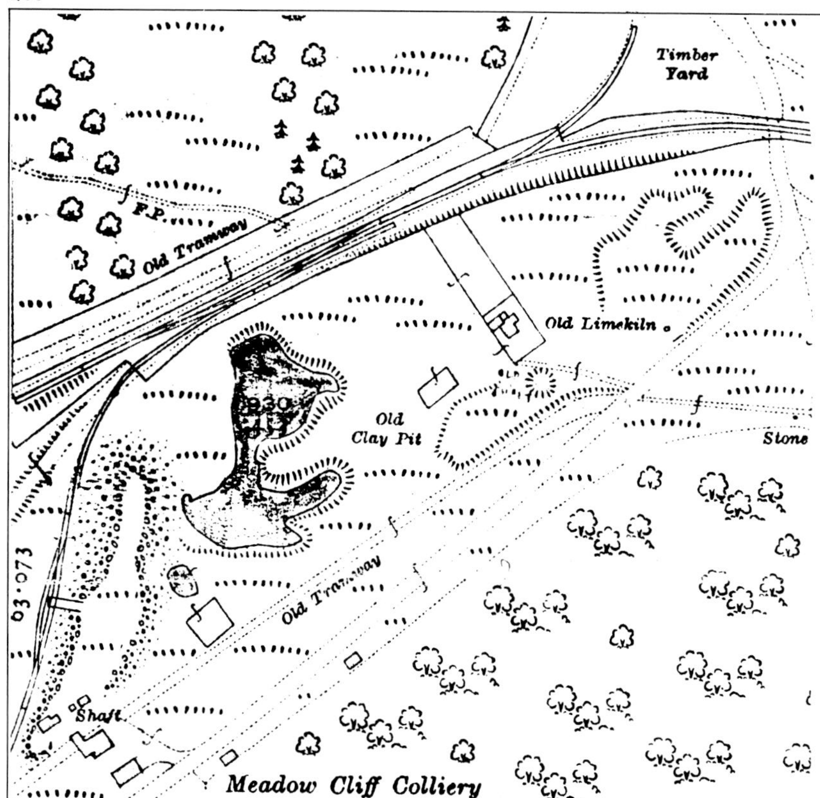

Another portion of the 1922 25-inch Ordnance Survey, slightly further to the west of that on page 264, revealing the site of Meadow Cliff Colliery and its siding. The pointwork and ground frame had previously served Nelson Colliery (see map on page 260), the abandoned formation of which is shown on the previous alignment to the west of the gate. *Crown copyright reserved*

The weighing machine being installed on the siding. It would appear that the building was secondhand, possibly the whole machine being acquired from elsewhere. The end of the Churchway branch can just be discerned in the background beyond the fence, with a 'throw-over' point lever just visible to the right of the figure standing on the pile of weights. *Cty. Daphne Booth*

The men from Meadow Cliff Colliery on the occasion of a presentation to the manager, Mr. Marfell, who features in the middle with his gift of a clock. *Cty. Daphne Booth*

A 'Heath Robinson' type pump at Meadow Cliff with the buildings behind now virtually complete. *Cty. Daphne Booth*

A more distant view of the site for Northern United than that on page 263, photographed in 1931 prior to development. The rough area of grass in the centre of the view marks the site of the sidings put in in 1872 for the East Slade Colliery. The screens building here, known as the Wooden House, was connected to the colliery by a rope-worked tramway, the route of which is apparent on an embankment in the field in the background. The embankment which carried the Hawkwell Colliery railway can be seen curving around on the extreme right along the edge of the trees.

Courtesy Marjory Oakey

NORTHERN UNITED COLLIERY

The Northern United, or No. 2 Area, gale was formed of the New Bowson, East Dean Deep, Holly Hill United and Richard Whites gales and was the last of the gales formed under the 1904 Dean Forest (Mines) Act to be developed. As already seen at New Bowson (page 242), the early attempts to work the deep measures were beset with problems and it was not until the gale passed into the hands of Henry Crawshay & Co. Ltd. from the Lydney & Crump Meadow Co. Ltd. that work began in earnest.

The idea of acquiring the Northern United gale was first raised in April 1930 when Arthur Morgan, Crawshay's Managing Director, pointed out to his Board that the Free Miners were disheartened and had little prospect of enjoying royalties from the working of the gale by the Lydney & Crump Meadow Co. It would appear that first news of the possible availability of the gale had come via William Meredith, Crawshay's manager at Lightmoor Colliery, who had been having discussions with Mr. J. J. Joynes, the manager at Cannop Colliery. Morgan ensured the possibility of its acquisition was recorded in the minutes. Meredith and Joynes thought that the best option would be for their respective companies to acquire the area jointly. This was particularly attractive to Meredith because if Cannop were to work the coal in the Northern United gale adjoining their existing area, they would also be burdened with all the water, thus allowing Crawshays to work the coal in their portion virtually free of water and pumping costs.

The following month, when a more detailed report was made to the Board by Meredith, the desirability of working jointly with Cannop was spelt out. As already seen at Eastern United (see page 133), a lot of coal in that gale would be lost if the coal in Northern was not worked, and drained, by Cannop. Meredith also reported that the Free Miners had given the Crump Meadow Co. three months in which to decide what to do, after which time they would force the forfeiture of the gale. He was firmly of the opinion that the best way of working the Northern United area would be by paying Crump Meadow a royalty on all coal raised to avoid the risk of paying for coal which did not exist or which was unworkable. Charles Hale of the Crump Meadow Co. had intimated that his company would be looking to sell the property for £67,000 but Crawshays felt that the most it would fetch was £25,000. Montague Maclean, for the Cannop Coal Co., would not entertain paying any lump sum for an area of Northern and was not prepared to go beyond 3d per ton on a royalty payment. Charles Hale regarded this as a ridiculous offer, so there the matter stood for several months with neither side prepared to move.

In August 1930 Crump Meadow offered Crawshays about 210 acres of the gale at £50 per acre, but this was rejected in favour of continued support for Cannop in only working the coal on a royalty basis. However, the real concern was still getting Cannop to work a portion of the gale and take all the water which would also enable Crawshays to work a valuable portion of the Eastern United. The deadline set by the Free Miners was to expire on the 22nd, Meredith, as their representative, claiming that if the gale returned to their hands, he would be happy to let Crawshays have the gale for £5,000. In September Crawshays suggested that they could work the area on a fifty-fifty basis with the Crump Meadow Co., whilst Arthur Morgan, unofficially, mentioned to Charles Hale that they might consider an outright purchase. It was hoped this might set something moving, especially as Northern United was the finest area of steam coal in the Forest. Eastern United had only another ten or twelve years left, so the Board might have been open to criticism from shareholders if a move were not made towards acquiring it, and if a third party stepped in to work Northern and later gave up, the water build-up could cause havoc at Eastern United.

In March 1931 it was reported that the Crump Meadow Co. were prepared to find about £20,000 for the development at Northern if someone else could be found to go in with them. As the amount concerned would only allow development to start in a small way, this did not find favour with the Deputy Gaveller. On 23rd July 1931 a meeting took place between the Boards of Henry Crawshay & Co. Ltd. and the Lydney & Crump Meadow Collieries Co. Ltd. at Lightmoor Colliery, when the final negotiations between the two parties took place. The Crump Meadow Co. asked £27,500 for the property and, whereas Crawshays were initially only prepared to offer £25,000, they subsequently offered £26,000 conditional on Cannop acquiring a portion of the area. Crump Meadow held out for more but suggested that if Crawshays raised their offer by £1,000 they would come down £500 and meet at £27,000, which they considered 'a great bargain', especially as a portion could be sold to the Cannop Coal Co. for £8,500. The plant already installed at the Bowson Pit was also included in the price (see page 246). The Crawshay Board accepted the price on condition that they be given an option for one month, during which time they would see what arrangement could be arrived at with Cannop. The option expired on 22nd August 1931.

On 26th August the draft contract for the purchase of the gale was signed and a 10% deposit paid. It was reported that Arthur Morgan had already had meetings with the Deputy Gaveller, Mr. Forster Brown; representatives of the Great Western Railway; the West Gloucestershire Power Co.; the Cannop Coal Co., and others. As a result of all this, Forster Brown had agreed to recommend to the Forestry Commission that the usual wayleave of a halfpenny per ton should be waived, which alone would save £8-10,000. The meeting with GWR officials had been cordial and he believed that there was every prospect of favourable treatment. The West Gloucestershire Power Co. offered special terms for the supply of current and Mr. Maclean of Cannop stated that his company intended to carry on working through the fault, and if they found the coal was satisfactory, they would be only too pleased to enter into negotiations for the acquisition of 300 acres of Northern United. Mr. Meredith had been asked to prepare plans and estimates for the complete layout of the colliery and was urging the immediate appointment of a manager on the site. It was decided that the colliery would be all electric and that some good secondhand equipment could probably be obtained from collieries that had closed and were being dismantled.

The gale contained about 1,698 acres, which it was estimated would yield some 10 million tons of coal. As some £60-70,000 would be needed for its development, it was decided that Arthur Morgan should enquire about an overdraft at the bank.

In October 1931 the plans produced by the GWR for the sidings at Northern were discussed. Although it seems to have been a firm rule of the GWR not to defray the cost of work done on any ground bar their own, they made an exception in the case of Northern, and the estimated cost of the sidings on Crown land, which amounted to £2,275 and £500 for work on railway land, was instead to be levied on traffic charges. The work to be done by Crawshays towards the sidings amounted to about £4,975, although if secondhand materials were used, the outlay was estimated at nearer £2,000.

Development work on the site of Northern commenced with the acquisition from the Crown of land on which to sink a new shaft. It had been decided not to use the old Bowson shaft, which was not in a particularly good condition, and to sink further west, thus avoiding the heavily watered area Bowson encountered. Initially, the Crown were loath to sell the desired plot as it was in enclosed land with trees growing upon it, but in November they were willing to sell if Crawshays would purchase the trees as well as the land. The Crown initially asked £50 for the trees, but Crawshays only offered £15. Subsequently the Crown came down to £25, and Crawshays increased to £20, but there the two sides stuck! An area of waste land required for a manager's house was also in dispute, the Crown asking 30/- a perch when land in the middle of Cinderford was selling for half that! The matter was finally settled in December with £30 being paid for the trees and 20/- a perch for the building site.

As well as sinking a new shaft, the old Hawkwell Colliery shafts were to be opened up to serve as a second way out and for ventilation purposes. Work on this had commenced by November 1931 under the direction of Mr. Joseph Morrison who had been appointed manager of Northern United. Prior to taking up this appointment, he had been manager at Foxes Bridge Colliery which had closed down the previous year. The Foxes Bridge Colliery Co. Ltd. was closely connected with Crawshays and thus it is no surprise that Morrison should have moved into the new position. A new headframe was erected and ready by the end of November, and in December Morrison, together with the electrician Mr. Hawden, visited the works of Messrs. Powell, Dyffryn & Co. in South Wales to look at an electric winder for Hawkwell. This was purchased very cheaply and

With Crawshays agreeing to purchase the Northern United gale in July 1931, work was soon able to commence at the old Hawkwell Colliery site. Once the old shafts were de-watered and cleared of mud, they were to be used as a second way out for Northern and for ventilation. In November 1931 the manager at Northern, Mr. Joseph Morrison, said that he hoped to complete the erection of the Hawkwell headgear by the end of the month. The headframes were built of pitch pine, imported through Lydney docks, and were erected by Jim Fox and Frank Niblet for the sum of £12. By comparison with the view on page 249 it can be seen that the Cornish engine house had been cut down and altered to act as a winding engine house. The headframe in front stood over the 8ft diameter shaft which formed the second way out. The top of the shaft was fitted with a heavy wooden lid which sealed the shaft so as not to interfere with the underground ventilation arrangements. The less substantial headframe beyond stood over a 6ft diameter shaft which was used as the 'upcast' shaft for the expulsion of all the stale air from the pit. The shaft was fitted with a 91 inch diameter Sirocco double inlet fan which drew air through the workings. The fan was first used in June 1937 when it was put to work slowly. The building on the right housed a weighbridge. *Cty. Marjory Oakey*

A view from the Mitcheldean–Monmouth road, looking over the new developments at Hawkwell. The brick buildings on the left were connected with the fan and ventilation arrangements. Large doors were fitted in the fan house tunnel which could be closed to enable the flow of air to be reversed if a major fire should occur underground. *Courtesy Marjory Oakey*

installed in the old pumping engine house which was altered to suit. It was hoped that the engine would be working early in March 1932. In April it was reported that work had begun on de-watering the shaft, which was 452 feet deep and 8 feet in diameter. Below the water the shaft was full of mud which also had to be removed, and mud was also present in the second 6 feet diameter shaft which was to be used for ventilation. The larger was to be the second way out.

The sinking operation on the main site at Northern was contracted out by the Francois Cementation Co. of Darlington, one of the largest firms of its kind in the country with an excellent reputation. The contract for the supply of electricity was signed with the West Gloucestershire Power Co. in November 1931, and in January 1932 a deal was concluded with the Metropolitan Vickers Co. for the supply of the main electric winder including transformers, engines and switchgear for the price of £2,200, which was £500 below their original quote. The bargaining was considerably aided by the influence of Sir Felix Pole who had become a good friend of Arthur Morgan. At the same time the contract for the concrete foundations, beds, pillars and bridge from the pit to the engine house, was let to Messrs. Hoboroughs of Gloucester for £1,800, again well below the original quote, thanks to the negotiating powers of Arthur Morgan. The concrete work was completed on 21st April 1932, but somewhere along the line a major error resulted in the surface works being laid out incorrectly. The whole arrangement was 90 degrees out, which was to cause problems later on in opening out the coal seam as the cages hung the wrong way round in the shaft. It is said that a gypsy had pointed out to Morrison that the whole thing was the wrong way round while the headframe was being erected.

At the same time as the concrete work was completed, work on de-watering the Hawkwell shaft was progressing. The method being used was cowling, and they had got to within four feet of the mud in the shaft when they had stuck. Sir Felix Pole stepped in to expedite the delivery of a new motor, which was required to power a recently obtained pump to help out with the water, and he used his influence again when a second pump was ordered from Messrs. Drysdale & Co. for the sum of £325, Sir Felix getting the cost of the electrical portion considerably reduced.

In mid-April 1933, when it was hoped that the work on sinking the Northern United shaft could soon begin, it was thought that some form of ceremony should mark the occasion. It was agreed that Miss Lisa Crawshay be asked to cut the first sod, after which a cold lunch would be served in the recently completed fitting shop. Mr. Arthur Morgan produced a list of about thirty guests and estimated that the whole affair could be carried out for under £50. On Thursday, 25th May 1933, therefore, about fifty eminent persons gathered at Northern to witness the cutting of the first sod by Miss Lisa F. Crawshay, after which the party adjourned to the fitting shop where a cold luncheon had been prepared by the proprietors of the Speech House Hotel.

It was anticipated that it would take six or seven months to sink the shaft over 200 yards and that to line it would take about 500,000 bricks. After the completion of the shaft, it was estimated that it would take another two to three years to open out pit-bottom and the main roadways underground before full production could begin.

The substantial concrete winding engine house, built by Messrs. Hoborough of Gloucester, was almost complete, together with other buildings around the colliery yard which were executed in red brick, but Hoboroughs declined the £1,000 contract for the offices which were subsequently built by Crawshays' own men.

The steel headframe was brought from the old Bowson shaft, having been put there by the Lydney & Crump Meadow Co., and a large electrical transformer had been installed nearby by the West Gloucestershire Power Co. to provide the electrical power which was to be used throughout the pit. A deep cutting had also been made to provide a convenient route for the loaded wagon road out of the screens. The *Dean Forest Mercury* reported on the scene as follows:

> 'The spot has a typical Forest setting, and on a warm mid-May morning, the surrounding woodlands were beautiful in their fresh spring-time garb. The grey of the huge concrete building, and the bright red brick of other erections, and, it may be said, the not unpicturesque character of the big transformer and other electrical apparatus for the uses of electric light and power, in no way spoils the general view.'

In August the shaft sinkers had gone down 25 yards, or one-eighth full depth, and the building of the permanent wall round the shaft had commenced. No problems had been encountered with the sinking passing through blue limestone shale. By the end of December, a depth of 160 yards had been reached, and in January 1934 consideration was being given as to how to open out the seam on the completion of the sinking. There were three alternatives, either to drive out from above the seam, from below it, or in the coal. The best course for opening out a new colliery was to sink below the coal and drive out, but as this was much more expensive, it was decided to drive out in the coal, although the shaft still had to be carried on down below the coal to form a sump and water hold. On Friday, 9th February 1934, it was reported in the local press that coal had been struck in the shaft, at a depth of 230 yards, during the previous evening, and by breakfast time the next morning coal was being brought to the surface.

Fortunately there were no fatalities during the sinking operation. At this time over 100 men were employed at Northern with preference having been given to men displaced from Lightmoor Colliery.

On reaching pit bottom at Hawkwell and exploring the underground roadways, it was found that they could not be used for the whole distance towards the new shaft, and so a new heading was driven. The Hawkwell shaft to be used as the emergency way out was covered by a lid made of 2-inch

The formal view of the guests at the ceremony of cutting the first sod in the sinking operations on Thursday, 25th May 1933. The ceremony was performed by Miss Lisa F. Crawshay using a silver spade, after which the party adjourned for a cold lunch served in the machine shop. Among the notables invited to the ceremony were several local politicians, Forestry Commission officials, officers of the GWR, and the owners of a number of coal factoring businesses. Included in the latter group were Mr. V. E. S. Burdess of the New Bowson Coal Co., Mr. Lowell Baldwin of Baldwins of Bristol, Mr. H. S. Morgan of the Dean Forest Coal Co., and Mr. J. Sully of Messrs. Sully & Co.

Cty. Marjory Oakey

The boiler used to raise steam for the shaft sinking plant can be seen in this view beside the winding engine house. *Cty. Marjory Oakey*

thick boards which lifted when the cage, which normally hung in the shaft, was raised. The second shaft was used as an upcast shaft to aid ventilation, and a 91-inch diameter Sirocco double inlet fan was installed to further increase the draught. It was the use of the second shaft for ventilation that necessitated the lid on the emergency exit shaft in order to prevent air being drawn down it.

Whilst development continued underground, the surface works were also put in hand. Consideration of the sidings had begun in 1931 but it was not until September 1933 that things began to move. The Great Western were no longer keen to provide siding space for wait-order coal and were consequently pressing for more siding space to be provided at Northern. In April 1934 revised plans of the

The main winding engine supplied by Metropolitan Vickers was driven by a 310hp electric motor but, typically, a spare motor was not purchased until May 1936. If the winder had failed prior to this, men underground would have had to walk to Hawkwell and be wound up the shaft there. In this eventuality, the pit would have been brought to a stand under the Mines Regulations, as with only one way out, no more than ten men could have been underground at any time. The lack of a spare motor for a period highlights the pennypinching attitude of Crawshays over Northern and the lack of spare parts anywhere at the colliery. *Courtesy Marjory Oakey*

sidings were produced together with a revised estimate of cost which now stood at £4,808 14s 0d, half of which was to be borne by Henry Crawshay & Co. It was payable immediately but refunded over a period of ten years by a rebate of 2d per ton on every ton above 187,627 conveyed yearly from both Northern and Eastern United Collieries. Crawshays were to provide some of the sidings themselves together with weighbridges and offices.

Pit-head baths were to be provided, especially as they were to be paid for by the Welfare Branch of the Mines Department, and at the same time it was planned to erect a lamp-room and an ambulance room but paid for by Crawshays. Although the cost of maintaining the baths was to be met by contributions from the workmen and from canteen profits, the work was not put in hand at the time and the Northern colliers had to wait many years

Development work in hand, with the headframe re-erected from Bowson and the concrete winding engine house complete. Some offices had been completed whilst those in the centre of the view were still being roofed. *Courtesy Marjory Oakey*

The main transformer station. Power was supplied by the West Gloucestershire Power Company whose generating station was alongside Norchard Colliery at Lydney. The 33,000 kV power line came in from the Steam Mills direction. *Cty. Marjory Oakey*

before they could return to their homes at the end of a shift having washed and changed. The most likely reason behind Crawshays applying for the baths at this time, especially if someone else would pay, was that they feared the Government would make pit-head baths compulsory.

With regard to other provisions on the surface, the Board could not agree on the type of screens to be provided. The Managing Director, Arthur Morgan, believed that an up-to-date colliery should be provided with the latest equipment, in this case a dry-cleaning plant for the coal similar to that recently installed at Cannop Colliery (see *The Severn & Wye Railway* Vol. 2, page 246). As this had cost about £14,000, the Chairman, R. C. Heyworth, felt that such a high cost should not be incurred until sufficient coal was being produced to pay for it. An ordinary set of screens like those at Eastern could be installed at a cost of £2,000-£3,000 and there had been no problem in selling the coal from there. Morgan's worry was that Cannop might break away from the price agreements in force and take most of the market with their dry-cleaned coals. The debate over the screens continued and in June Morgan is recorded as saying that it 'was deplorable that a Company of this kind should be crippled for funds for development'. Another of the directors, F. Washbourn, pointed out that the company was not losing any trade 'as the demand could be supplied from Eastern United', which led the Chairman to remark that in view of the market they might have developed the colliery too soon. The matter was pressing as in the very near future coal would be being produced in quantity from Northern, and if there were no screens or sidings, work would have to stop.

The roadway from the Hawkwell shaft broke through in October 1934 which meant that work could begin in earnest on coal production, so the provision of a skeleton siding and whatever screening plant was to be installed became even more urgent.

As winding increased at Northern, it became apparent that the current consumed by the winding engine was rather heavy. This was put down to the fact that the load was unbalanced as there was only one cage, or bond. When descending the shaft, this was fairly light, but in ascending it was heavy, especially as there was no descending cage to help balance things out. Consequently it was agreed to obtain quotations for installing a double bond and in November the cost of doing so was put at about £582.

The matter of spending money on the screens and sidings appears to have come to a head in December when three courses of action were laid before the Board of Crawshays.

1. To stop the development and put in a caretaker. This would cost an estimated £6,000 per year.
2. In view of the fact that £84,915 had already been spent and that a further £10,000 would be required to completely finish development work, consideration should be given to completing the equipment of the colliery to enable an output of 50,000 tons per year. The colliery would then be in a position to produce coal at any time. The estimate for this was £6,000, after which the colliery could be put on a caretaking basis.
3. To complete the development and work the colliery to such an extent as would wipe out the loss which would be sustained by keeping it idle. To do this it would be necessary to secure new trade, possibly by winning road-borne business, and if 50,000 tons could be sold each year, then the colliery would pay its way.

Eventually, after much discussion, it was decided to go for the third option, and the cost of completing the works approved as follows: £4,000 for screens, £500 further expenditure on the sidings, £500 for pit cars, and £580 for installing the double bond in the Northern shaft. For a wages bill of about £600 a week, it was thought that an output of 1,000 tons would cover costs, and if the colliery could produce 1,250 tons a week or 60,000 tons per year, then it would make a profit of about £4,500 at 1/6d per ton.

With work at the Hawkwell end of the colliery practically stopped, it was decided that the men could be transferred to the Northern United end, which would effect a considerable saving as more coal could be handled there. It was thought that a market could be found for 60,000 tons per year providing Northern could be granted a sufficient standard tonnage quota under the Forest of Dean Coal Mines Scheme of 1930. Under this scheme each colliery was granted a specified tonnage of coal and fined a fixed amount per ton for the over-production if sales exceeded this figure. As Northern United was a new mine, it had no standard tonnage and it was hoped that Crawshays could not be refused a quota for a developing colliery.

Following the decision to work Northern, tenders were sought for the provision of a set of conventional screens, and in January 1935 the contract was awarded to Nortons, Tividale Co. which came in at £3,848, with erection work

A closer view of the headframe and winding engine house before the winding cable had been put on. Shaft sinking had therefore probably not yet commenced. *Courtesy Marjory Oakey*

commencing in May. Having previously decided to push hard for road-borne trade, it is surprising that no provision was made in the design of the screens for land sales. Consequently they had to be redesigned to include a conveyor for loading road vehicles, and a cutting had to be made for a road down to the screens. This road was 16 feet wide to enable two lorries to pass. Work on the railway sidings had begun in November 1934 after the GWR had asked the colliery company to drain the ground on which they were to stand as it was 'somewhat marshy'. After this was done, a bed of ashes was laid down and levelled. In March 1935 the GWR were seeking permission to remove Schofield's Siding (see page 262) to make way for the new arrangements. It is possible that any materials which had been delivered by rail during the development work at Northern were unloaded at this siding, and, as some coal had been produced from Hawkwell, it is feasible that it could have been loaded here. The following month the GWR agreed to carry out the work on Crawshays' portion of the sidings at a cost of £2,550 which included two weighbridges. As the estimated cost of the weighbridges was £780, the net cost of the sidings would have amounted to £1,770 if the colliery company found their own weighing machine. Mr. Morrison obtained quotations for suitable weighbridges and found he could save £100 on the railway company's quote, and there was also the possibility of obtaining a secondhand one for £170, thus saving £200. Crawshays also considered installing a weighbridge on the loaded wagon siding only and waiting until the machine from Lightmoor Colliery became available for taring the empty wagons. Morrison was against this as he feared it might lead to losses through false or incorrect tares on wagons, so it was decided to proceed with the sidings and leave the question of the weighbridges until a later date.

Meanwhile, underground difficulties were being experienced with the roof which consisted of a thick layer of clod over the coal. In March 1935, for example, two carts of dirt were being taken out of the pit for every one of coal. In one part the cost of the traditional pillar and stall working was proving prohibitive and thus experiments were made with longwall working which was leaving a better roof. It was decided that if the trial proved successful, then the sooner a coal-cutting machine was installed the better. Pillar and stall working was where the coal was divided up into fairly narrow blocks and large pillars of it were left to support the roof. Once the barrier had been reached, work on pillaring back to the pit bottom commenced, whereby the pillars themselves were worked and the roof allowed to collapse behind. However, this system was not really suitable for thin seams or where the roof was soft. In the longwall system, which was adopted for Northern, the coal was extracted in a long face (normally 30-50 yards long) which was gradually moved forward whilst the space behind the face was filled in to save sending rubbish to the surface. In this system of working, the collier undercut the coal all the way along the face and supported it on wedges. The roof behind was kept up on two rows of props, behind which the rubbish was stacked. When the wedges were removed, the coal was either blown down or fell of its own accord. It was then cleared into tubs and taken to the surface. Once the face was cleared of coal, it was advanced forward and the whole process began again.

In June 1935 further details of the arrangements underground were discussed when the question of dipples was raised. Two pairs of dipples would ultimately be necessary but Crawshays thought they might get away with driving only one pair at this time. Mr. Meredith, who by this time had been replaced as manager at Lightmoor and was acting as mining adviser to the Board, felt that from a mining point of view it would be best to drive both pairs of dipples and also to drive them to the barrier as quickly as possible in order to get to the deepest part of the workings while Cannop were still working in the area and draining the coal. However, it was considered more sensible to drive a set of dipples on the Hawkwell side of the colliery first as they were nearer the rock there, being on the land side. Coal could be pulled up the dipples, a haulage of about 400 yards, and then dropped down to the Northern shaft for winding to the surface. One thing that had to be watched was that coal from that area was wet and care had to be taken not to let it prejudice sales; the wettest coal was used to supply the workmen's allowance. The Hawkwell dipples were pushed on with all speed, the men working three shifts on their drivage. The management were also given authority to begin the second set of dipples if the trade position warranted it.

At the same meeting it was mentioned that with the experimental longwall working, 1,200 tons less dirt had been wound during the month of May than in April. It was also thought that a coal cutter would be most useful. The surface arrangements were also discussed and it was hoped that they would be complete by the time of the company's annual general meeting in August, which indeed they were.

The first coal was put through the screens in late August. Mr. Meredith, who visited the colliery at about this time, thought that the screens were the best in the Forest, if not the country, and was confident they should get little complaint of bad screening. He also took a trip underground where he was pleased with the success in working the longwall method and estimated that in three or four months time the colliery would be raising 1,000 tons a week and showing a profit.

The sidings were first used on 4th September 1935, although the two single-lever ground frames controlling them had been brought into use on 25th March. The private siding agreement itself had been signed on 18th May. The sidings gave accommodation for 60 empties and the colliery company agreed to continue tipping waste material to provide suitable ground for the extension of the empty wagon sidings if they were required in the future.

The operation of traffic to and from the colliery required the use of two guards, the train being propelled along the Churchway branch from Bilson. The leading vehicle had to be a brake van with the verandah end leading and the guard was required to carry a horn to warn any person of the approach of the train. He also had to be prepared to stop the train by exhibiting a red flag or light if necessary.

On arrival at the colliery the brake van was placed at the end of the Churchway branch, clear of the colliery sidings. The empty wagons were then propelled up the gradient into the empties sidings, a man walking in front to guide them in. Once the wagons were berthed, the engine returned to collect the brake van which was left just above the loaded road connection while the loadeds were drawn out. These had been gravitated down through the screens and clear of an overbridge which was of insufficient height to allow an engine to pass. The maximum permitted load for uncoloured engines was 15 empties from Bilson to Northern and 40

Northern United viewed from the Mitcheldean–Monmouth road prior to the Second World War. The building to the left of the headframe amidst all of the pit timber was the saw mills. *Collection Maurice Bent*

loadeds on return, and, because the line fell away to Bilson Yard at 1 in 41, the wagon brakes had to be pinned down before any movement took place.

In October 1935 the double bond in the Northern shaft was in use and working satisfactorily and about 450 tons of coal a week were being raised. Each ton cost 15s 7.55d to get to the surface whilst the selling price was 13s 9.17d, which gave a loss of 1s 10.38d per ton, an overall loss for the colliery during the month of £207 17s 2d. Following on from the decision made in June, a coal cutter had been purchased and in November it was reported that 75% of the output from the colliery was machine cut. The trade position was so good that the company had far more orders than Eastern and Northern could supply, and an opportunity had arisen to supply a further 600 tons a week from Northern to a South Wales steelworks. To increase the output, two more coal cutters were ordered. The November cost sheets reveal that 3,157 tons of coal had been sold from Northern and a profit of £99 10s 0d had been made. The company had evidently made the correct decision in opening Northern rather than mothballing it.

The colliery had been brought into production for under £100,000, much less than the cost of developing Eastern United. However, not all the equipment was new; things such as the headframe from Bowson had been acquired and re-used. There was also the mistake made in laying out the colliery, which had still to be dealt with, especially as output increased. In the initial purchase discussions, the whole matter of obtaining the colliery hinged around the Cannop Coal Co. buying a portion of the Northern United gale, but when, in January 1936, it was reported that they had applied to purchase 300 acres, Crawshays were not so keen to sell – they no longer needed the money! Also the area of coal Cannop applied for was some of the best, and the directors of Crawshays decided that they would instead offer 240 acres in a different direction including some faulty ground which was expensive to work. At the same time Cannop was trying to obtain an area of coal from Eastern United, but all of these negotiations fell through when Cannop purchased an area from the Princess Royal Collieries Co. The area concerned was at the lowest point of both the Northern and Eastern United takings and thus Crawshays had achieved their aim of getting Cannop to pump all of the water without actually having to sell any of their coal!

Problems over the sending of coal from Northern arose in March 1936 due to insufficient siding space. The GWR occasionally ran an extra train to the colliery each day, but then the traffic department stopped the locomotive coming into the Northern United sidings as they had not received a maintenance certificate from the maintenance department. It took three days to obtain a temporary certificate and this only extended to the use of the middle two sidings and was conditional on the sidings being extended as quickly as possible to give more empty wagon storage. The work was put in hand immediately and in December 1936 the GWR submitted an account for £827 for work and materials. The average output during early 1937 was 25 wagons per day which meant that the siding accommodation was ample, but by June things were getting a little tight with empties being kept at Bilson until required. The colliery then requested specific wagons for despatch, which entailed considerable extra shunting. The increase in empty wagon storage space at the colliery was almost completed, giving room for an extra 20 wagons and alleviating the problem at Bilson, although tipping continued to allow even further siding extensions in case they were needed in the future.

In April 1936 water entering the top end of the underground workings was reported as highly charged with sulphuric acid, which it was considered was likely to eat away the steel pipes in the column up which the water was pumped in the Northern United shaft. The makers of the pipes reported that the water was the worst they had known and would not guarantee their pipes against it, their only solution being to have the pipes back and line them with vulcanised bitumen. This course of action would have been prohibitively expensive and impractical as the pipes were in daily use and water pumping could not be stopped. The acid water had previously been neutralised by the addition of lime, but this treatment was stopped on 28th

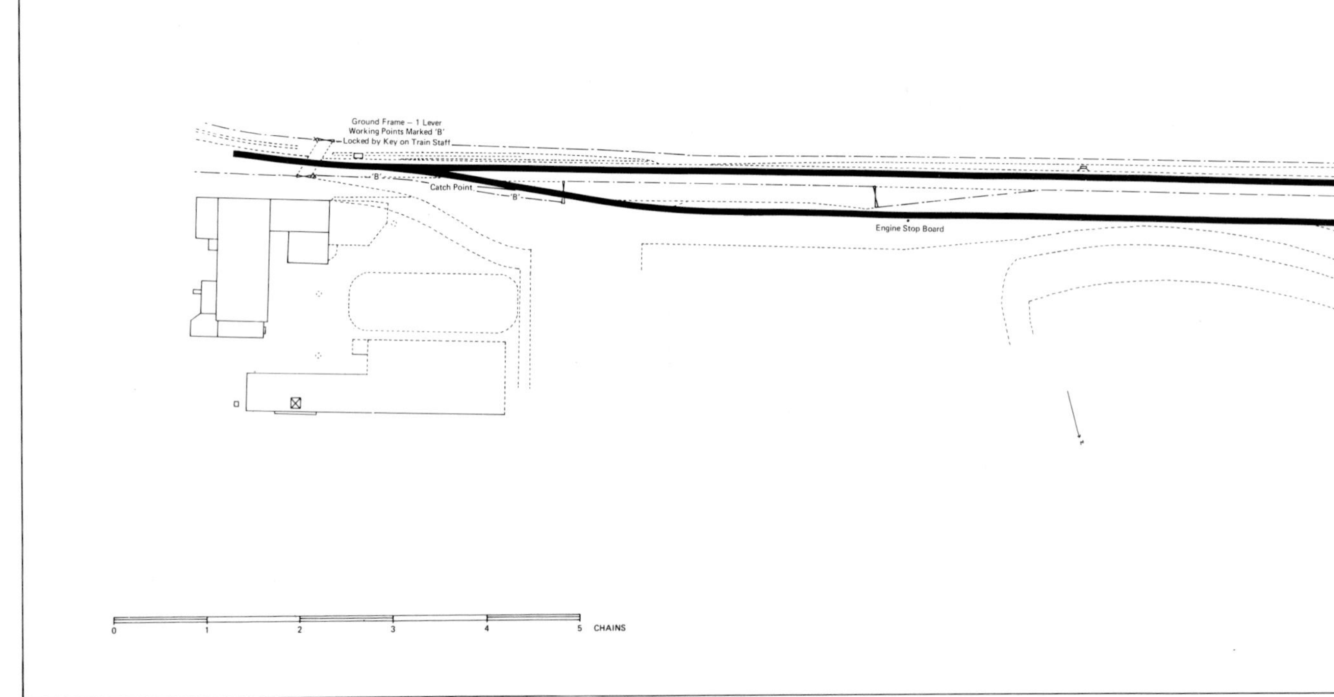

March due to considerable wear in a pump attributed to the abrasive action of the lime sediment. The colliery manager, Morrison, was against the termination of the lime treatment as the acid water threatened the safety of the pit, but the damage to the pump highlighted another problem at Northern. Crawshays had developed the mine as cheaply as possible and, in keeping the running costs down, had neither provided a duplicate pump nor any spare parts to replace those worn. At other Forest collieries, it would simply have been a matter of going to the stores, but at Northern it was a question of waiting three weeks for the parts to be delivered. In the meantime the pump could fail or the acid might eat through the shaft column – either way the colliery would be drowned out.

Various suggestions for dealing with the water included a column of cast iron pipes which would not be affected by the acid in the Northern shaft, or pumping the water from a 'hold', or pond, at Northern to Hawkwell where it could be pumped to the surface instead, or even creating a series of 'holds' whereby lime added in the top one could settle out as it passed through the subsequent ones.

A sub-committee, formed to investigate the problem, visited Northern and had one of the pipes in the shaft column taken off and inspected. Inside was a thick layer of sludge which, when wiped away, revealed no damage to the pipe itself. At a second meeting another pipe was taken off at a point most likely to be damaged, but again it proved unharmed. In the meantime Morrison had requisitioned for 750 yards of 4 inch diameter pipes to conduct the water to Hawkwell, but luckily the order had not been processed. The Managing Director pointed out that the shaft column should have been inspected before the pipes requisition was put in and before any other action was taken.

Only a month later, water samples showed distinct traces of alkalinity and by July there was very little acid present

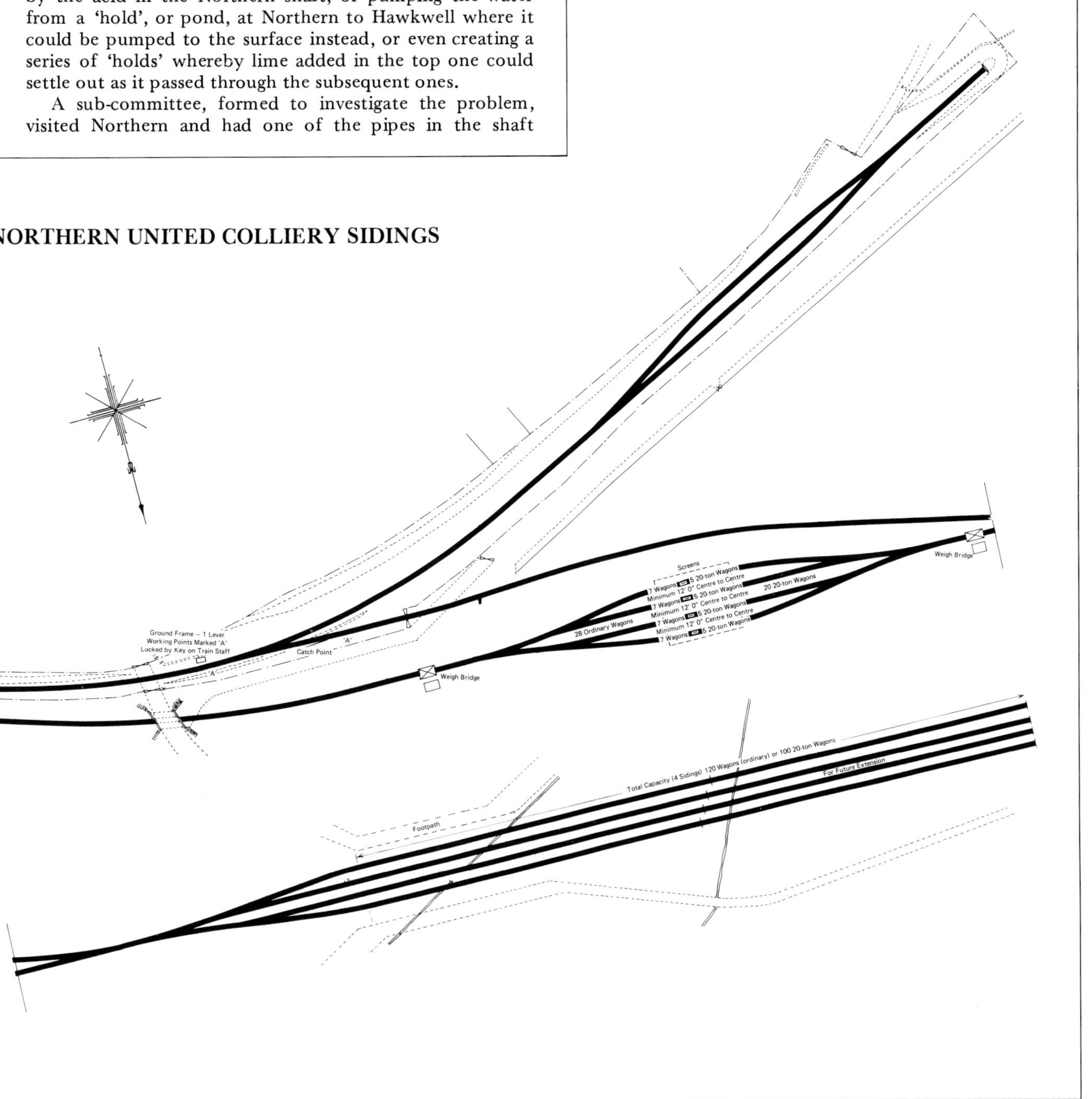

in the water. Thus, after much discussion and disagreement, the problem had resolved itself.

Another concern at this time was the type of timber being used for roof supports at Northern. Following a complaint from the mines inspector, Morrison wanted to order a different grade at 3s 6d to 4s more per ton than that already in use. Morrison was worried that if there was an accident and the grade of timber used had not been improved, the mines inspector would criticise him very strongly. The inspector had wanted to write to the company on the matter, but Morrison persuaded him otherwise as a letter of that kind could be used in evidence. Apparently, some of the timber in use did not last a day and had broken before the men left it. The employment of soft timber was the idea of another director, D. N. Lang, who believed that with large lids, when the roof came down, it would subside bodily and thus the ash content in the small coal would be reduced. No doubt the cost also entered into the equation. One outcome of the discussions was a decision to use steel arches in the main roadways and an order was placed for a regular monthly quantity.

As more coal-cutting machines were purchased and the output from Northern increased, the colliery's quota came into question. When Northern opened, the standard tonnage awarded under the Forest of Dean District Coal Mines Scheme, 1930, was 15,000 tons. In August 1936 application was made to increase this to 85,000 tons as 1,500 tons a week were being produced. This was opposed by other Forest collieries, but an increase to 21,856 tons was sanctioned. Immediately afterwards, a further application was made and the matter was taken to arbitration, which resulted in Northern's quota being raised to 55,000 tons.

Any further review was said to depend on the position of Lightmoor Colliery. It had always been thought that Crawshays would shut the pit in the early 1930s and use the tonnage allowance from there for Northern, but they kept it going and had thus increased their market share. Despite this, an extra 20,000 tons was granted in April 1937 and a further 10,000 tons in March 1938.

Whether Morrison had blotted his copybook over the acid water and soft timber questions is unknown, but in January 1937 the Board felt that an under-manager should be appointed at Northern, and Albert Wood was transferred from Lightmoor. One problem at the time was that the dipples were not being driven fast enough for the Board, and thus coal faces could not be opened out in the most desirable way but instead were worked to give an instant return on investment. The ideal method of working would have been to drive the pair of dipples down to their fullest extent, that is to the barrier, and then retreat from the coal faces, allowing the roof to collapse behind. At Northern this was not done and faces were taken off the dipples as soon as possible, which gave the problem that once the coal had been removed, the roof over the roadways had to be supported to keep them open to give access to faces further on. Often a 10ft high roadway would be squashed down to 5 feet or less, and roadmen would be employed to dig out the floor to restore the roadway. In April 1937 the second pair of dipples still had not been started, although Morrison promised action shortly. The dipple on the Hawkwell side, known as H Dipple, was progressing slowly.

Although five coal-cutting machines were in use by this time, the expected increase in output did not come. The central selling committee for the Forest of Dean, who had taken over all coal sales from the Forest's collieries in August 1936, was overselling Northern United coal during 1937 on the assumption of greater output and had taken an order for 15,000 tons, delivery of which was to commence in November. In August Morrison claimed that in three months he could increase output by 1,800 tons a week, but would require an additional 140 men to do so. Besides

A Northern United wagon built by the Gloucester Railway Carriage & Wagon Co. Ltd. and photographed in November 1938. Twenty-five new 12T wagons were ordered in September 1938 on hire purchase terms spread over 7 years at a cost of £155 per wagon. The livery was black, with white letters, shaded red.

GRC&W Co.

Another view over the colliery from the road, showing more of the office buildings on the left. Note the large stock of pit timber. In October 1939 it was reported that Crawshays faced an enormous increase in the cost of pitwood. They had been paying the Forestry Commission 24 shillings per ton but it went up to 40 shillings per ton. In November they had purchased 87 acres of timber on the Dinmore Manor Estate in Herefordshire from the Yorkley Coal Co. for the sum of £1,000 with a guarantee of 2,000 tons of pitwood. This gave a supply of timber at 32s 9d delivered against the set control price of 50s 0d per ton. *Collection Maurice Bent*

doubting that such a number of skilled men could be found in that time, the Board wanted to see the increase in output achieved without extra manpower and at a cheap rate, and to strengthen the team at Northern 'a good engineer', William Wood, was appointed from Arthur & Edward Colliery that November.

Although in the middle of 1938 slack time was being worked, it was decided that the dipples should be driven on with all speed regardless of 'play days'. By July, work had commenced on the second pair of dipples, known as J Dipple, on the Brierley side of the pit. In November it was reported that a conveyor had been started in the longwall face to take the coal from the face to a main roadway for loading into tubs.

In January 1939 trouble was being experienced with the roof in the longwall, with about 10ft of clod over the coal before the rock was reached. Absenteeism ran high, with 426 man shifts lost in January, and in February the under-manager, Wood, returned to Lightmoor to cover for the manager there who was off sick. This was a portent of things to come as absenteeism was to become a serious problem at the pit. Throughout 1939 a series of reasons was proffered by Morrison to the Board for the low output from Northern, which included the bad roof, water, holiday periods and a shortage of skilled labour. To add to the pit's difficulties, and the cost per ton of coal, the start of the Second World War brought an immediate increase in the cost of pit timber from about 24/- to 40/- per ton, and in December a huge stone, some 50ft long and 20ft thick, fell from the roof in the conveyor place and brought down the roof for over 50 yards, bringing work to a halt.

The start of the war also signalled the start of even heavier absenteeism from Northern, with over 1,000 man shifts being lost in most months. Some of the men apparently thought that if output was kept down, they would not be called up for service, whilst others stayed away to have a good time before being called up. Men were also leaving the pit to work in Government factories where wages were higher. However, there was a possibility that colliers from other coalfields might be transferred as a result of bombing and that some French and Belgian colliers might also arrive.

May 1940 marked the start of several months of loss recorded at Northern. One of the contributory problems was that although it was intended to keep the Forest pits at work on Saturday afternoons, the men objected and did not report for work. This resulted in heavy falls in coal places which had been left by the Saturday morning shift in anticipation of timbering during the afternoon. This, of course, resulted in lost time on the Monday morning in clearing up. In August 1940 the Board gave the question of the problems at Northern serious consideration. The manager agreed with them that the results were very unsatisfactory, attributing them to three things. Firstly, there were the conditions brought about by the war, with some men leaving to work in Government factories for high wages, and others not working regularly in order (or so they thought) to safeguard their positions. This latter aspect was connected to the second of the manager's problems, absenteeism, which in turn caused problems with the third worry, the bad roof. This made absenteeism an even more serious matter than just a loss of production because every shift which had coal faces standing and no men to do the packing and timbering was liable to bad roof falls. Although Eastern United was also suffering badly from absenteeism, Eastern was under the rock, so the problem with the roof did not occur. The Board found it difficult to accept that absenteeism was to blame for the poor showing at Northern as the same problem occurring at Eastern did not result in any financial loss. Morrison's reversion to thicker and better quality pit timber than that previously recommended by the Board, also had an effect on financial performance but he was putting safety before profit. Morrison hoped that he would not be blamed for the conditions over which he had no control, but the Chairman remarked that Mr. Morrison did not seem to be able to meet the difficulties and that another man may have avoided them. The Board did not want to be too drastic as Morrison had given them long service, but the shareholders would want to know the cause of the losses, and if another man could make the colliery pay, they would be expected to employ him.

The Board wanted Morrison to endeavour to get on better with his men. He was a disciplinarian but did not always bring the best results as one also had to be a tactician to get the best out of the Foresters, and working one of the shifts underground without an overman did not help. The Board also felt that Morrison was keeping up his output at the expense of his roadways, especially the drivage of the dipples, yet, when output fell, the Board also complained, so Morrison was constantly moving his men from one job to another.

It was thought that some improvement in the men's morale might be brought about by 'riding them' down the dipples at the start and end of a shift, thus saving them a walk. To do this the main dipples would have to be improved, about 900 yards having to be ringed with steel arches at a cost of 30/- a yard. Man riding, which it was hoped could be introduced by November, could increase output from 37 cwts to 41 cwts a man.

The following month was no better. The August Bank Holiday had affected output, absenteeism was bad, three falls of roof had occurred, and air-raid warnings on three nights had stopped the men from coming to work. However, a third conveyor had been put into use which increased output by 2 cwts per manshift and reduced costs by one third per ton, but this slight improvement came too late for Morrison. The Board decided to terminate his employment, although he was given the option of resigning. The official view was that another manager might make a better go of the colliery and get on better with the men, but Morrison was clearly held in respect at Northern where all of the men contributed to his leaving present. The men understood that Morrison had disagreed with the Board and resigned over a safety matter, and they may not have been far wrong as it appears that his reluctance to cut corners in the drive for productivity and profit led to his fall from grace with the Board. Morrison left Northern on 23rd September 1940.

He was replaced by Mr. Edward Gerrard, whose first job was to have the sump at the bottom of the Northern United shaft cleaned out so that it could hold ten hours inflow of water. A total of 283 carts of dirt were removed, which gave an additional capacity of 26,000 gallons.

One small wartime incident occurred on 22nd October 1940, when a bomb fell about seven yards from the screens. Luckily, it landed in soft earth but the explosion lifted about 18 tons of dirt over the sidings. No damage was done to buildings or personnel.

November saw the first profit made at the colliery for six months, but a loss was recorded again in December. The dipples had been standing since September and, although it was May 1941 before drivage recommenced, they had been tidied up, and in November 1940 man riding was introduced in the No. 2 Dipple, as promised. The men still had to walk from pit bottom to the top of the dipples but then they were able to ride down, kneeling on a riding trolley, six at a time.

The appointment of the new manager had not brought about great changes or an upturn in fortunes. In May 1941 the Board again discussed the position of the colliery and, with no prospect of increasing the workforce, the question of winding coal on one shift only per day was raised. The average coal got per man per shift at the coal face at this time was 39.75 cwts. Taking other underground workers into account, the figure reduced to 20.85 cwts per man, and by the time surface workers were included, it came down to 15.2 cwts per man employed. Winding coal on two shifts left some men on the surface idle at times waiting for coal. By winding coal on one shift only, some surface workers could be put to work elsewhere, thus reducing expenses.

The drivage of the dipples was causing concern again in June 1941. As already mentioned, they had stood for about eight months until the drivage of No. 2 Dipple recommenced on 19th May. Between then and the end of the month, only five yards were driven which the Board considered insufficient progress. Failing a considerable increase in the rate of drivage, they would be too late arriving in the deep as Cannop would have finished work in the area and water would percolate through, flooding Northern workings. It was felt that the dipple should be put on three-shift working and not only should no men be taken from there to replace absentees elsewhere, but if a man was absent from the dipple he should be replaced. The question of the dipples had haunted the colliery from the very outset. From Day One of the colliery the decision should have been made to drive the dipples to the barrier and then open out the coal faces and retreat them to pit bottom, but Crawshays were reluctant to spend money at Northern, and in their desire to see the colliery make money, the future prospects were squandered for a quick return.

The other problem dating from the commencement of Northern was that the colliery was started the wrong way round, and to remedy the situation in October 1941 it was decided to move the steam winding engine from Lightmoor Colliery (which had closed in 1940) to Northern and re-erect it there. This would have given the opportunity of putting the pit the right way round but although it is believed the engine was taken to Northern, nothing was done with it.

The men's comfort at Northern was improved in March 1943 with the opening of a new canteen, the erection of which had commenced the previous August. However, there was still no sign of a pit-head bath even though the matter had been raised again in December 1939 and the Miners Welfare Committee approached for sanction.

In March 1943 complaints were received of bad coal from Northern, and the manager of the Swindon Gas Works, who also represented the Severn Valley Gas Co. and the Oxford Gas Co., made it clear that if the dirty supplies

The Northern United Colliery canteen opened on 1st March 1943. Railway crews who used it particularly remember the cakes provided here. On one occasion a driver, on going across to the canteen for the usual order of buns, discovered that the price had increased by a penny. He was told that it was 'for the paper bag', so on his next trip he returned with a neatly folded paper bag, hoping to save a penny!
Cty. Dean Forest Mercury

continued, coal would have to be found elsewhere. He said they had installed plant specifically to take Forest coal and he wanted 70,000 tons the current year and 100,000 in the next. The loss of this account would have been a serious matter for Crawshays. In May 1946 further complaints were made about the ash content in the coal and Gerrard stated that unless the men underground were watched, they were not particular and he got no co-operation from them.

Since September 1943 the colliery had been making a profit, but this ended in February 1946 when decline set in once more. Unfortunately, the colliery remained in this state for the rest of its life. When the collieries were nationalised on 1st January 1947 it no doubt came as a great relief to Crawshays that they no longer had to worry about Northern. The old company continued in business long enough to wind up its affairs and the last Board meeting was held on 2nd December 1947.

The National Coal Board brought about some improvements to the colliery in 1952 when a coal washing plant was added to the screens, although, like a lot of other equipment at Northern, it was secondhand, having come from a colliery at Cwmtillery, South Wales. On 16th August the same year came the long-awaited opening of the pit-head baths. In 1955 the whole of the pit top was reorganised with some labour-saving devices, such as rams to push the tubs off the cage, together with a conveyor from the pit-head to the screens which replaced the tub route. The head-frames at Hawkwell were also replaced with steel structures.

However, the Forest of Dean coal-field was beginning to decline, especially with the district being 'cared for' by

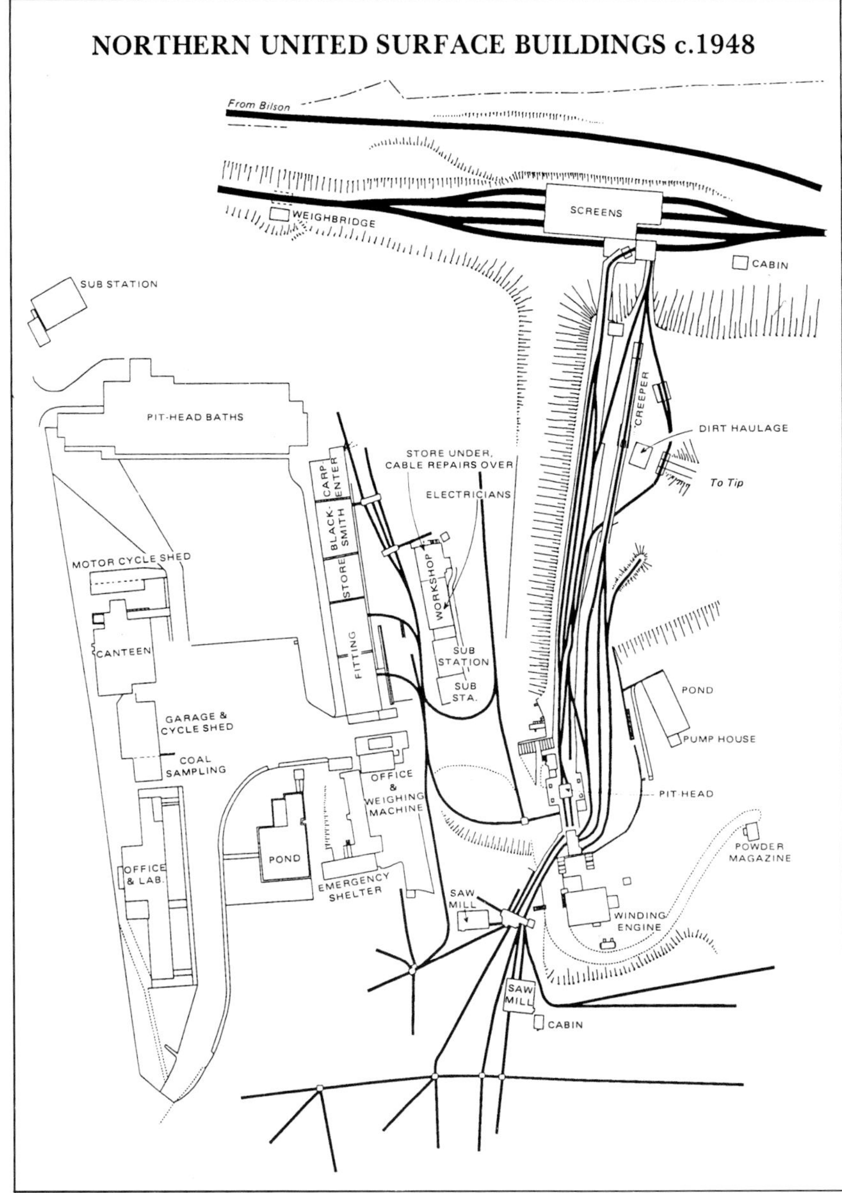

NORTHERN UNITED SURFACE BUILDINGS c.1948

The pit-head, photographed on 11th July 1948, with journeys of empty tubs awaiting return underground. The loaded tub roads to the screens were under the curved corrugated-iron roof. Notice how the ground around the pit-head was made up. To the right of the headframe can be seen the office and weighbridge for land sales. The building in front of the trees, with the colliery clock set into the roof, housed the main offices. The bare hillside of Heywood in the background was on the far side of the railway up to Drybrook. *L. E. Copeland*

A journey of carts at the pit-head. *Collection Maurice Bent*

Top: The end of the empty cart creeper at the pit-head.
Collection Maurice Bent

Left and above: These pictures show the last tub of coal to be raised at Northern United on Christmas Eve 1965, with Bert Hiatt.
A. K. Pope

South Wales, which sent many men to inspect the Forest's collieries but who did not understand the area and its working practices. The closure of Eastern United, as already mentioned, came in 1959 together with Arthur & Edward Colliery at Lydbrook, from where 210 men were transferred to Northern. When Cannop Colliery was closed in September 1960, it was feared that the water would soon affect the Northern workings and, even though some pumps were installed at Cannop, the end was in sight. Strangely, 1960 was the only year under the NCB that Northern made a profit. Redundancies began at Northern in 1964 and the final shift was worked on Christmas Eve 1965, bringing unemployment to 215 men. At its peak Northern had employed 700.

While the colliery stood idle over the Christmas and New Year holidays, the air soon became bad, and water filled Hawkwell so that the few men who returned to recover equipment from underground were unable to do so. The cables on the cages were cut both at Northern and Hawkwell and the shafts were soon filled up.

The closure at Northern marked the end of deep mining in the Forest of Dean, leaving the Free Miners to continue the coal mining tradition as they always have done. One question that might be asked is why did Northern United continue working for so long when it was making a loss? The answer might lie in the early closure of Eastern United. By shutting the profitable pit first and keeping the loss-maker going, the entire coalfield would show a loss to justify closing the Forest coalfield.

Four views underground. *Top left:* The ubiquitous canary in its cage to give early warning of gas. *Top right:* The J Dipple haulage engine. *Bottom left:* Another, smaller underground haulage. *Bottom right:* A journey of tubs at pit bottom.

Cty. Forest of Dean Caving Club and Maurice Bent

Having been propelled all the way from Bilson Junction to Churchway, the brake van was left beyond the connection to the Northern United empty sidings at 6 miles 3 chains, as shown here, and the empties propelled up the 1 in 41 gradient into the colliery's private sidings, with a man walking in front . . .

Below: . . . then the engine returned to collect the brake van and take it back down to the connection with the loaded road.

2–6–2T No. 4564 at the same point in the procedure on another occasion. *Rev. D. A. Tipper*

The screens viewed from the footplate while a rake of empties was being propelled into the sidings. The two wagons in the foreground were 'internal user' vehicles kept within the confines of the colliery. *R. H. Marrows*

57XX pannier tank No. 8701 drifting back past the screens after placing its wagons in the empty sidings. *A. K. Pope*

The line passing the screens. The corrugated-iron structure attached to the original brick screens was the washery acquired from Cymtillery in South Wales in 1952. *A. K. Pope*

Looking towards the empties roads on 6th October 1946. The gantry behind the screens allowed wagons to be lifted for repairs to wheelsets, axleboxes, etc. *L. E. Copeland*

The four empty wagon roads were laid on specially built-up ground. The purpose of the narrow gauge line running alongside and also crossing over and heading off down alongside the tip is unknown. 11th July 1948. *L. E. Copeland*

The rear of the screens with the wagon gantry on the right and a couple of 'Jubilee' skips on the narrow gauge line. 11th July 1948. *L. E. Copeland*

The buffer stops at the end of the empties roads. The extension of sidings shown on official plans was never required. *A. K. Pope*

Empty wagons about to pass under the screens. The weighbridge for these on the left was provided in 1937. The pannier was heading back towards the Churchway branch after placing more empties in the sidings. *R. H. Marrows*

A view from the dirt tip over the screens and looking eastwards down the Churchway branch. The covered tub route from the pit-head can be seen running into the screens. The rails heading up the tip carried the waste tipping cart which was filled from the colliery tubs via the tippler at the base of the tip. The haulage engine for the waste tipper was housed in the building behind the tippler. This photograph, taken on 11th July 1948, also shows the cottages which remained of the Nelson Green brickworks, on the extreme right above the screens.

L. E. Copeland

Road access to the screens for loading land sales coal came in on the right. The internal user wagons on the left were used for land sales.
John Suckling

A closer view of the screens on the same occasion. *John Suckling*

The lorries shown here, an Albion and two Bedfords, were all collecting land sales coal, showing how popular road transport was becoming. *R. Dagley Morris*

This picture, looking down the loaded wagon road from the screens, shows a rake of wagons which had just passed over the loaded wagon weighbridge. The weighman here for many years was Leslie Yorke. *R. Dagley Morris*

Looking back up the loaded truck run on a day when Les Yorke obviously had a good warming fire going in the weigh house. The engine on the left was collecting the brake van from the end of the Churchway branch ready to go and fetch the loaded wagons. *R. H. Marrows*

The loaded run passed under a Forestry road, the height of the bridge precluding locomotives from passing any further up the sidings. 27th June 1948. *L. E. Copeland*

Taken from the gate of the Forestry road crossing over the Churchway branch, this view looks towards the Hawkwell brickworks. 27th June 1948. *L. E. Copeland*

Another view taken from the bridge but showing more of the loaded truck road. *R. Dagley Morris*

Loaded wagons being collected in December 1963. *R. H. Marrows*

A chilly day in December 1963 with just a few wagons of coal from 'Northern' being pulled out of the loaded road. When clear of the points, the brake van was gravitated onto the train. Warmed by a traditional coal-fired stove, the van was a cosy retreat during the winter months.
R. H. Marrows

This view shows the 1955 rebuilt area around the pit-head and, beyond, the washery. *Collection Maurice Bent*

The second exit at Northern was the Hawkwell shaft previously seen on pages 272 and 273. The metal headframe replaced the timber ones after 1955. December 1965. *R. H. Marrows*

The old S & W tramroad formation was followed by the pole route on the right of this view, looking towards the end of the Churchway branch on 27th June 1948. Nelson Colliery was off to the left, the loop enabling traffic to and from the colliery to be shunted or perhaps run round. Unfortunately, we have not been able to trace any recollections of procedure here. The stop board had been erected by July 1938 when the line had been examined for the heavier '57xx' class pannier tanks and the rotting sleepers at this extremity were considered dangerously weak.

L. E. Copeland

The end of the Churchway branch, again on 6th October 1947. *L. E. Copeland*

This panorama of the Cinderford (left) and Whimsey (foreground) lines curving away from Bilson Junction was taken looking south from the embankment of the Cinderford Extension in the early morning of 26th March 1948. The signal in the foreground was the up fixed distant for trains from Whimsey to Bilson.
L. E. Copeland

THE WHIMSEY BRANCH

The Whimsey branch and its subsequent extension to Mitcheldean Road had a complex story which has been outlined on page 6, but the line began as a broad gauge branch of the South Wales Railway serving Whimsey Colliery approximately three-quarters of a mile from Bilson Junction.

The plate girder bridge carrying the Cinderford Extension over the Whimsey branch, still looking south. This picture was taken from the top of the fixed distant for Cinderford goods, looking towards Bilson Junction on 28th August 1947. *L. E. Copeland*

'57xx' class 0–6–0PT No. 7723 returning from Whimsey with empty bitumen wagons and about to pass under the bridge featured in the previous view. Hollyhill Wood features in the background of this picture taken on 7th September 1959. *John Marshall*

The down fixed distant for Cinderford Goods stood adjacent to the level crossing where the lane leading to Cinderford Old Severn & Wye station crossed the line. Broadmoor Brickworks features on the right of this picture taken on 6th October 1946. *L. E. Copeland*

After leaving Bilson Yard, the Whimsey branch swung to the north-east and was crossed by a plate girder bridge carrying the Cinderford extension before reverting to a more northerly course. Shortly afterwards the line first crossed the site of a canal which once took coke from Broadmoor to the Cinderford Ironworks and then a level crossing with the remaining portion of the Bullo Pill tramroad. This had run parallel to the railway along the eastern edge of Bilson Green and skirting Hollyhill Wood. Here it crossed to the western side of the railway on the level. A tramroad branch to Churchway had formerly forked left here and headed westwards across an embankment which formed a dam to impound water for use at an iron furnace at Soudley. The pond dated from at least 1635 when it was described as being 720ft long with a sluice and 'ground trowe'. The furnace at Soudley was out of use by 1650 but the pond remained and was later used in conjunction with the ironworks at Cinderford, although in later years it gradually silted up. The pond was known locally as the Dam Pool, but in 1875 following flooding, the dam was breached and the area behind it became a rather marshy expanse as the remaining water escaped. It was the bursting of the dam which sounded the final death knell for the tramroad to Churchway. After the building of the broad gauge line, the tramroad branch was retained to provide through communication to the Severn & Wye at Churchway and the western side of the Forest. However, the Churchway tramroad was probably little used after the opening of the Severn & Wye Bilson branch in 1873, so when the bursting of the dam occurred, the line was not repaired. The plates on the rest of the line had been removed by 1878. However, the tramroad to Whimsey, which paralleled the railway on the western side, survived longer.

HAYWOOD COLLIERY

Shortly beyond the tramroad crossing, a short siding trailed southwards on the east side of the railway, latterly serving the Haywood Colliery. A short siding had been provided from the beginning of the broad gauge line, the South Wales Railway sanctioning a siding to 'Mr. Hart's colliery' in December 1854. This was completed by August 1855 when Messrs. Tredwell submitted their account for its construction. It was built to serve an interchange wharf with a tramroad siding for the Paragon & Spero Coal Mining Company. Paragon and Spero were two adjoining gales on Bilson Green served by a branch tramroad off the Bullo Pill tramroad. Traffic was thus brought down the branch from the colliery (possibly sanctioned in 1856) and then along a short stretch of the main Bullo Pill tramroad to the siding. In 1841 Paragon was being worked by the Cinderford Iron Company which achieved an output of 846 tons that year. Only 218 tons were raised in the following year and the returns for 1843/4 were nil. The year 1845 saw a figure of 1,039 tons which dropped to 985 tons in 1846. The colliery was working two pits, Land and Deep Paragon, winning coal from the Churchway High Delf, Rocky and Lowery seams.

In 1841 Spero was in the hands of James Cowmeadow and was working the coal in the Lowery seam. When the two gales came to be worked together is unknown but in April 1857 the Paragon & Spero Coal Mining Co. Ltd. was incorporated to take over the lease of 'certain collieries now possessed by certain people carrying on the business of mining for coals under the Cost Book principle by the name of the Paragon & Spero Coal Mining Co.' The new company had a capital of £20,000 in £10 shares but never proceeded to business and was wound up in 1858. It may have been at this date that the leases of the two gales were terminated and the gales passed back to their registered owners. It seems likely that the Spero siding, as it was known, fell into disuse around this time, but was later extended to serve the Haywood Colliery.

The 1841 Awards confirmed the Haywood Gale in the possession of Moses Teague, a Free Miner. He had applied for it before this date but his application was not granted. However, in conjunction with William Crawshay, he commenced work to gain the coal from the Coleford High Delf. In March 1841 the Haywood Colliery Pit was described as being worked by Messrs. Crawshay & Sons. The pit was 70 yards deep down to the Hill Delph coal. There were two engines at work, an 18in high pressure pumping engine and a 10in high pressure winder. The 300 tons or so of small coal being raised per month were used to supply Crawshay's own engines, probably at the Cinderford Ironworks and possibly at the winding and pumping engines at Crawshay's various iron mines around the Cinderford area. It seems that the opening of the colliery was not complete at this time and production figures for the 1840s tend to bear this out as they climb from 1842 onwards. The actual figures are as follows:

Year	*Tonnage*
1841	1,510 tons
1842	3,975
1843	3,772
1844	3,725
1845	5,428
1846	4,149

Work at the colliery may have stopped for a while during the late 1840s or early 50s when Crawshays began to take their coal from their newly opened Lightmoor Colliery but by 1863 it had obviously restarted and was progressing well, as in that year Henry Crawshay was granted a licence from the Crown for a road or tramway which became known as Crawshay's Tramroad. Linking the various interests of the Crawshays in the Cinderford area, it ran from the Buckshaft Iron Mine at Ruspidge in the south to the St. Annals Iron Mine in the north serving the Cinderford Ironworks and Haywood Colliery en route whilst a branch served Lightmoor Colliery.

Work at the colliery may have ceased again for a period and not restarted until 1873 when the registered owner of the gale was Edwin Crawshay, the youngest son of Henry,

A closer view of the crossing, pictured on the same occasion. The Bullo Pill tramroad had run parallel to the Forest of Dean branch, but along the eastern edge of Bilson Green, skirting Hollyhill Wood and crossing the Whimsey branch on the level at this point on its way to Whimsey Colliery. The embankment seen on the opposite side of the crossing once carried a tramroad branch to Churchway. The main tramroad to Whimsey survived intact until c.1907-8, but had been out of use for many years by then. *L. E. Copeland*

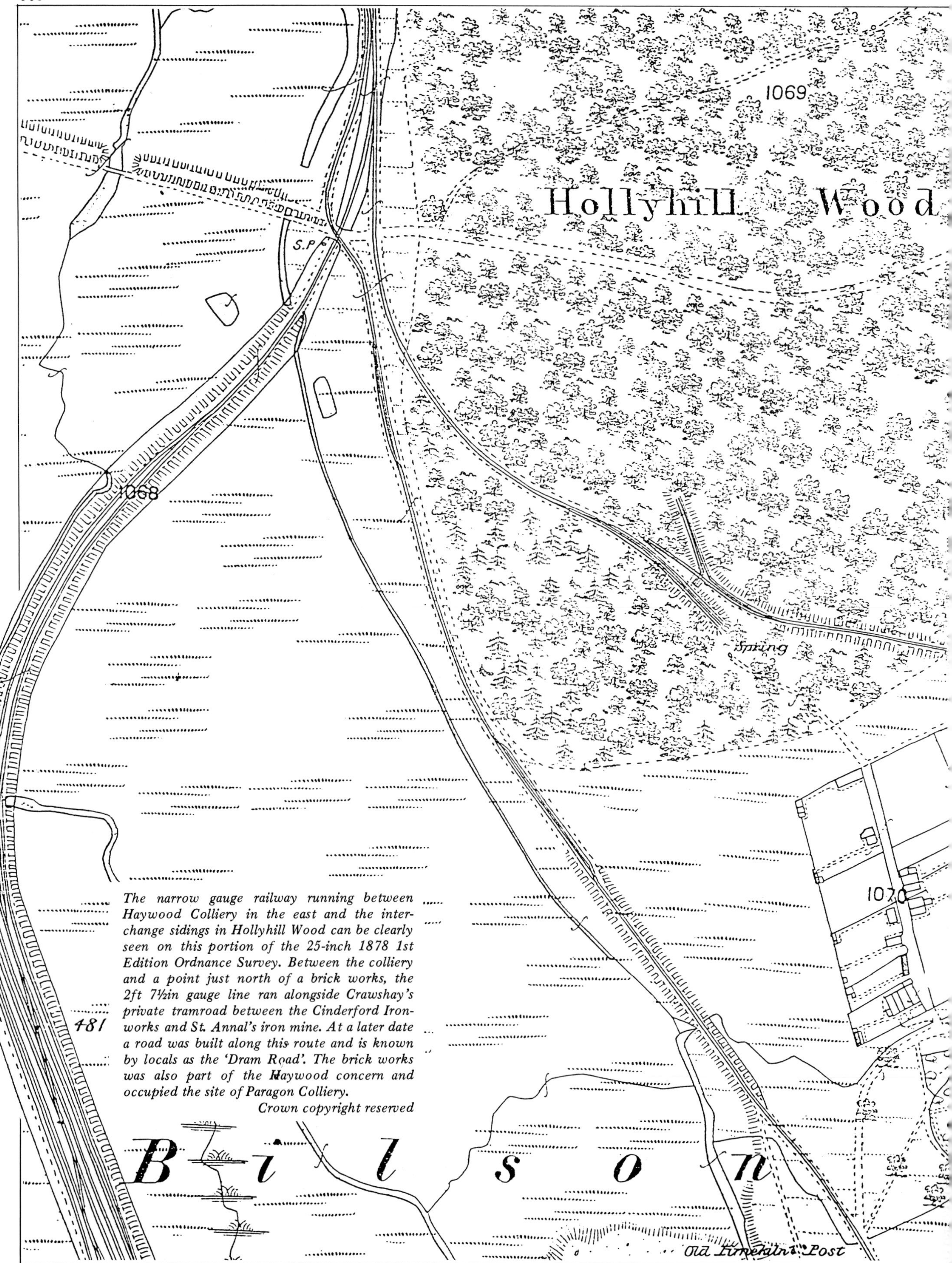

The narrow gauge railway running between Haywood Colliery in the east and the interchange sidings in Hollyhill Wood can be clearly seen on this portion of the 25-inch 1878 1st Edition Ordnance Survey. Between the colliery and a point just north of a brick works, the 2ft 7½in gauge line ran alongside Crawshay's private tramroad between the Cinderford Ironworks and St. Annal's iron mine. At a later date a road was built along this route and is known by locals as the 'Dram Road'. The brick works was also part of the Haywood concern and occupied the site of Paragon Colliery.

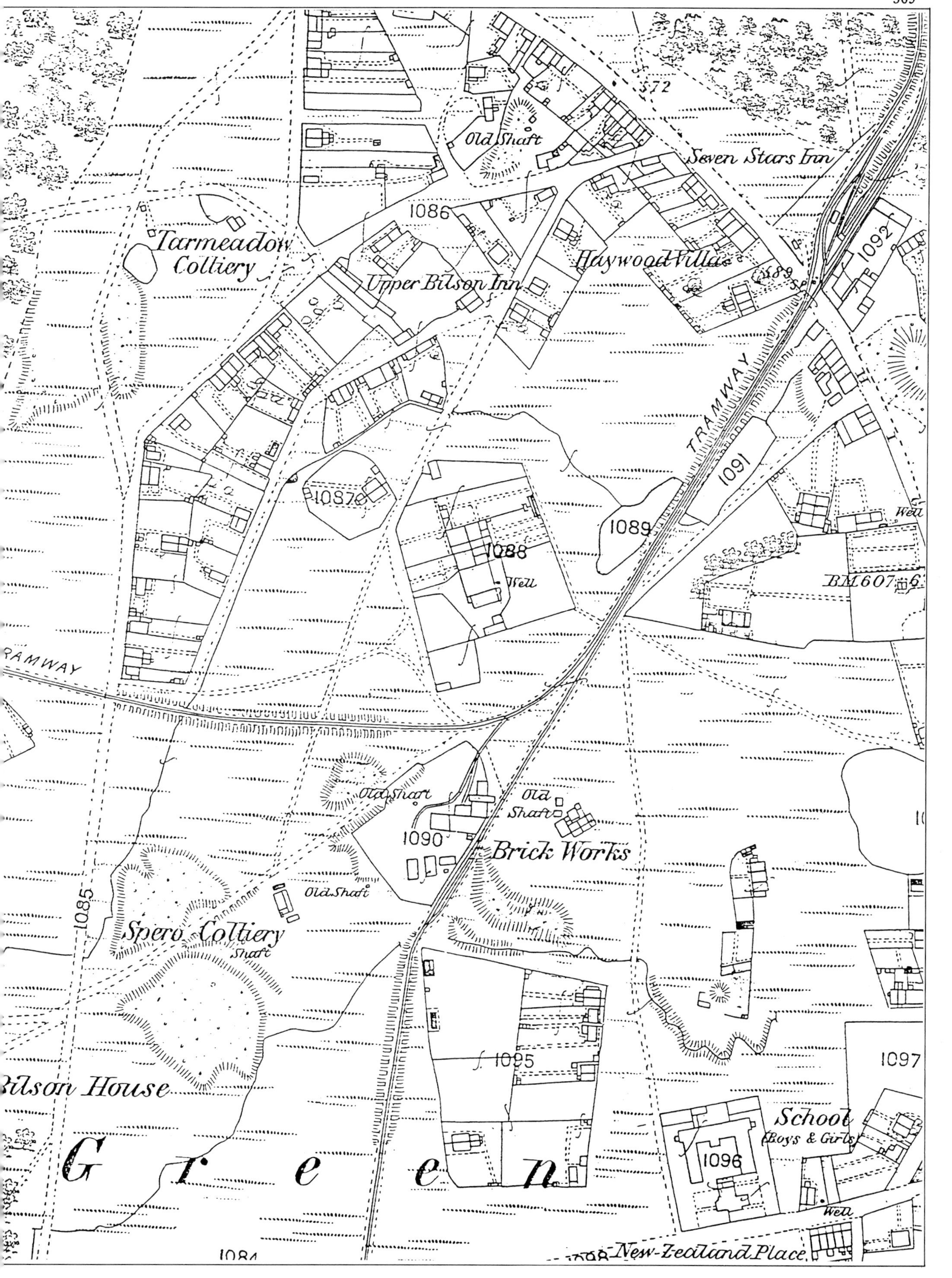
572
Old Shaft
Seven Stars Inn
1086
Tarmeadow Colliery
Haywood Villa
1092
Upper Bilson Inn
TRAMWAY
1091
1087
1088
Well
1089
Well
BM607
TRAMWAY
Old Shaft
Old Shaft
1090
Brick Works
Old Shaft
1085
Spero Colliery
Shaft
1095
1097
Bilson House
School
(Boys & Girls)
1096
Green
Well
1084
New Zealand Place

who was chairman of the Littledean Woodside Coal Co. With a registered capital of £25,000 in £5 shares, this company was working Haywood in conjunction with the Addis Hill gale to the north. In that year they also added the Smith's Delight gale.

Smith's Delight was granted in May 1873 to Thomas Smith who had applied for a pit on the deep side of Haywood Pit to win the Coleford High Delf, or Hill Delf, coal. There were objections to this grant on the grounds that a strip of coal 58 chains long and 1 chain wide was too narrow to be worked independently. Crawshay, however, undertook to win the coal by sinking his Haywood Pumping Pit to the required depth.

At a meeting of the Littledean Woodside Coal Company in May 1874 it was reported that 'not withstanding that the company's trade is a local country one, having no outlet at present to send coal to other markets, they were able to declare a dividend at the rate of ten per cent'. A large extension of business was expected with the completion of a railway then under construction to link the colliery to the Forest of Dean branch of the Great Western Railway. Built to the same 2ft 7½in gauge as Brain's Tramway at Trafalgar Colliery, the new railway ran alongside Crawshay's Tramroad before curving away across Bilson Green to Hollyhill Wood where interchange sidings were constructed, together with a set of screens, on a siding curving off the Whimsey branch from near the dam. The interchange appears to have been built with several levels possibly in the hope of some incoming traffic.

The *Dean Forest Mercury* for 7th October 1876 reported that the Coleford High Delf seam had been cut in the Haywood Colliery. It was possibly the addition of the Smith's Delight gale which had made the working of the Coleford High Delf possible at Haywood as the seam was fairly deep and therefore uneconomic to work in small areas. The company had erected extensive machinery and were looking for a large output of coal. The colliery was the second on the eastern side of the Forest to work the Coleford High Delf in the deep, rather than at the outcrop, the first being Hawkwell Colliery which hit the coal a month earlier (see page 248). It was also reported that the company owned a 'brick manufactory' which was located at the Paragon Colliery a short distance to the south-west of Haywood Colliery. The 1878 25-inch Ordnance Survey shows a connection from the line between Haywood Colliery and its interchange sidings to Paragon Colliery and its associated brickworks. As already mentioned, in 1841 Paragon was held by the Cinderford Iron Co. and thus would have passed into the hands of the Crawshays.

The Littledean Woodside Co., however, soon found it necessary to borrow money from the Standard Building Society which evidently was not sufficient as the company went into liquidation in 1882. Edwin Crawshay continued on until 1885 when the building society itself was wound up and, as Haywood was mortgaged to them, there was a threat that the concern would be sold. To stave this off, Crawshay induced friends to inject some capital and the Haywood Colliery Co. Ltd. was formed.

Incorporated on 25th March 1886, the company had a capital of £5,000 in 1,000 £5 shares to acquire the Addis Hill, Haywood and Richard White gales from Wallace Hadingham of Newnham, Frederick Morgan of Ruspidge and Charlotte Crawshay, Edwin's wife. It was these three who had baled out Edwin over his debt to the building society. There was an indenture in 1883 between Crawshay and the building society for £3,750 (this would have been after the collapse of the Littledean Woodside Coal Co.) As mentioned above, Edwin Crawshay continued on alone, hence his debt to the building society, but in December 1885 the building society itself was in difficulties so the trustees issued a writ against Edwin who had been unable to pay the £2,500 which he had agreed to. To relieve him of this debt, the three mentioned above came to his help and on the formation of the new company each received 167 shares plus £500.

Despite a fresh financial start, the company did not prosper and was wound up voluntarily in September 1888. In April 1890 all hope of the colliery being worked again was removed. It was reported in the *Dean Forest Mercury* that the whole of the plant, engine house, boilers, sheds, etc., together with the 'towering' stack, had been sold at

This picture, taken from the top of the distant signal featured on the opposite page, shows the course of the tramroad to Bullo. The curved embankment on the left had carried the broad gauge Spero siding to an interchange wharf with a tramroad siding for the Haywood Colliery. *L. E. Copeland*

auction by Messrs. Alexander of Cardiff and were to be razed to the ground. Apparently between 80 and 100 men working at the colliery were affected by the closure. At the same sale, held at the Lion Hotel, Cinderford, the Addis Hill gale was also sold for the sum of £200 to Mr. Richard Hadingham.

It is likely that the siding off the Whimsey branch fell into disuse with the closure of the Haywood Colliery and had certainly been removed by 1896 as no mention is made of crossing it when the Severn & Wye's Cinderford Extension was being planned (see *The Severn & Wye Railway, Vol. 2*, Pope, How & Karau, Wild Swan Publications, 1985).

WINNING COLLIERY

The siding here may well have been provided upon the opening of the broad gauge line but certainly prior to 1857, when an early gradient profile shows a siding serving Mr. Goold's Winning Pits. The Winning or Winner Colliery formed part of Bilson Colliery and later part of Crump Meadow. All were originally owned by Edward Protheroe with Aaron Goold acting as his agent in the Forest of Dean. Goold appears to have been working the collieries on his own account by 1847 and trading as Aaron Goold & Co.

The two shafts at the Winning Colliery were alongside the Churchway branch and by c.1833 were the only ones of the four forming Bilson in use. They were described as being 130 yards in depth and were working the Churchway High Delf coal. Underground the coal was won by the pillar and stall method with 16yd wide stalls and 5yd wide pillars. The coal was taken from the face to the shaft in hods which were on wheels and carried 4 cwts.

In 1841 the colliery had a 30in cylinder condensing double power engine and was producing 63,100 tons per year, the coal being disposed of to the Cinderford furnaces and to Bullo Pill.

In February 1864 it was reported in connection with a dispute with the neighbouring Bowson Colliery, that the Winning Pits belonged to Messrs. Goold & Heyworth and that the Churchway High Delf coal in the area had been exhausted. Local legend has it that when the shaft at Bowson, which was the first real attempt to win the Coleford High Delf in the deep, cut the Winning workings, the shaft sinkers were met by Goold's men and a fight broke out underground.

Whether much coal was being won from the Winning Pits after this time is unknown, but the 1878 25-inch Ordnance Survey shows a tramway running eastwards from the shafts to the Duck Colliery where the siding off the Whimsey branch was located. Possibly the pumping engine at Winning was being used in conjunction with Crump Meadow Colliery and the tramway was in use to take coal to the boilers.

DUCK COLLIERY

The Duck Colliery, or Broadmoor, was on the Broadmoor Engine gale which also formed part of the Bilson Colliery. One of the first references to the colliery was in the *Gloucester Journal* for 1st June 1839. It was reported that when 23-year-old Thomas Williams was at work at a coal shaft named Duck's Pit, he slipped and fell to the bottom of the pit, a distance of 60 yards and was killed on the spot. He had been occupied in fastening a chain to a skip wagon in which the coals were hauled to the surface.

In 1841 the colliery was working in the Lowery seam, the High Delf being worked out. The colliery was worked by a 22in cylinder condensing double power engine and 10,500 tons were produced annually.

Both the Winning Colliery and Duck Colliery followed through the same ownership, passing from the Goold's to the Bilson & Crump Meadow Collieries Co. Ltd. in 1874 and in October 1884 to the Lydney & Crump Meadow Collieries Co. Ltd. Whereas it is likely that little coal was worked from the Winning Pits after the 1860s, Duck Colliery remained in production. It would appear that it was leased to Messrs. Jenkins & Parsons prior to 1884 as in that year Messrs. J. Chivers & Co. of Hawkwell Tinplate works were worried about damage which might be caused by Messrs. Jenkins and Parsons of the Duck Colliery. The following year Jenkins and Parsons were in trouble, having trespassed into the adjoining Victory gale owned by Goodrich Langham.

In June 1888 the Lydney & Crump Meadow Collieries Co. Ltd. were applying to the Crown for permission to burn 200-300 tons of coke on the pit bank at Duck during the following three months. It was stated that the coke was to be used for the purpose of drying hops. The Crown were

A closer view of the down distant signal for Cinderford Crossing as shown on page 306 (but now fixed at Caution). This photo shows the signal in a rather neglected state in September 1959 for it had ceased to have any real function after the withdrawal of passenger services. *A. K. Pope*

worried about the possible damage to timber in the nearby Hollyhill Wood but it was pointed out that the coal to be burnt was from the Starkey seam which was a much cleaner coal than 'the rubbish from the Coleford High Delf'. The Crown gave their permission and the production of coke continued on an annual basis until 1893.

In 1898 the Great Western licence from the Crown for the Forest of Dean tramroad expired and it was agreed that the Lydney & Crump Meadow Co. would take over the portion of line from Bilson to Duck in order to move pit timber from their saw mills at Bilson to Duck. However, this was not done as the tramroad was said to be in very poor condition and there was not much coal left in Duck Pit. The date at which the tramroad was actually removed on this stretch is uncertain, but as a bridge was built to allow it to pass through the Cinderford loop, it is likely that it was still in situ in 1908.

Duck Colliery continued working and in 1908 *Potts Mining Register* records that it was owned by the Lydney & Crump Meadow Collieries Co. Ltd. and that 60 were employed below ground and 11 above. On 13th May 1910 the *Dean Forest Mercury* reported a break-in at the colliery engine house in which the oil engine was damaged. The engine was further in the wars in November 1911 when on Monday the 7th, a fire broke out at about 10 o'clock in the morning. The *Dean Forest Mercury* report of the fire gave several details of the colliery. At the pit-head for some time there had been a 30 or 40 horsepower oil engine for the purpose of underground haulage by means of cables. The engineman was one James Davis and, on the morning in question, by some means the ignition valve failed to act and oil from the small supply tank ignited and escaped. The engine house was soon in flames and ashes but luckily no-one was injured and there was a good supply of water on hand with plenty of helpers. The possibility of a greater disaster was avoided by the removal of a large storage tank of petrol just outside the building. Attention then moved to the screens, pit-head gear, etc., which were saved by playing the company's hose continuously on them. Not much hope was held out for the engine house or its contents for, although the massive engine was for the most part saved, it had become red-hot and was believed to be greatly damaged, if not useless. As the pit supplied a great part of the local and 'country' trade, steps were immediately taken to make the underground arrangements as effective as possible so the colliery should not be stopped.

Duck Colliery ground frame (5 miles 40 chains) on 26th June 1933 by which time the siding was serving Broadmoor Brickworks. *L. E. Copeland*

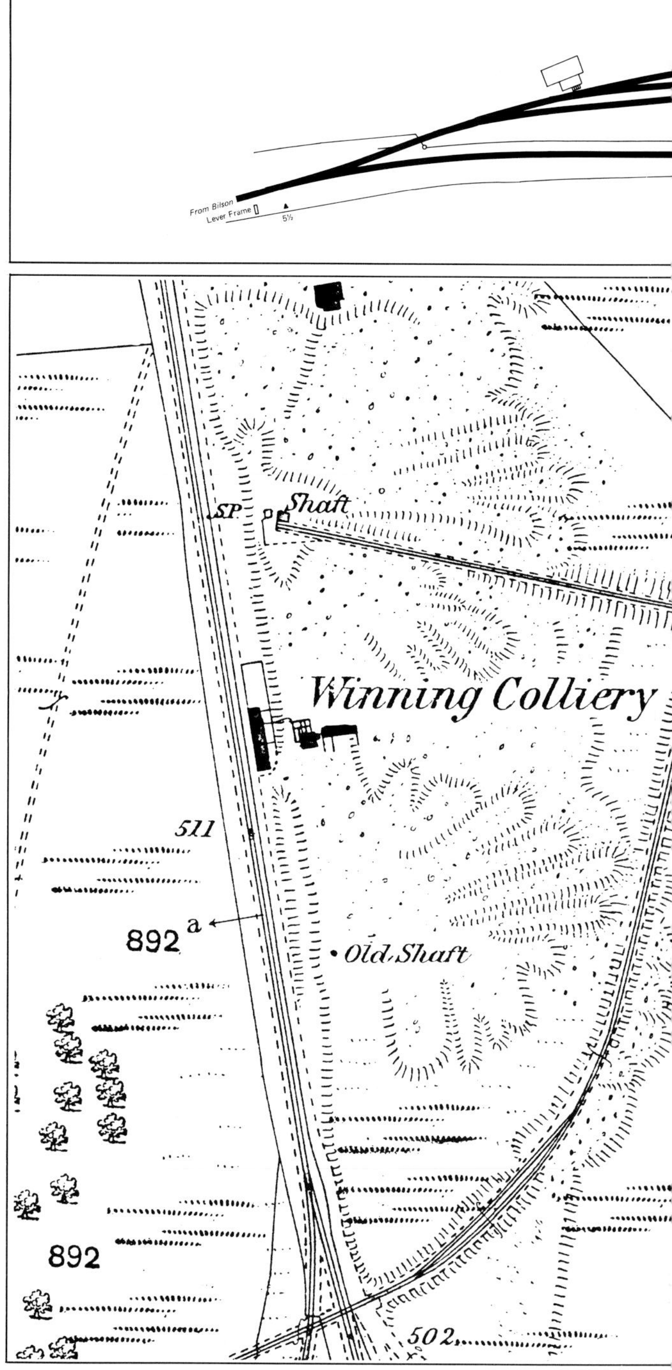

Whether the fire sparked a redevelopment at the colliery is uncertain but a new engine house was erected in 1915, possibly housing a steam engine. At the same time the siding arrangements at the colliery were improved by the addition of a second connection to the GWR and two sidings, authorised in August 1915. The GWR minutes for December 1892 record permission to extend rails to join the GWR for better working of the colliery, but exactly what this refers to has not been established.

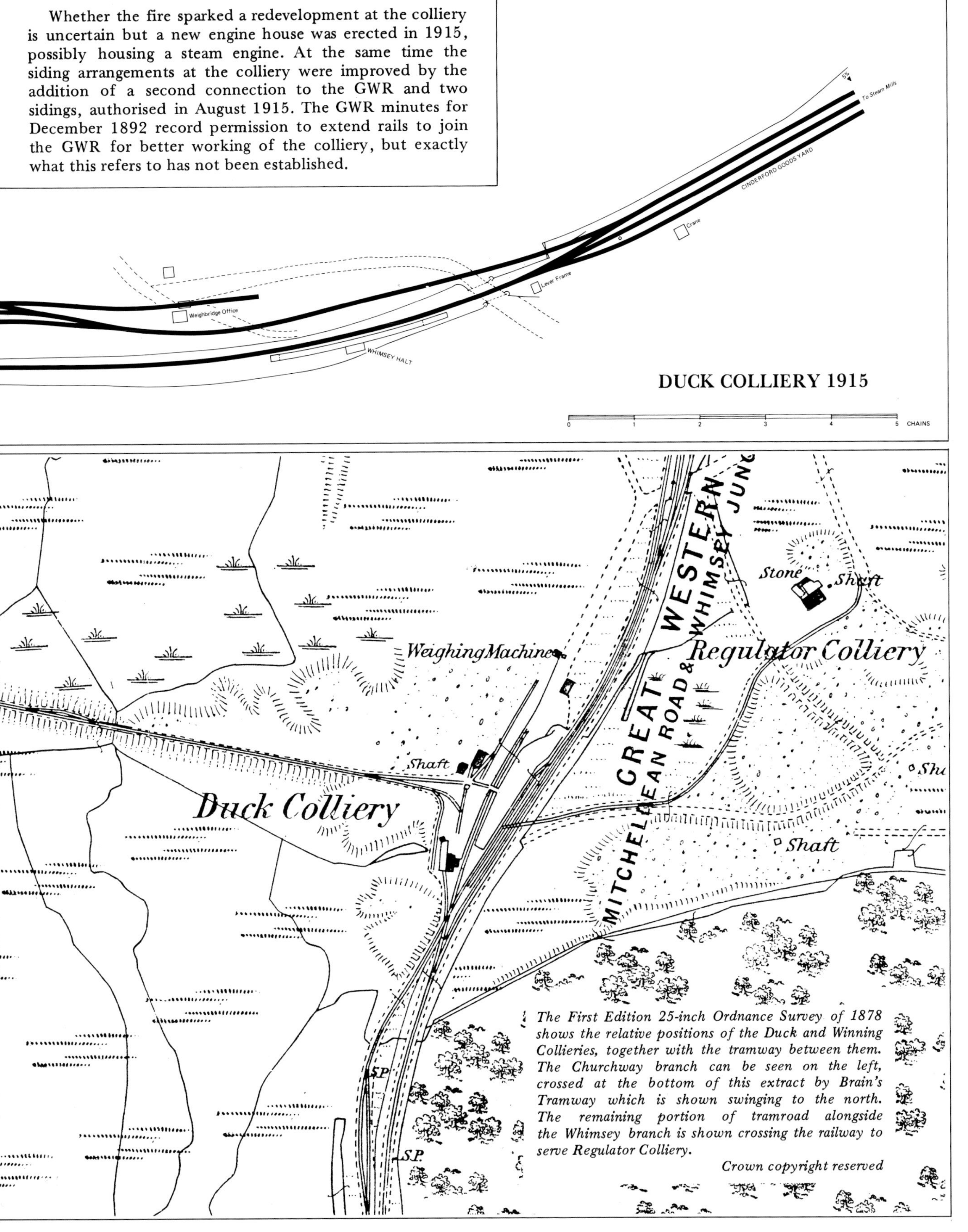

The First Edition 25-inch Ordnance Survey of 1878 shows the relative positions of the Duck and Winning Collieries, together with the tramway between them. The Churchway branch can be seen on the left, crossed at the bottom of this extract by Brain's Tramway which is shown swinging to the north. The remaining portion of tramroad alongside the Whimsey branch is shown crossing the railway to serve Regulator Colliery.

Crown copyright reserved

BROADMOOR BRICKWORKS

Some of the buildings connected with the Duck Colliery took on a new use in 1922 with the establishment by the Lydney & Crump Meadow Collieries Co. of a brickworks. In May 1923 an advert appeared in the *Dean Forest Mercury* advising that bricks were now available at the works. Expansion was evidently in hand in July when a good bricklayer was required for building a further kiln. The works were set up at Duck to use the material in the colliery waste mound – a diversification for the colliery company whose Crump Meadow Colliery was coming to the end of its active life.

In April 1938 the works were again being extended and modernised when the company announced the electrification of the works and the erection of a continuous kiln and stack with new brick-making machinery. At an estimated cost of around £6,000, the improvements would raise the output from 2,500,000 to 6,000,000 bricks per year. At the same time an application was made to the Crown for

Two views of the private siding serving Broadmoor Brickworks on 27th October 1946. Driver Bob Trigg remembers 'Duck Colliery never produced much coal – just the odd wagon or two'. Broadmoor Brickworks was served by up trains on their way back to Bilson.

L. E. Copeland

Broadmoor Brickworks, obscured by the surplus steam escaping from the safety valves of an up train rattling down the bank towards Bilson on 6th April 1962. *A. K. Pope*

permission to use the waste tips at the Winning Colliery, and a tramway was laid along the embankment which had previously formed a connection between the two sites. In October the buildings and machinery were given as:

> 'Old Engine House in brick and slate, 24ft x 28ft x 20ft, built about 1915, in use as a storeroom.
> One large kiln to hold 38,000 bricks, said to be 23 years old.
> One office 10ft x 10ft
> Mixing shed 80ft x 20ft in timber and corrugated iron. Old boiler house adjoining.
> Drying shed on south side for 50,000 bricks.
> 5 kilns of which 3 are to be dismantled.
> New power house 8ft x 15ft, brick and corrugated roof.'

From the above description it would appear that the electrification of the works had been already carried out. The old engine house once contained a single cylinder steam engine fed by a Lancashire boiler which may have replaced the old engine when the site was still in use for colliery purposes. Certainly the date of the 'old engine house', 1915, ties in with development work at the colliery, as does the date given to 'one large kiln' said to be 23 years old, which would give a building date of 1915 also. It is possible that the Lydney & Crump Meadow Company were producing bricks for their own use at Broadmoor prior to 1922 and in that year decided to market their bricks following the virtual closure of a nearby brickworks at Hawkwell (see page 252).

In 1946, following the nationalisation of the coal industry, the colliery-owned brickworks were inspected and at Broadmoor it is recorded that the works were using shale from the tips at Duck, Winning and Crump Meadow, which it was estimated would last for another thirty years. Coal for the works was brought from the Lydney & Crump Meadow Company's Arthur & Edward Colliery at Lydbrook where about half a percent of the brickworks' output was used. The management at Broadmoor was entirely separate from that of the colliery, and the brickworks were valued by a valuation panel.

The works continue in use at the time of writing.

REGULATOR COLLIERY

The siding to Regulator Colliery was provided soon after the opening of the line on the broad gauge. It stemmed from virtually the end of the Whimsey branch and, as depicted on a plan of 1856, curved away to the south-east and terminated at a loading wharf.

The Regulator was one of the older workings in the area and in 1833 it was owned by Mr. Bennett who was working it by means of two pits, the Regulator Pit, which was 90 yards deep, and the Oak Pit at 70 yards deep. The workings were in the Churchway High Delf and were drained by an engine which drew the water out in buckets. The output was twenty-two tons per day which was mainly sold locally.

By 1841 parts of Regulator Nos. 1, 2 & 3 were being worked by a firm called the Cheltenham Protector Coal Company which had been sold to them by James Bennett who retained the rest. The portion worked by Bennett included the Regulator, Waterloo, Oak and George's Folly gales and it was probably in connection with these that the siding was put in.

In 1841 there was a 22 inch double condensing engine at the colliery and the shafts were 90 yards deep. The output of coals was 20 tons per day from the Starkey and 10 tons from the Lowery, which gave an annual output of 9,000 tons. It was observed that a steam engine on the No. 3 shaft which was not then at work would be sunk on down to the Churchway High Delf seam.

The portion of Regulator held by Bennett had been surrendered by 1865 and it is likely that the siding was removed around this time. It had certainly gone by 1878.

WHIMSEY

A unique view of the northern gated entrance to the brickworks and colliery in 1933 with Cinderford Goods just visible beyond. This second connection to the GWR was added in 1915 but was evidently removed by 1946. The signal visible was the down distant for Steam Mills Crossing Ground Frame. Cinderford Crossing GF was just out of view to the right, with the crossing behind the photographer. The site of the disused Whimsey Colliery (see map on p. 321) was on the left. *Baxter, cty. Railway & Canal Historical Society*

When the broad gauge railway was completed and opened in 1854, Whimsey was one of the two northernmost points, the other being Churchway. The line terminated alongside Whimsey Colliery; however, this appears to have closed soon afterwards and it seems that most of the railway traffic originating here in the early days came from elsewhere. The original FODR tramroad from Bullo Pill had also terminated at Whimsey until it was extended by private tramroads to Nailbridge in 1834 and to Westbury Brook Iron Mine in 1842. Although largely replaced by the new railway, the tramroad system was kept intact from Cinderford Bridge to Whimsey and beyond until around 1908, serving the iron works, iron mines and collieries in the area, and was in fact extended to Wigpool Iron Mine shortly after the broad gauge line was built.

A tramroad wharf was provided at Whimsey for transferring traffic onto the broad gauge but, unfortunately, no early trackplan showing this has yet been discovered. The earliest known plan of Whimsey is the 25-inch Ordnance Survey of 1878, by which time a portion of the Mitcheldean Road & Forest of Dean Junction Railway had been completed northwards from Whimsey. The through line ran between a loop siding on the up or western side and a dead-end siding to the east, and it is tempting to speculate that the Mitcheldean Road line was formed by simply extending the headshunt for the existing loop and that the formation hardly changed as a result, but this cannot be confirmed. The dead-end siding terminated at a loading bank, whilst the loop siding had a loading bank with a tip arrangement at its northern end. The tramroad ran close alongside this siding, between it and the by now disused Whimsey Colliery, and the loops which served the interchange facilities are shown adjacent to the loading bank. The up loop siding was also known as 'Dowlais Siding' from the destination of the Westbury Brook iron ore traffic, a name which lasted well after the closure of the iron mine.

When Whimsey was selected as the site for a new goods station serving Cinderford in place of the one at Ruspidge, the necessary expenditure, estimated at £500, which included a second junction with the existing siding, was authorised on 31st October 1883. The following January, C. W. Whalley's tender of £343 was accepted for the construction of the goods shed, offices and the provision and fixing of the crane. The new station, to which the name Cinderford Goods was transferred from Ruspidge, was officially opened on 1st September 1884 and remained the GWR's principal goods station for the town even after the opening of the new joint station in 1900 (see *The Severn & Wye Railway* Vol. 2), as the income from this was shared with the Midland Railway.

The first station master at Whimsey is believed to have been a Mr. D. Burford, who retired from there on 17th February 1893 after 40 years service in the area. Originally based at Awre Junction on the South Wales main line, Mr. Burford moved to Cinderford Bridge in February 1874 and later to Whimsey. He was succeeded by a Mr. Jones, who lasted only four years before moving to Llantrisant.

Further changes at Whimsey included the provision of a private siding from 1911 for Williams' saw mills (later the

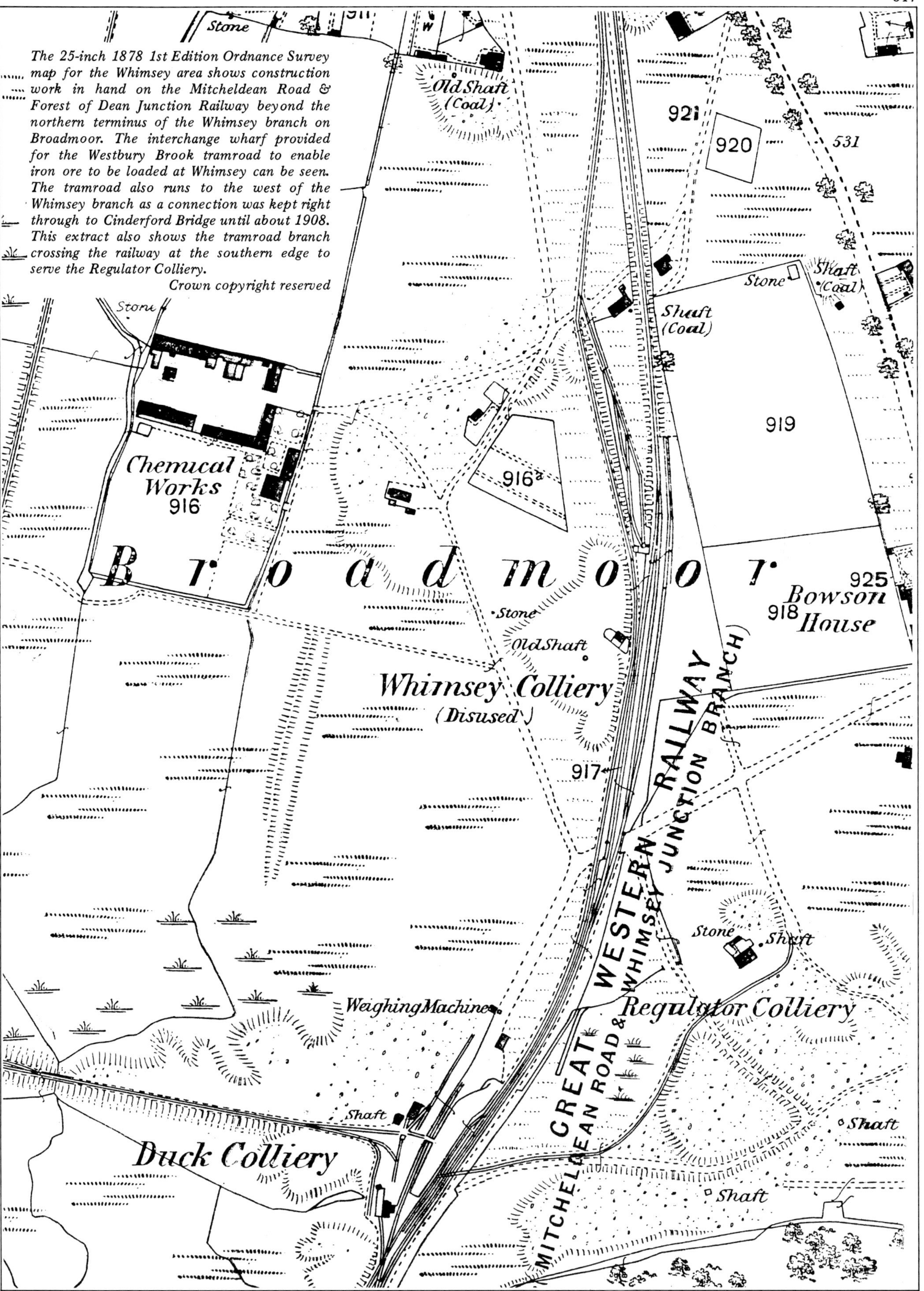

The 25-inch 1878 1st Edition Ordnance Survey map for the Whimsey area shows construction work in hand on the Mitcheldean Road & Forest of Dean Junction Railway beyond the northern terminus of the Whimsey branch on Broadmoor. The interchange wharf provided for the Westbury Brook tramroad to enable iron ore to be loaded at Whimsey can be seen. The tramroad also runs to the west of the Whimsey branch as a connection was kept right through to Cinderford Bridge until about 1908. This extract also shows the tramroad branch crossing the railway at the southern edge to serve the Regulator Colliery.

This early 1920s view of Whimsey yard is the best known view of the sidings and rear of the goods shed, which has what appears to be a GWR one-horse lorry backed up to the loading bay. The Dean Forest Timber Company's premises can be seen on the right, outside the railway boundary and, in the foreground, the short siding and brick-built carriage landing believed to have been provided in 1913. As this view shows, the siding was squeezed in between the existing siding and the boundary fence at minimum cost, resulting in somewhat less than the standard 6ft clearance between tracks. This extra siding held just two wagons and seems to have been removed by 1946. *Collection Keith Alford*

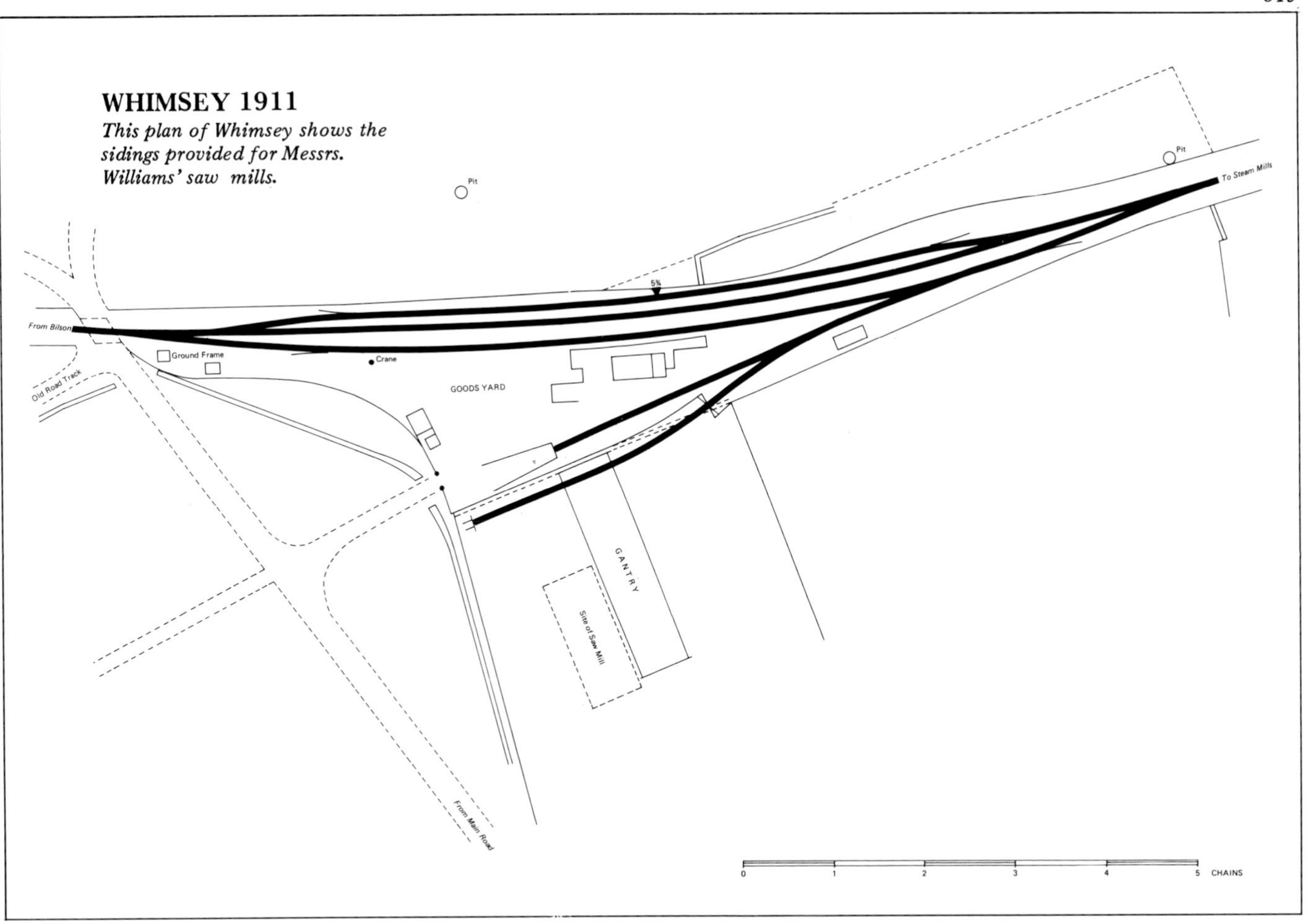

WHIMSEY 1911
This plan of Whimsey shows the sidings provided for Messrs. Williams' saw mills.

Dean Forest Timber Company) on the eastern boundary of the site. Originally served by a single siding, the 1922 Ordnance Survey shows two lines inside their plot at right-angles to each other. A short siding and carriage landing dock was also provided off the existing goods yard siding c.1913.

The 1908 timetable shows five departures from Cinderford Goods between 9.00 a.m. and 4.08 p.m., including one round trip to Speedwell which ran as required, but by 1927 this had reduced to two turns plus a working to Drybrook Quarries which was not timetabled to stop at Whimsey. By the late 1940s the sawmills had closed and much of Cinderford Goods traffic was by that time dealt with at the joint station in Cinderford, where the sharing of income was abolished upon nationalisation and the transfer of the Forest lines to the new Western Region of British Railways. As a result, Cinderford Goods station was little used, but new life was breathed into the site when Berry Wiggins & Co. Ltd., whose registered office at one time was in Stratford, East London, and later at Field House, Fetter Lane, London, established a bitumen distribution depot there in 1949. It was estimated that about 5,000 tons of bitumen per annum would be received at Whimsey for transfer to road tankers, bringing a revenue to the railway of some £5,000.

With the closure of Drybrook Quarries in 1953 and the abandonment of the line north of Whimsey soon after, Berry Wiggins' traffic formed a major part of the traffic on the Forest of Dean branch in later years, and practically the only traffic after the closure of Northern United Colliery at the end of 1965. When Berry Wiggins transferred their bitumen operation to a new depot in Lydney at the end of 1966 this effectively spelt the end for the branch, which closed seven months later.

WHIMSEY COLLIERY

This was the point to which the branch was originally built. Whimsey Colliery was started in 1737 when it was known as Major Wade's Suff, suff being a corruption of 'sough' or water outlet. By 1833 it was known as The Whimsey or Major Lough (*sic*) Colliery and was galed to Thomas Meek and partners but was not working. By 1841 the gale was in the hands of James Teague, James Bennett, Thomas Brain and John Williams and was working the coal in the Brazilly and all veins above. The colliery was obviously still producing when the broad gauge was laid but apparently closed soon afterwards. The 1878 25-inch Ordnance Survey marks the colliery as 'disused'.

ALL OFFERS SUBJECT TO EARLY REPLY AND BEING UNSOLD ON RECEIPT OF ORDER.

TELEPHONE NO. 33 — ESTABLISHED 1865 — TELEGRAMS: "OAK, CINDERFORD."

MEMO. FROM

THE DEAN FOREST TIMBER CO., LTD.

English and Foreign Timber and General Builders' Merchants.

GOVERNMENT CONTRACTORS.

SAW MILLS,
CINDERFORD,
GLOS. 27th March 1926

STATION & PRIVATE SIDINGS: CINDERFORD G.W.R.

Messrs. Bruton, Knowles & Co.,
Auctioneers,
Gloucester.

WILLIAMS' SAW MILLS

Messrs. Williams & Co. was an old established timber business, formed in 1865, with a mill in Foundry Lane, Cinderford. In January 1910 the concern was turned into a limited company, Williams & Co. (Cinderford) Ltd, the proprietors being Ernest Williams, William Gardner, Thomas Shill and Philip Evans. The first three were described as timber merchants and all lived in Cinderford whilst Evans was a colliery manager from Lydbrook. The authorised capital of the new company was £7,000 in £1 shares, the majority being used to pay the directors for their interest in Williams & Co. On 4th January 1910, the day after the company was incorporated, £2,000 of debentures were issued by way of a first mortgage, whilst in February a second mortgage of £1,000 was taken.

Business appears to have been brisk, the mill working night and day through the year to cope with demand. This annoyance to neighbouring residential property, and the occurrence of a fire in March which gutted a portion of the mill and led to calls for the formation of a fire brigade in Cinderford, probably prompted the company to acquire a patch of land alongside Cinderford Goods station.

In November it was reported that the new mill was in the course of erection and that the power for the works was to be a Tangye 95 hp gas engine which, together with a suction plant, was designed to use the waste products from the mill rather than anthracite as normal. This plant was the first of its kind erected by Tangyes and cost £1,000. A private siding was constructed outside the boundary at Cinderford Goods under an agreement of February 1911. The cost of construction was £73 0s 1d which was advanced by Williams to be returned to them as a 5% rebate on traffic charges for five years, or, until the actual cost had been refunded.

The new mill, reported to be in working order in June 1911, was described as 'capacious'. It was 120ft long by 80ft wide and contained a number of circular saws, benches and one 'very large' rack saw. The output from the mill included oak railway wagon scantlings; key wood; oak, ash, elm and beech planks; elm and larch cart boards; cleft oak gates; pales; spokes; ladder rungs; and sawn oak field gates and posts.

In September 1911 a third issue of debentures raised a further £600 and in the following January fourth debentures were issued for a further £1,000. Whether the company was by now in financial problems is unknown, but in April 1913 two of the original directors, Gardner and Shill, retired and in May Daniel Walkley, who had become a director in November 1910, appointed himself receiver under powers contained in holding twenty of the second mortgage debentures of £50 each. In April 1914 it was announced that the company was to be wound up and by July this was completed with the property being disposed of.

The works were taken over by the Dean Forest Timber Co. to which the private siding agreement was transferred in October 1914. The transfer document stated that although the siding had been completed, no traffic had passed over it and only £42 had been paid towards the cost.

Daniel Walkley remained connected with the Dean Forest Timber Co. and became manager. The proprietor appears to have been one Morgan Jones. It would also

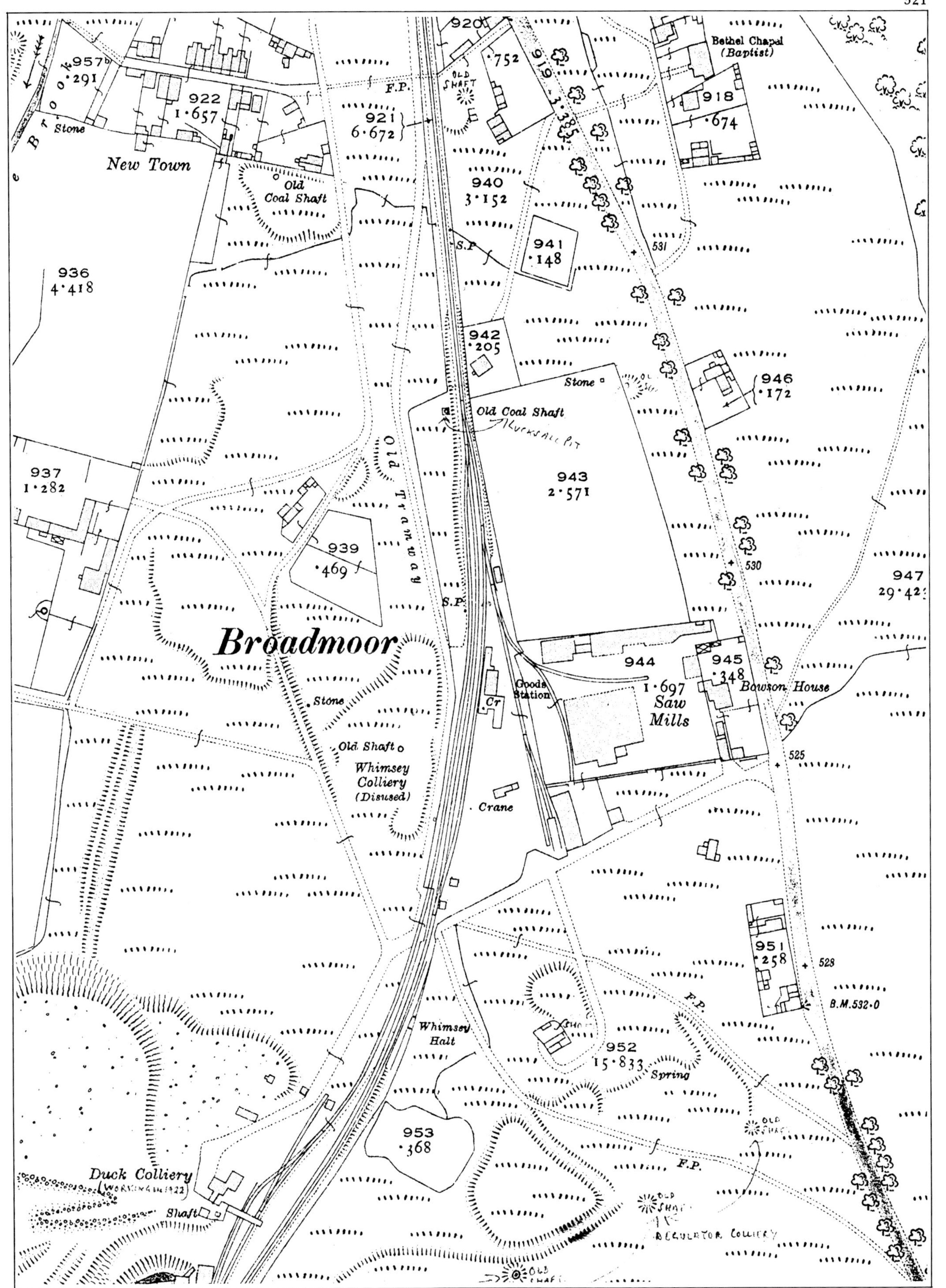

This extract from the 25-inch Ordnance Survey for 1922 shows the later arrangements at the saw mills.

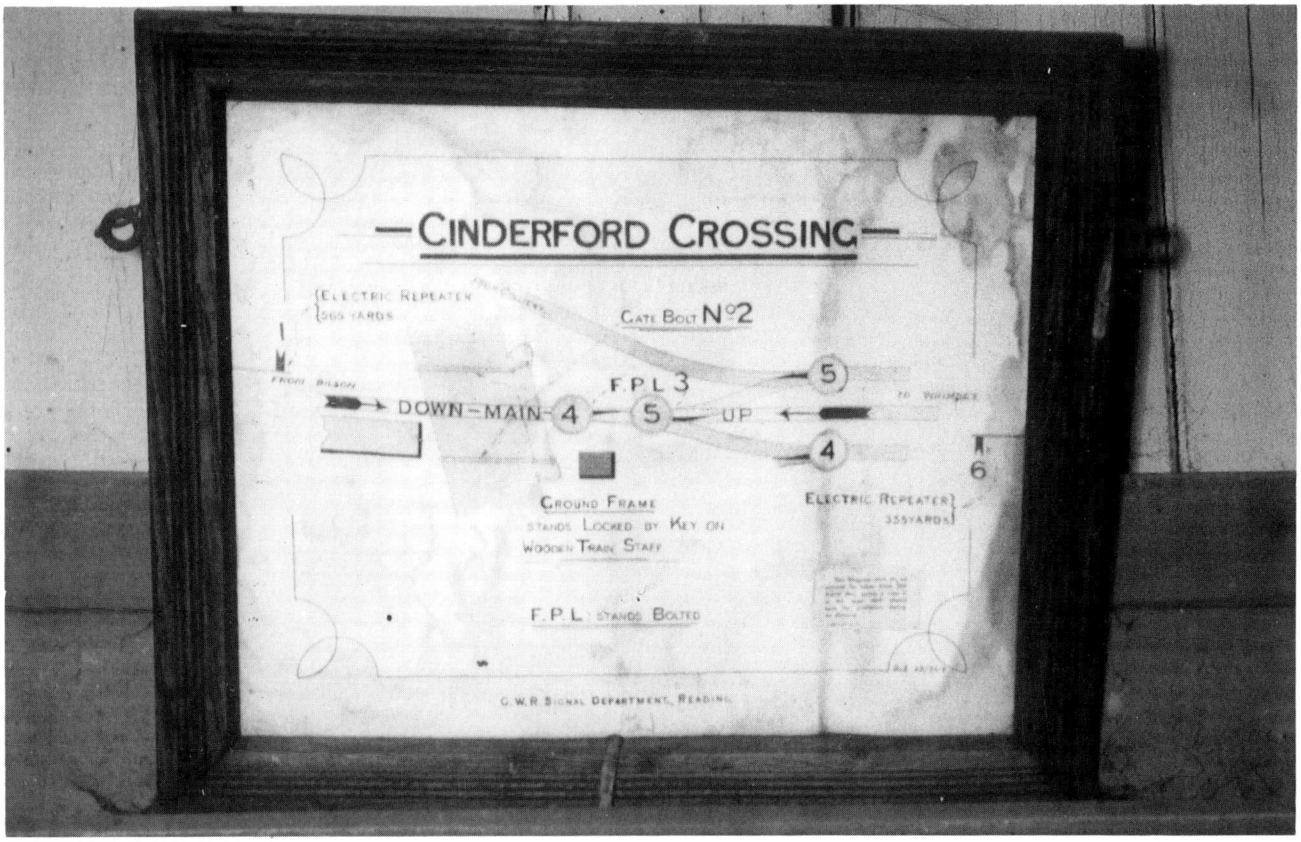

The diagram for Cinderford Crossing which still showed the line coming in from Duck Colliery at the top left, years after the connection was removed. The diagram was drawn in 1907 and remained in the ground frame until closure. *A. K. Pope*

Left: The interior of the ground frame, showing the 'stud locking' frame with six levers at 5¼in centres. The two wire tensioners behind the frame allowed the crossing keeper to take the slack out of the wires operating the Distant signals. However, since the signal worked by the No. 6 lever was only 355 yards from the cabin, this adjuster was seldom used. *Right:* An external view of the ground frame. *L. E. Copeland*

appear that William Gardner was a part of the new concern as in August 1918 he was signing a cheque for an extra area of land at Whimsey.

By 1922 as well as being 'English and Foreign Timber Merchants', the company had become factors of all kinds of building materials. Their letterhead also announced that they were 'Government & Railway Contractors'.

The 1922 edition of the 25-inch Ordnance Survey shows two sidings within the works yard, splitting after passing through the gate which protected the Forest of Dean branch from straying animals. Railwaymen remember traffic being brought in for the saw mills on 'Macaw' bogie bolster wagons but unfortunately no other details have been discovered.

The saw mills were up for auction on 30th/31st March 1926 when most of the equipment and materials were disposed of. Included amongst the lots in the auction catalogue were the Tangye engine and a 5 hp Garratt traction engine and timber trailer. The site was purchased by Messrs. Joiner who operated a saw mills at Camp Mill, Soudley, and a general contracting company including steam rolling. A traffic report in June 1946 gave a siding for J. Joiner & Sons Ltd., Cinderford, as being defunct for 20 years. It is likely that the site remained vacant until Joiners moved from their Soudley site in 1952 to Whimsey the move being virtually complete by September. The reason given for the change of site was that 98% of Joiners' output went by rail. In November it was reported that it might be necessary to extend a siding at Whimsey to accommodate wagons for the saw mills. It was believed that a gantry crane was to be erected alongside the siding but whether this work was carried out is unknown. Whimsey yard had been taken over by Berry Wiggins who established a bitumen distribution depot there. This had been set up in 1949 and occupied most of the available siding space.

Cinderford Goods station in the 1940s. 'Dowlais siding' on the left had served the interchange wharf for the Westbury Brook Tramroad which conveyed ore from the Westbury Brook and later Fairplay iron mines, and, as shown on the signalling diagram, the Crossing Ground Frame had once extended to a 'colliery'. Occupation Key box No. 6 beside the catch point is just visible behind the sign beside the gates. The distant signal in the background was the down distant for Steam Mills Crossing Ground Frame. Point discs working with the blades of the trap point were provided on both of the loop sidings.

L. E. Copeland

OFFICIAL DRAWING OF WHIMSEY GOODS SHED

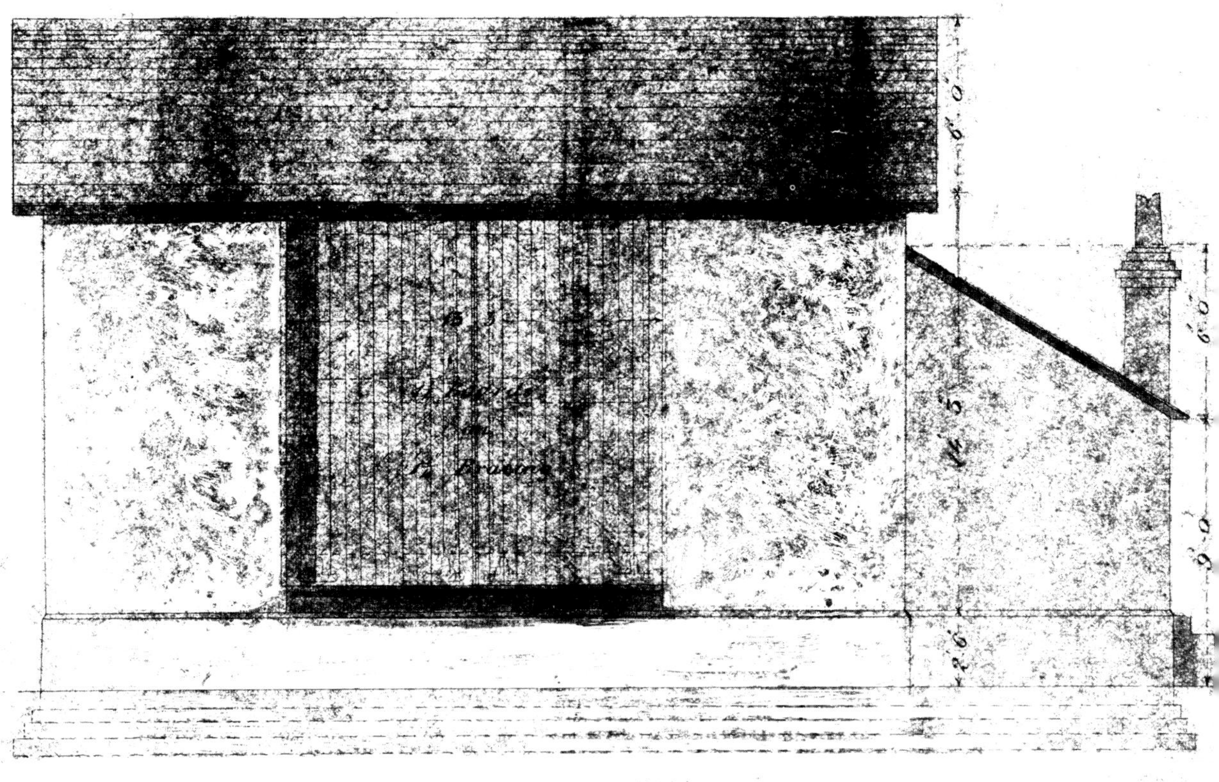

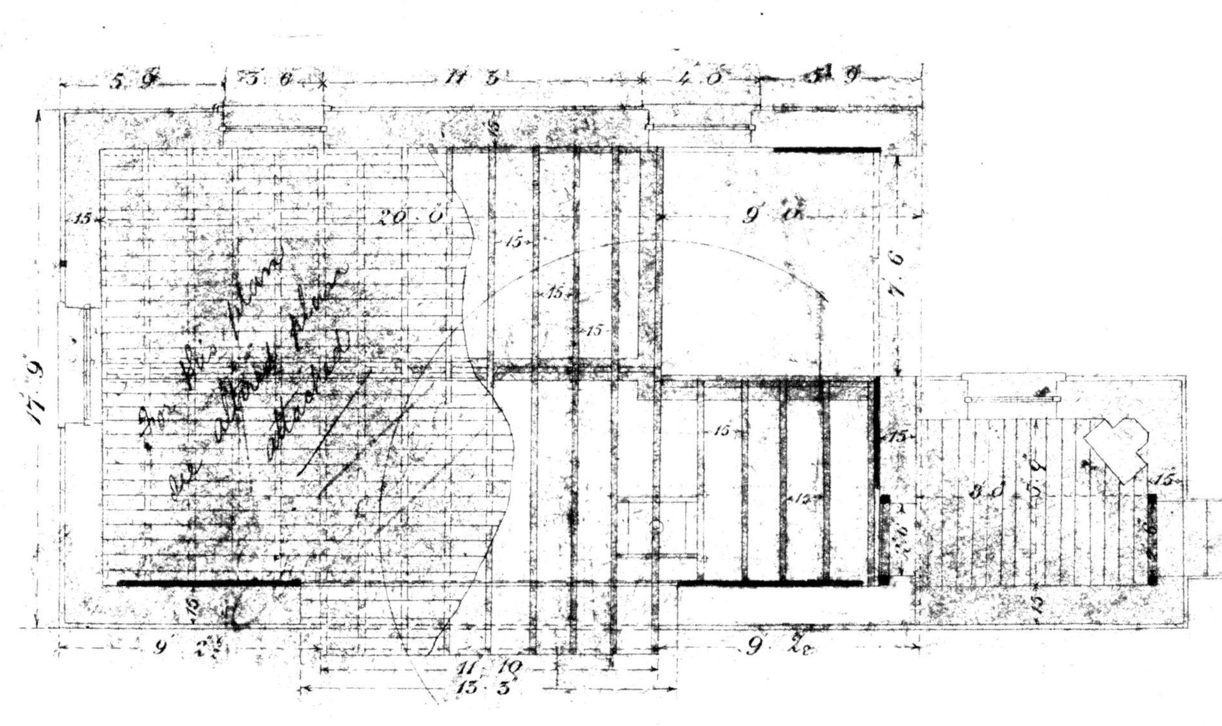

WHIMSEY

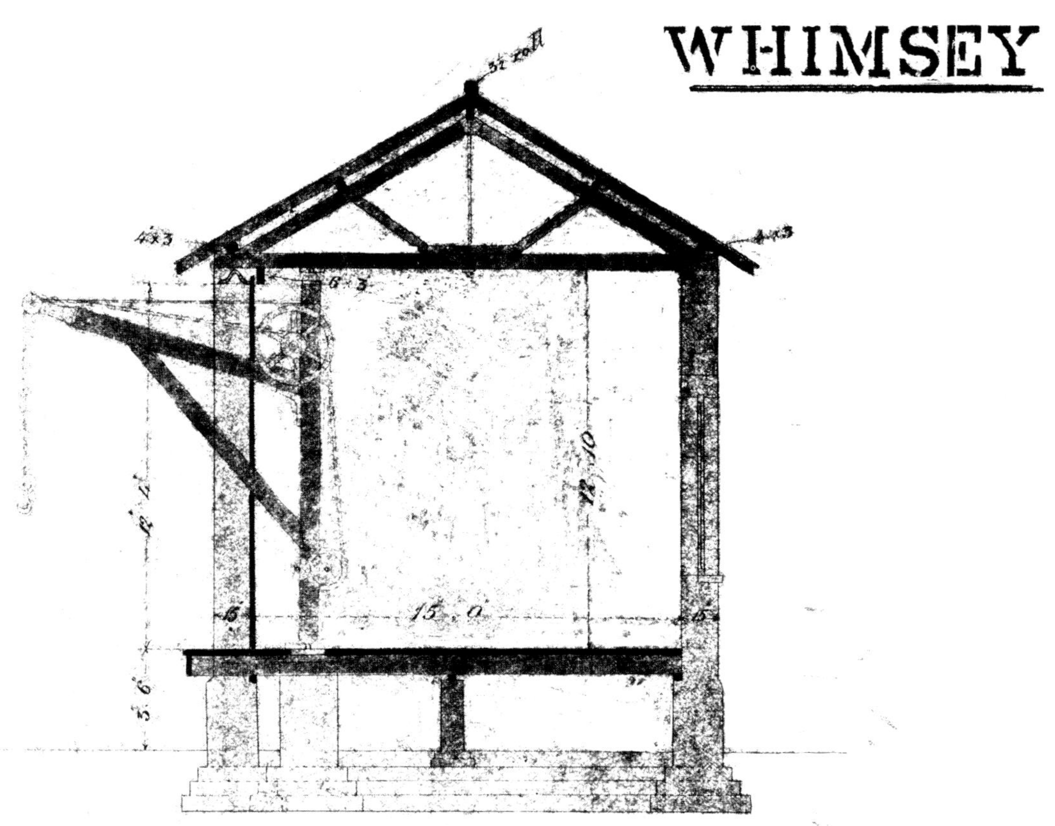
5½ roll
4×3
4×3
6×3
12 4
12 10
15
15 0
15
3 6

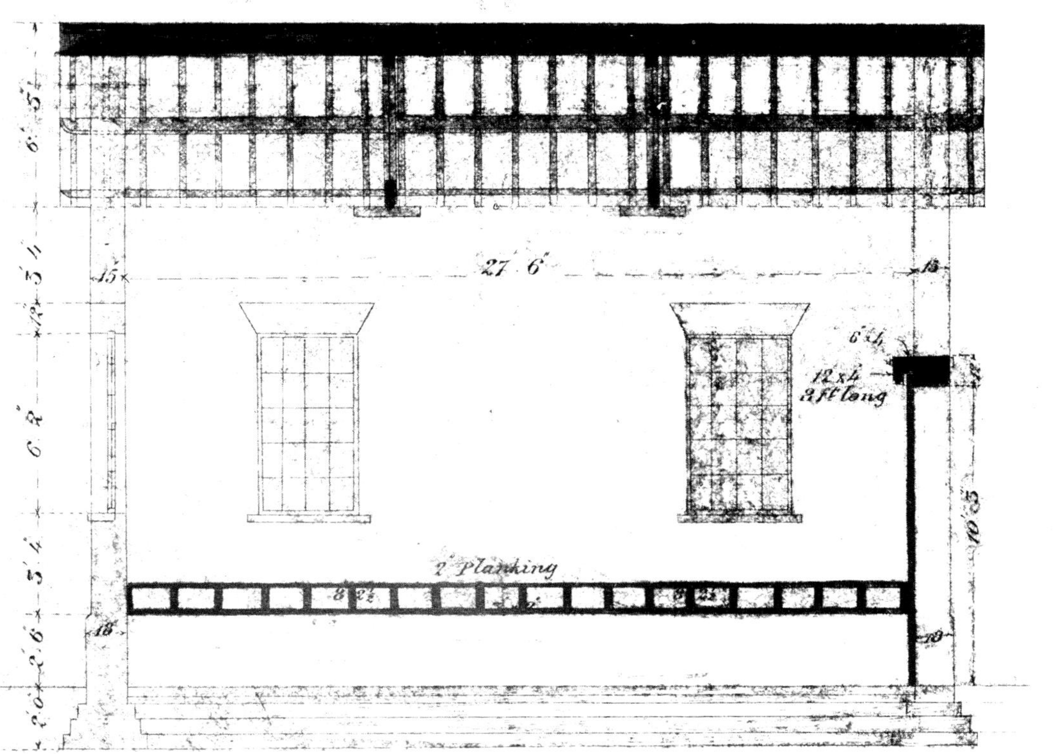
6 5½
3 4
27 6
15
15
6 4
12×4
8 ft long
6 2
10 5
3 4
2 Planking
8 2½
2 6
18
10
2 0

The stone-built goods shed and sleeper-topped platform on 27th October 1946. The sawmill, previously situated outside the boundary fence on the left, had long gone but the derelict private siding may have still been in situ at this time. Cinderford Goods was busy in the 1920s with the receipt of general goods, and the odd truck of coal and timber for the saw mills. Crown timber was also loaded here, often onto 'Macaws' using the 6-ton crane shown on the opposite page. There had also been a smaller 1½ ton crane on the far end of the platform for more general use and this is just visible on the edge of the picture on page 320. By the time this picture was taken, most of Cinderford's goods traffic was more sensibly dealt with at the joint station, and crews remember that the sidings here were only served occasionally, hence the rather lonely appearance of the site in these views. The offices in the background beyond the goods shed date from the opening in 1884 and were erected alongside the original boundary to the site. The extra land was acquired in October 1913. *L. E. Copeland*

Looking south towards Bilson with Holly Hill Wood and Broadmoor Brickworks on the horizon and the course of the tramroad served by Dowlais siding apparent in the foreground. The buildings on the left were a PW hut and Cinderford Crossing ground frame cabin. Whimsey Halt was situated on the left-hand side, immediately beyond the level crossing, but frustratingly, despite tireless searches, no pictures of it have yet come to light. *L. E. Copeland*

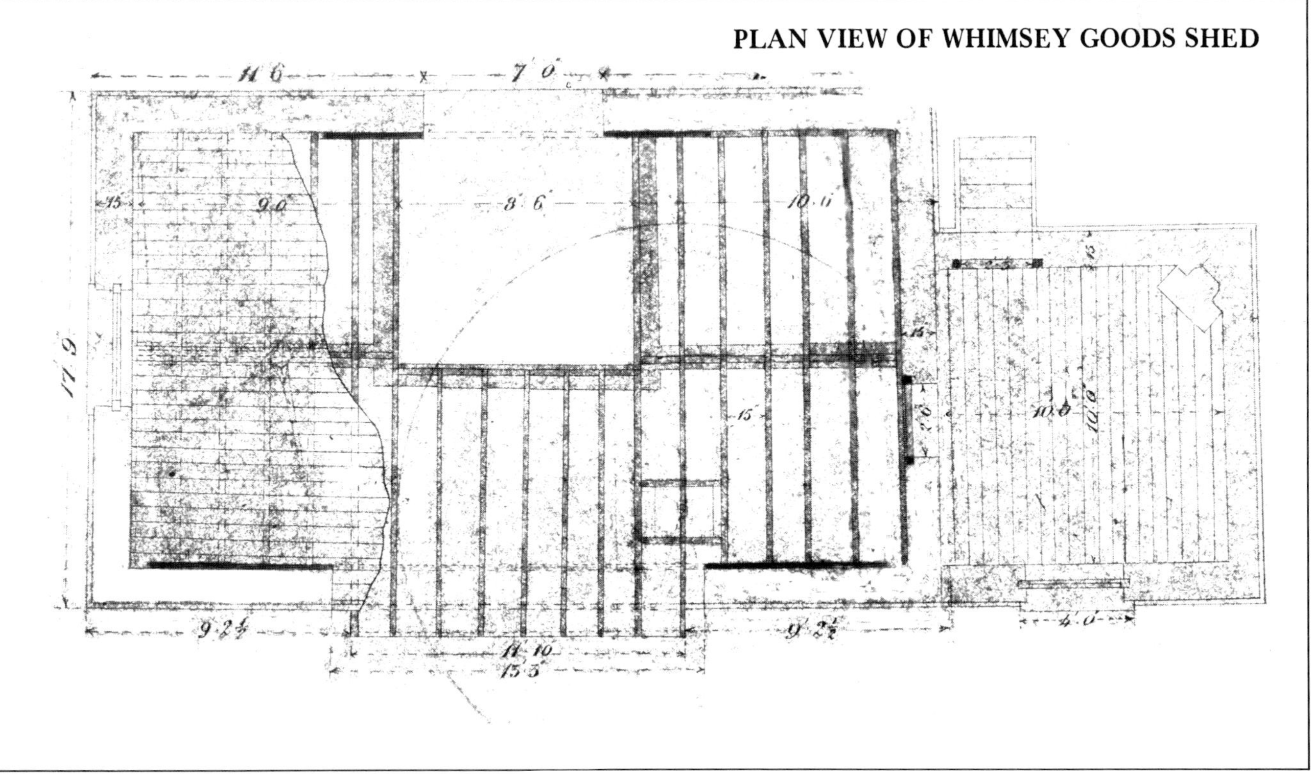

PLAN VIEW OF WHIMSEY GOODS SHED

Another view of the tramroad course alongside Dowlais siding on 27th October 1946. The signal was the down distant for Steam Mills Crossing. *L. E. Copeland*

The northern end of Whimsey yard, or Cinderford Goods as it was officially known, with Steam Mills Level Crossing in the distance. The distant signal visible in the centre of the photograph was the up distant for Cinderford Crossing Ground Frame, only 355 yards from the crossing. Note the point disc signal working with the switch blade of the trap points, an unnecessary luxury, but two of these point discs survived at this location until February 1953.

L. E. Copeland

A closer look at Cinderford Goods Siding Ground Frame featured in the previous view, but shown here on 26th June 1933. *L. E. Copeland*

In 1949 Messrs. Berry Wiggins & Co. Ltd., whose registered office at one time was in Stratford, East London, and later at Field House, Fetter Lane, London, took over the little used Cinderford Goods station for a bitumen heating plant. Boilers were installed to provide steam in order to liquify the bitumen which was delivered in tank wagons from Sharnal Street on the Isle of Grain, Kent. At Whimsey it was transferred into road tankers for distribution. It was estimated that about 5,000 tons per annum would be received at Whimsey, bringing a revenue to the railway of some £5,000. About five or six 20-ton tank wagons were brought up at a time, the traffic being referred to by local railwaymen as the tank invasion! *Collection A. K. Pope*

Taken on separate occasions, these views show how the Goods station was completely taken over by Berry Wiggins. *A. K. Pope*

Hardly a scene that would spring to mind in association with traditional Forest industries, but familiar enough throughout the British Railways era. Not only did Berry Wiggins provide local employment, but, had it not been for their depot, this short branch from Bilson Junction would surely have disappeared c.1950.
D. A. Tipper

Cinderford Crossing Ground Frame. The up distant signal was taken away in August 1955. The down distant signal was abolished three years later, and replaced by a stop board just south of the level crossing gates.

A closer view of the level crossing in June 1961. *R. H. Marrows*

This picture shows a train of tank wagons with brake van still attached standing on the running line shortly after arrival at Whimsey on 7th September 1959. The engine, a '57XX' class 0–6–0PT No. 7723, is seen here waiting to shunt out the empties. Cinderford Goods Siding ground frame is in the foreground.
John Marshall

BERRY WIGGINS' DEPOT, WHIMSEY

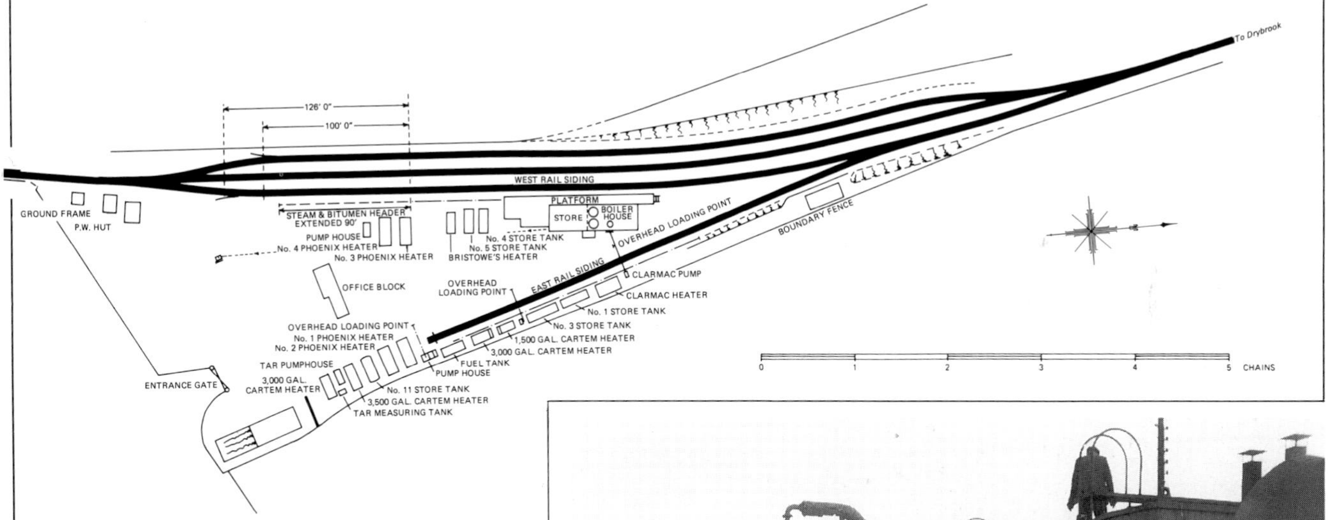

Contrasting with the earlier views on page 330, these pictures show the depot in maturity with storage tanks in position.

A. K. Pope

0–6–0PT No. 4614 drawing wagons up the 1 in 69 gradient on the climb out of Whimsey on 6th January 1964. At this time the line to Steam Mills was retained purely as a headshunt for servicing Berry Wiggins' yard. *A. K. Pope*

Lydney driver Vic Rees easing a few tank wagons back towards the old goods shed. *A. K. Pope*

A final look at Berry Wiggins activity with this view across Broadmoor towards the building which once housed Broadmoor Chemical Works, on 14th May 1965. *A. K. Pope*

Looking northwards towards Steam Mills from alongside the road from Cinderford, with the level crossing prominent in the centre of the view. The mill beyond, which gave the settlement its name, was owned in the early 1840s by Timothy Bennett who titled himself a 'miller, corn and flour factor, maltster and coal merchant'. In the late 1880s it was owned by Thomas and Francis Wintle. After closing as a mill, the building was used by a machine tool factor and then as a storage area for Rosedale Plastics of Cinderford. On the extreme left the tall, thin chimney marks the premises of Messrs. Teague & Chew, engineers and iron founders. The firm was founded in 1888 by Moses Edward Teague. Soon the works were producing steam engines for colliery use, including winding and pumping plant. Local users were Lightmoor and New Fancy Collieries. The pumping engine house at Hawkwell Colliery features in the background above the works and, to its right, Hawkwell Row. *Cty. Roger Hale*

STEAM MILLS HALT

This view, looking down the main street at Steam Mills, could almost have been taken from the level crossing. *Collection A. K. Pope*

STEAM MILLS HALT AND LEVEL CROSSING

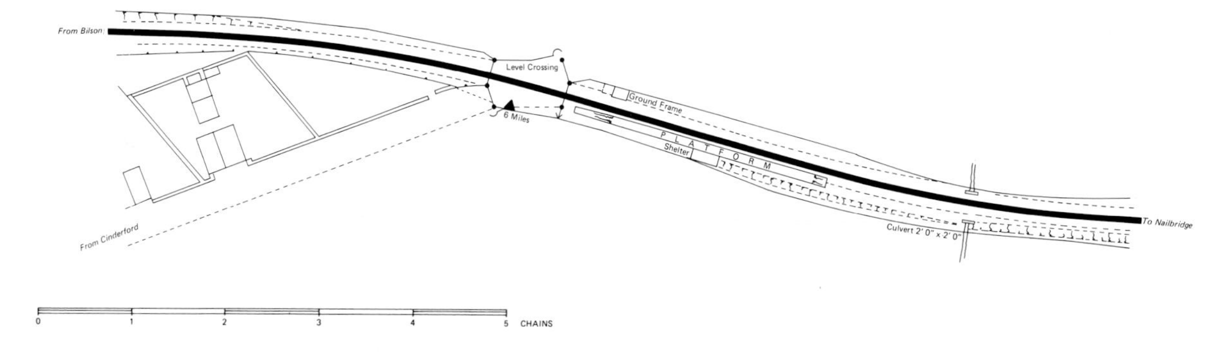

Steam Mills Crossing, looking towards Nailbridge, on 4th November 1907, the first day of extended services to Drybrook.

Lens of Sutton

The only known view of the Steam Mills Halt (7 miles 7 chains) which can just be seen behind the fencing on the right. The halt served a small settlement at the bottom of Cinderford, colliers from here travelling to work by train each morning and returning on foot. An unusual feature here was the arrangement of the gate posts, enforced by the acute angle at which the road crossed over the railway (see the plan on the opposite page).
Collection Paul Karau

A later view of the crossing with replacement gates, typically unmatched, on 27th October 1946. *L. E. Copeland*

A closer view of the ground frame cabin (6 miles 2 chains) taken on 26th June 1933. In later years the gates were opened and closed by the guards, but as there were only two or three wagons at this time, they didn't have far to walk.
L. E. Copeland

The up distant for Steam Mills features in the centre of this postcard view taken from the Mitcheldean–Monmouth Road close by Forest Church. *Collection I. A. Pope*

As can be seen in this series of photographs, the stretch of line between Steam Mills and Nailbridge was heavily engineered. On leaving Steam Mills Crossing Halt, the line climbed at 1 in 42 on the embankment seen here. This view was taken from the formation of Bishop's Tramroad, built under a Crown licence of 12th July 1834, but probably completed prior to this date, which ran from Whimsey to Nailbridge (see page 348). In 1841 Sir Josiah Guest was constructing a tramroad from his iron mines at Edge Hill to a junction with the Bishop's Tramroad at this point. When the Mitcheldean Road & Dean Forest Junction Railway was constructed, it crossed the Westbury Brook Tramroad, by the skew overbridge seen here. The bridge, at 6m 30ch, dated from 1907 when the steel main girders with steel trough flooring were placed on the stone abutments. Details of the earlier structure are unknown but the bridge may have been of timber construction. The span was 11ft 3in on the square and 16ft 4in on the skew. The trackbed of the Bishop's Tramroad northwards from this point was later used by Brain's Tramway, built in 1869 as an extension of the line from Trafalgar Colliery to Bilson Yard (see *Severn & Wye Railway* Vol. 2, pp. 291-296). The extension ran to Brain's Golden Valley Iron Mine at Drybrook. *L. E. Copeland*

The next two underbridges, just visible in the distance in the previous view, maintained access to quarries. That nearest the camera had a central pier to support the span which crossed an access track at the point at which it divided into the quarries, thus one track passed either side. Again the superstructures dated from 1907, the bridge in the foreground, at 6m 34½ch, had two spans of 12ft (13ft 6in on the skew) whilst that beyond, at 6m 36ch, was 12ft 6in on the square and 12ft 10in on the skew. 13th July 1947. *L. E. Copeland*

Beyond the second quarry access bridge, the line was crossed by the Mitcheldean–Monmouth road, originally a turnpike road and one of the original routes through the Forest of Dean. The arch at the lower level allowed the Bishop's Tramroad and later Brain's Tramway to pass under the road. Notice also the retaining walls at this point holding up the embankment. These undoubtedly had to be provided due to the close proximity of Brain's Tramway which was the line in existence when the Mitcheldean Road & Dean Forest Junction Railway was constructed. *L. E. Copeland*

Looking south from the Mitcheldean to Monmouth road at Nailbridge on 27th October 1946, showing all three bridges and the substantial nature of the embankment. The Steam Mills Crossing up distant signal can be seen in the distance. *L. E. Copeland*

Looking east from the road into the quarries served by the tracks under the railway, and showing the back of the P. Way hut also seen in a previous view. *L. E. Copeland*

NAILBRIDGE HALT

The northern side of the short tunnel through which the Mitcheldean Road and Forest of Dean Junction Railway burrowed under the Mitcheldean–Monmouth Road. The line climbed from Steam Mills on gradients of 1 in 339, 68, 42, 206 and 72. The lower and smaller bore had accommodated Brain's Tramway which was laid on the course of the Bishop's Tramroad to Newbridge Engine Colliery. Between the tunnel and the house on the left, Brain's Tramway split, a branch on this side of the railway following the Bishop's Tramroad route to Mitcheldean Colliery and serving Speedwell Level and the sidings. The main line to the Golden Valley Iron Mine at Drybrook passed under the railway by means of the underbridge whose abutments can be seen to the right of the house on the left. *L. E. Copeland*

NEWBRIDGE ENGINE COLLIERY

In April 1833 the Forest of Dean Railway was approached by William and Henry Bishop who enquired about the possibility of extending the tramroad from its terminus at Whimsey to their colliery at Nailbridge, a distance of about 1,600 yards. This application was declined, and so, at a cost of about £700, the Bishops built the line themselves under a licence from the Office of Woods, dated 12th July 1834. The Bishops, together with Charles and George Meek, were joint proprietors of the Newbridge Engine Colliery. In the first half of 1833 they sold an eighth share to Henry Nichols and an eighth to Thomas Atkinson, and on 31st July 1834 a further eighth was sold to Thomas Hopkins of Chatham, Kent.

By 1835 affairs at the colliery had taken a downwards turn and instead of receiving an eighth of the profit, Hopkins found that the concern was in an embarrassed state with debts of about £1,700. By this time Hopkins had invested some £1,000 and in August 1836 he agreed to pay all liabilities – £5,670 18s 7d – even though the colliery was only valued at £4,290. This arrangement appears to have given Hopkins effective control of the works but he only worked it for about 18 months, during which time he made an abortive attempt to sell out to Edward Protheroe for £3,500.

The 1841 Awards show that Thomas Hopkins held two eighth shares, Francis Bishop of Littledean, one eighth; Joseph Bennett and Joseph Webb, as assignees of William Bishop who had become an insolvent debtor, two eighths; James and Harriet Powell, both of Lydney, representing the deceased Thomas Powell, one eighth; Alfred Ceal and John Coleman, as assignees of Thomas Atkinson, a bankrupt, one eighth; and Henry Nichols, one eighth. From this it can be

Harrow Hill and Nailbridge Halt (6 miles 54 chains) probably during the late 1920s. The small bridge, visible behind the corrugated iron pagoda waiting shed, once accommodated the Brain's Tramway branch to the Golden Valley mine near Drybrook. Hale & Co.'s builders yard in the foreground of this view occupied the site of Speedwell Colliery. *Collection A. K. Pope*

An earlier view of the halt, around the time of the Great War, with Brain's Tramway to Speedwell in the foreground. The tramway also features (just) behind the builders' shed in the previous view. *Collection A. K. Pope*

seen that several of the partners from 1833 were still involved with the colliery although the financial status of some of them was doubtful!

The works themselves were in a bad way. When Joseph Bennett was in possession, he had allowed them to fill with water, whilst in 1842 Henry Nichols took twenty men and nine tramroad wagons and lifted the tramroad. It was said that he took the tramplates to Coleford and sold them. Nichols also attempted to remove 'two engines' from the colliery, presumably the pumping and winding engines. The whole of the proceedings of the colliery were in a mess and it was Hopkins in Chatham who was paying. With the assistance of the Crown he managed to get the gale forfeited and on 23rd April 1849 it was re-granted to Richard James, a Free Miner nominated by Hopkins, who immediately conveyed it to him, thus giving Hopkins total control over the colliery that had cost him so dear.

Hopkins now held the gale until 1859, apart from conveying it to his son Joseph for a short period while Hopkins senior was ill and fearing the worst! Throughout this period the colliery remained silent and full of water.

In 1859 the colliery was sold to Richard White and by September he was said to have commenced work to re-open it. He had also applied to the Crown for permission to re-lay a tramway to Whimsey using the route of the Bishops' line, but was informed that a Mr. Woodhouse had recently been granted a licence for a portion of the formation on which he had relaid the plates for the use of Pluckpenny Colliery as far as the junction with a branch to Westbury Brook. This latter line had been laid around 1842 along the line of the removed Bishops' tramroad until branching off eastwards up the Gorbrook towards Edge Hills. It would seem that this was done without the knowledge of Thomas Hopkins who was later to write to the Crown: ' . . . the trustees of the late Sir John Guest had laid down plates on a part to bring down iron mine to the locomotive line of railroad'.

In September 1860 White wanted to sink a new pit at Nailbridge and also to have some land at Gorbrook, south of Nailbridge, in order to erect a pumping engine which would allow him to work the eastern part of the gale. Little work was done and by midsummer 1861 arrears of dead rent on the gale stood against him, and in May 1864 he was in chancery.

By August 1871 the registered owners of the gale were Charles Ward of Bristol and 'the representatives of his late partner'. The colliery itself was still full of water.

In August 1875 the Newbridge Engine Colliery Co. Ltd. was incorporated to acquire the interests of John Anstie who had entered into an agreement in July to lease the colliery. The company never traded but in January 1876 the Mitcheldean Colliery Co. Ltd. was formed. A Charles Phillips had acquired Anstie's interests and now sold them to the new company whose authorised capital was £5,000

After lying unused for some years, the line from Whimsey was opened as far as Speedwell in 1885. This view, looking west towards Ruardean Hill from the foot of Harrow Hill, shows the line passing the future site of Nailbridge Halt and the tramways on both sides of the line. Ruardean Hill was heavily quarried and the waste tip in the middle of the picture was from Speedwell Colliery. *Collection A. K. Pope*

in £5 shares. In November 1877 the capital was increased by 1,200 new £5 preference shares and in September 1878 £6,000 worth of first mortgage £20 debentures were issued to pay off 'certain pressing claims'. It is highly probable that no work was actually done at the colliery as in May 1884 it was stated that the colliery had not worked since June 1879. The company was dissolved in October 1885.

The company may have leased, or even sold off, the colliery as early as 1882 to Jacob Chivers, the owner of the neighbouring Small Profit gale which he worked as Hawkwell Colliery (see page 248). In June 1885 it was said that Chivers was preparing to win the coal in Newbridge Engine gale through Small Profit. It can be assumed that the ownership of Newbridge Engine then followed the same pattern as Small Profit, passing to A. C. Bright and then A. C. Bright & Co. Ltd. until surrendered in 1898.

In September 1898 Newbridge Engine was re-granted to John Wilce who entered an agreement with the New Bowson Coal Co. to take what coal they could. The gale was returned to Wilce by July 1906. In August it was reported that Mr. Wyatt had acquired the gale; as he had also taken an interest in Eastern United (see page 133), it is likely that nothing came of it, and by March 1907 the gale was in the hands of Thomas Burdess.

In October 1918 the gale was purchased by Albert Jones to form part of Harrow Hill Colliery (see page 355).

A similar view taken after the opening of the halt and featuring Speedwell Sidings in the right distance. *Collection A. K. Pope*

SPEEDWELL SIDING

At the end of 1881 Mr. Goodrich Langham of Coleford took a lease of the west wing of Speedwell Newbridge Colliery and proceeded to open the works with the financial assistance of Richard Searle of Newport. By February 1885 the colliery was putting out coal and, in order to provide a siding connection, the unused rails of the Mitcheldean Road and Forest of Dean Junction Railway were brought into use from Whimsey as far as the colliery. In November 1885 Goodrich Langham took five 8-ton wagons on hire from the Gloucester Wagon Co. and in the same month signed a private agreement with the GWR for a siding which cost £209.

The Speedwell gale had first been worked in the 1730s when it was described as Speedwell, near Tresser Mill in Ruardean Hill. The 1841 Awards listed the galees as Samuel Baker and William Frankis, a merchant, both of Gloucester. The coal was in the Hill Delf vein and lay under Ruardean and Harrow Hills. By July 1862 a Mr. St. Patrick appears to have been the galee as he was agreeing to new rents. It was not recorded who Langham leased the portion of the gale from.

Once the colliery was opened and in production, Langham persuaded Searle's son Edgar to join him as a partner and traded as Langham & Co. They soon ran into difficulties over the ventilation of the colliery and to alleviate this they drove a heading to the disused Ruardean Hill pit which they claimed was on the gale. The colliery then worked for three and a half years with output increasing until it reached over 13,000 tons in 1889. In November 1888 it had been said that Mr. Langham & Mr. Searle were working the Speedwell Newbridge Colliery 'in a substantial way' and were outputting about 1,000 tons per month. In February 1890 they were applying to the Crown for permission to burn coke at the colliery. Towards the end of the year Mr. T. B. Brain, the owner of the adjoining Pluckpenny gale, claimed that the Ruardean Hill pit was on his gale and blocked it by building a cover over the top, much to the chagrin of Langham & Co.

With the much-quarried face of Ruardean Hill in the background, this postcard view of Nailbridge was taken looking south-west towards the junction of the road between Nailbridge and Ruardean and the road to Drybrook in the foreground. *Collection N. Parkhouse*

Looking west over the bridge carrying the Drybrook to Nailbridge road over the line to the north of Nailbridge Halt. The parapet of this bridge can be seen to the right of the horse and cart. Speedwell siding is on the right, the Trafalgar wagons being stabled there for land sales.
Collection A. K. Pope

In September 1892 the partnership between Langham and Searle was dissolved. It would appear that Searle continued work as a result of the dispute over Ruardean Hill pit. He purchased the Pluckpenny gale from Brain in January 1893 and obtained leave from the Crown to work the barrier between the two gales. However, this brought about some debate with Langham, who had retained his interest in the east wing of Speedwell, together with the adjoining Prosper gale, and was now attempting to get money from Searle for the coal in the barrier which, he claimed, belonged to the gale as a whole.

In view of the increased area of coal and the expected additional output, Searle laid in extra siding accommodation in 1894, a PSA being signed on 19th July 1894, by which time the siding was complete, the materials being supplied by the GWR, and built screens to satisfy the output which had for some time past averaged over 4,000 tons per month. In October 1893 the Speedwell Newbridge Colliery Co. purchased thirty new 10-ton wagons on seven years deferred purchase from the Gloucester Carriage & Wagon Co. In January 1896 the company was having difficulties in paying their bills to the GC&W Co. and by April 1897 the company was in the hands of trustees who may have sold the vehicles back to Gloucester as that month they took thirty secondhand wagons on monthly hire.

On 11th June 1897 the effects of the colliery were auctioned off. Included in the sale were a 10 HP portable engine, a winding drum and gear, 120 pit carts, 2,000 sleepers and 11 young pit horses and ponies, and in August 1897 it was reported that Messrs. Searle, of Maindee, Newport, were to give up Speedwell and Pluckpenny gales. The land occupied by the siding was transferred to the Trafalgar Colliery Co. for the sum of £250, the siding agreement having been made over on 22nd July, and it appears they also occupied some buildings. The gales themselves were surrendered.

The wharf reopened for business on 1st September 1897 when the Trafalgar Co. appear to have been using it for land sales traffic. It may have been the acquisition of the wharf which led to the final demise of the Drybrook section of Brain's Tramway. Following the acquisition of Trafalgar Colliery by Messrs. H. Crawshay & Co. Ltd. and the Foxes Bridge Colliery Co. Ltd., Speedwell siding was transferred to Crawshays who continued to use it for land sales.

In June 1917 permission was given to the owners of Harrow Hill Colliery to load coal here, an arrangement which probably continued until the Harrow Hill Colliery's own siding was completed in 1924.

In June 1928 a government inspector condemned the weighbridge at Speedwell Wharf and the tenants had to temporarily continue with a scoop machine which was unsatisfactory. Crawshays considered moving a weighbridge from their Eastern United Colliery, but whether this was done is not known.

In December 1929 it was reported that the GWR had asked Crawshays to bear the expense of necessary repairs to the siding connection amounting to about £275. Crawshays declined, so the railway company carried out the work anyway and increased the rates on traffic to and from the siding by 2d per ton to recoup expenditure. Crawshays felt this was a much more satisfactory arrangement as the 2d

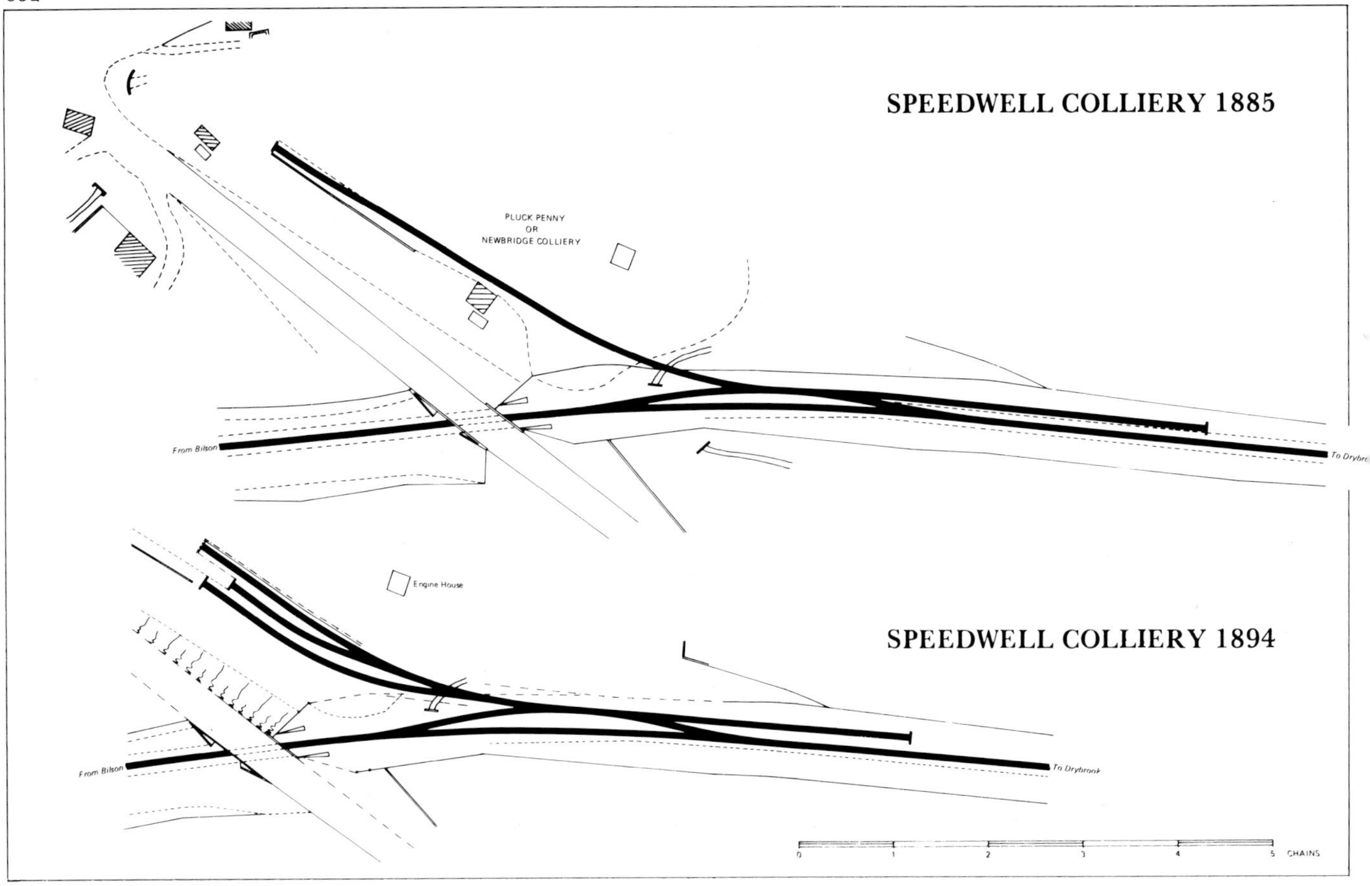

SPEEDWELL COLLIERY 1885

PLUCK PENNY
OR
NEWBRIDGE COLLIERY

From Bilson

To Drybrook

SPEEDWELL COLLIERY 1894

Engine House

From Bilson

To Drybrook

0 1 2 3 4 5 CHAINS

per ton was borne by those using the siding and not by them!

On 28th May 1930 the GWR agreed that Crawshays could allow Messrs Tom and Tom Parker, trading as T. Parker & Sons, coal merchants, High Street, Drybrook; Bernard Henry James, coal merchant of 4 New Road, Lydney; and Frederick George Hale and John Hale, trading as Hale & Co., builders merchants, to use the siding.

On 10th May 1937 Crawshays applied to terminate the siding agreement as they were delivering supplies from Lightmoor to the wharf by lorry instead. Their nearby Northern United Colliery was also offering land sales. The redundant connection, together with Speedwell Middle and South ground frames were subsequently taken out of use in January 1938.

Speedwell Colliery South ground frame on 26th June 1933.
L. E. Copeland

The bridge on which the horse and cart were standing in the previous picture features on the right of this view, taken after the removal of Speedwell Siding, which lay at the end of the colliery waste tip on the right. The arch on the left allowed Brain's Tramway to Drybrook to pass under the road. *B. Baxter, cty. Railway & Canal Historical Society*

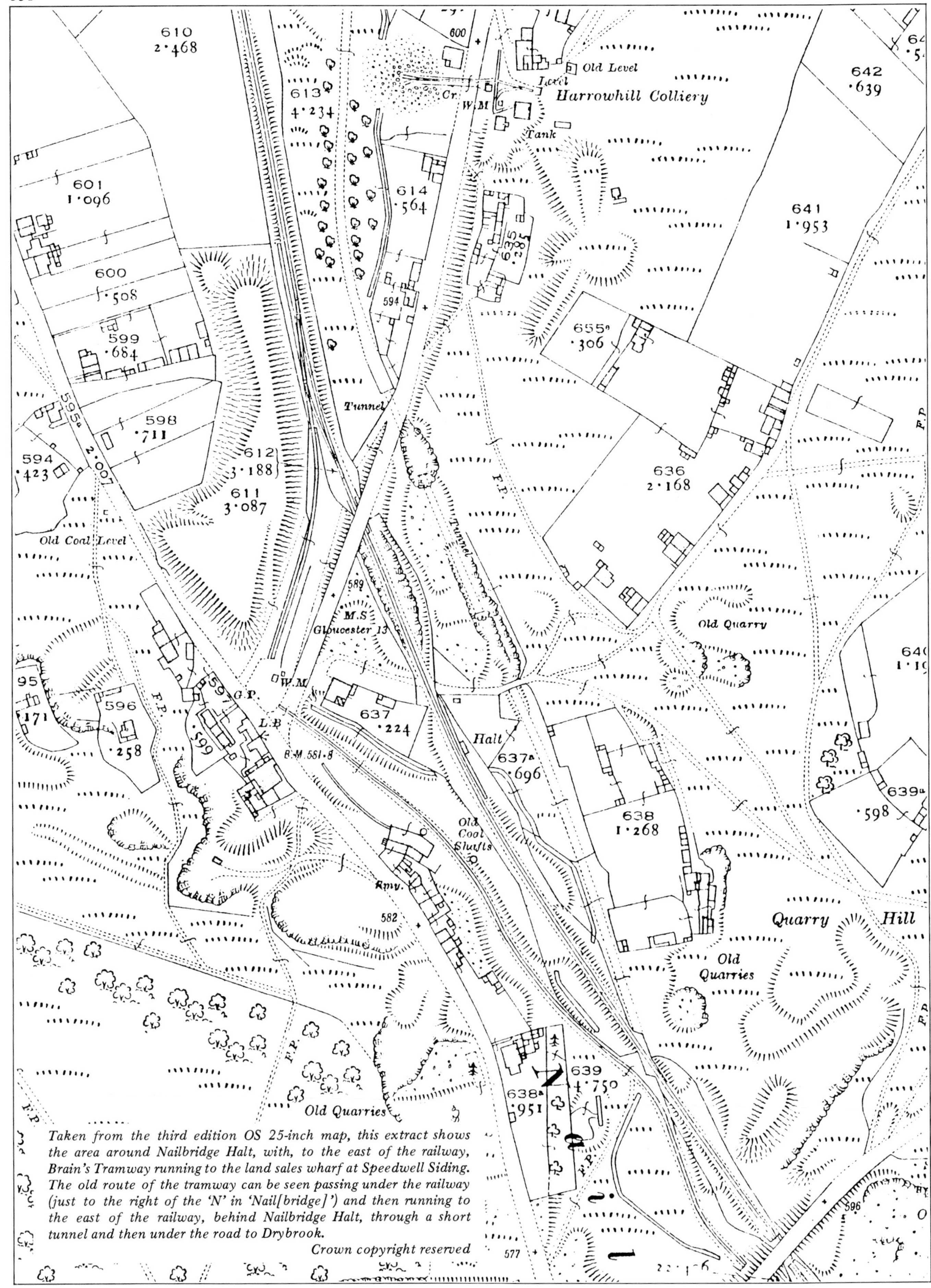

Taken from the third edition OS 25-inch map, this extract shows the area around Nailbridge Halt, with, to the east of the railway, Brain's Tramway running to the land sales wharf at Speedwell Siding. The old route of the tramway can be seen passing under the railway (just to the right of the 'N' in 'Nail[bridge]') and then running to the east of the railway, behind Nailbridge Halt, through a short tunnel and then under the road to Drybrook.

Looking west across to Ruardean Hill, this view shows the northern connection to Speedwell Siding before the installation of the adjacent sidings for Harrow Hill Colliery in 1924. The ground frame shown was known as Speedwell Sidings North, later renamed 'Middle'.
Collection A. K. Pope

HARROW HILL COLLIERY

On 3rd March 1916 Mr. Albert Jones purchased the mining rights on Prosper gale situated on Harrow Hill for the sum of £225. Prior to coming to the Forest, Jones had been a mining engineer at Trimsarn, near Kidwelly. His starting capital took the form of shares in various companies which were deposited at his bank in order that he could raise loans upon them. The total capital thus available to him was about £1,500.

In September he added to his interests when he took a forty-year lease on the east wing of the Speedwell Newbridge Colliery. This may have depleted his resources as by the end of the year Jones's capital was exhausted. He looked elsewhere for finance and on 1st December entered into partnership with William H. F. Hill and Sydney Thomas. The agreement was for a term of twenty-one years, Hill investing £1,006 for a one-fifth share and Thomas chipping in with £160. Together they traded as the Harrow Hill Colliery Co.

In October 1918 a further £300 was expended on the purchase of the Newbridge Engine Colliery but this was the last act of the partnership which was dissolved in December 1918. Hill was said to have been taking over a family business but, whatever the reason for dissolution, Jones bought his partners out with a handsome premium, Hill receiving £1,250 and Thomas £210. These payments put a further strain on Jones who decided that, although the colliery had not yet made a profit, he would continue on.

Speedwell Sidings Middle ground frame cover on 26th June 1933. *L. E. Copeland*

The gated Harrow Hill Sidings shown here evidently shortly after completion in 1924. The embankment and bridge over the Drybrook to Nailbridge road supported the tramway connecting Harrow Hill Colliery with the private siding. On the left centre of the view a timber trestle bridge connects a level on Ruardean Hill to the siding.
Collection A. K. Pope

A view of Harrow Hill Colliery prior to the installation of their siding in 1924. The large tip in the right foreground was from Speedwell Newbridge Colliery.
Collection N. Parkhouse

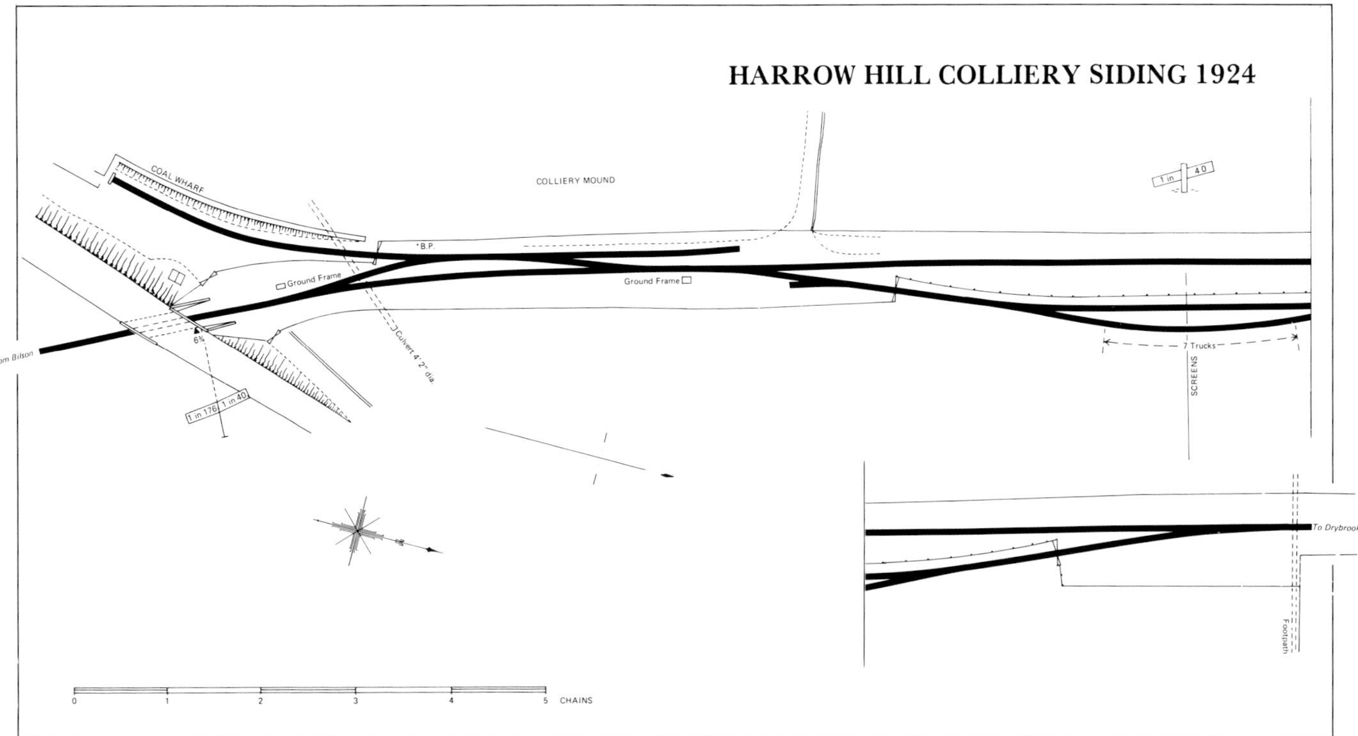

To allow him to do so, he hoped to form a limited company in order to raise capital but this did not come to fruition and instead he relied on loans from various members of his family.

Jones continued working the colliery at a loss, a state of affairs not helped by a coal strike in October 1920 and a three-month dispute in 1921. During these periods the colliery officials and one or two others managed to keep the workings free of water whilst the rest of the 197 men employed were supporting the strike.

In April 1921 Jones acquired a further gale, Gorbrook No. 3, which was so far unworked, but this was insufficient to turn his financial position around. In the six months ended 30th September 1922 the loss made was £1,623 13s 10d, for the next six months £1,762 3s 10d and for the six months ending 30th September 1923 £1,086 10s 4d. In August it was reported that the company owed £215 to Henry Crawshay & Co. Ltd. for siding charges at Speedwell. Crawshays appear to have resigned themselves to the opinion that a large proportion of this would be unrecoverable. This state of affairs could not continue and in October Jones entered into an agreement with a local colliery owner and coal agent, I. W. Baldwin of Ruardean. The colliery was to be worked by Baldwin who would pay Jones a royalty of 4d on every ton of coal sold. Baldwin was to pay all other costs and work the colliery for as long as he could make it pay, subject to a week's notice. It would seem that one of Baldwin's first moves was to cut the wages bill as in November it was reported that sixty men were employed, 130 less than in 1921. In November 1923 Jones filed a petition against himself for bankruptcy. The Official Receiver decided that the agreement with Baldwin could continue.

Just prior to Baldwin taking over, Jones arranged for a private siding to be provided for the colliery. Coal had previously been hauled to the nearest railhead at Speedwell Siding at a cost of 2/- per ton. Despite the difficulties at the colliery, construction of the siding went ahead, the GWR authorising £900 for the work (£730 Chief Engineers plus £170 Signal Engineers Dept.) which was completed by November 1924. The two sidings both had connections either end, the southern connection to the main line being worked by the existing Speedwell North ground frame whilst the northern connection was controlled by a new Harrow Hill North ground frame (some sources state that Speedwell Siding North ground frame was renamed Harrow Hill South ground frame, but the picture on page 355 shows that it was actually renamed Speedwell Sidings Middle ground frame. The sidings were gated at each end, a point which locomotives were on no account to pass, the keys for the gates being attached to the train staff. Outwards traffic was to be removed via the southern connection whilst ingoing traffic used the northern end.

To bring the coal to the siding, the colliery company erected a bridge which spanned the Nailbridge–Drybrook road and an embankment across a field to another structure where coal was discharged directly into the railway wagons below via a chute.

Baldwin obviously decided that he could not carry on as in March 1924 it was reported in the *Dean Forest Mercury* that the sale of the plant and equipment at the colliery was pending. On 12th July 1924 the colliery was conveyed by the Midland Bank and Jones's trustee to the Wigpool Coal & Iron Co. Ltd. who also took over the siding agreement for the, as yet, unfinished sidings.

The managing director of the Wigpool Coal & Iron Co. was Captain H. A. Pringle, a mining entrepreneur who, upon acquiring the Harrow Hill Colliery, immediately set about completing the sidings, purchasing the old siding from the Meadow Cliff Colliery (page 267) for £60 for materials.

In July 1927 it was reported that Harrow Hill Colliery had temporarily closed two months previously and that in the meantime the underground roadways had suffered badly. In October 1929 it was reported that Pringle was bankrupt having acquired a large number of Forest coal and iron gales and having also been involved in a local gold mining adventure. The private siding agreement for Harrow Hill Sidings was terminated in 1931.

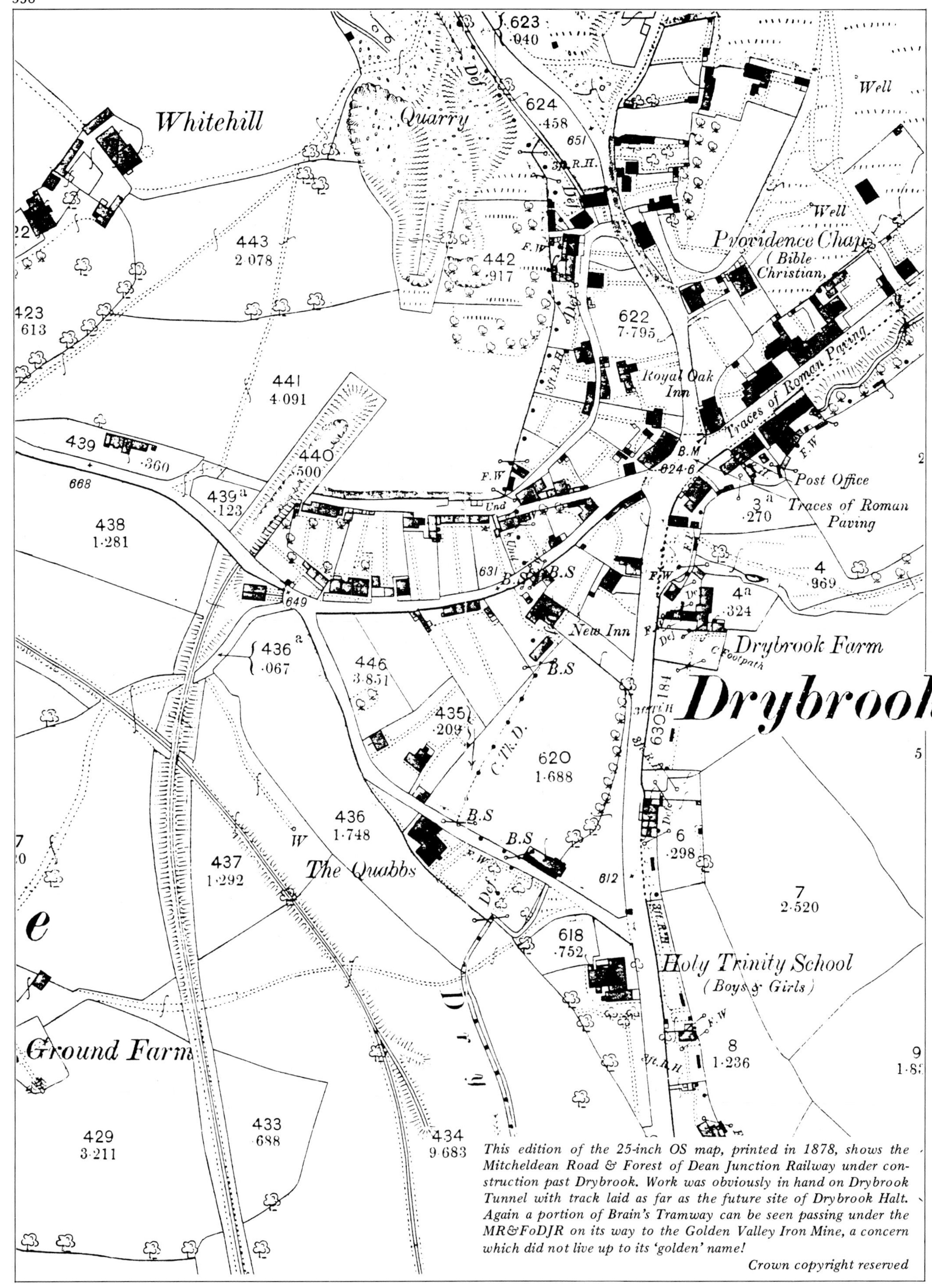

This edition of the 25-inch OS map, printed in 1878, shows the Mitcheldean Road & Forest of Dean Junction Railway under construction past Drybrook. Work was obviously in hand on Drybrook Tunnel with track laid as far as the future site of Drybrook Halt. Again a portion of Brain's Tramway can be seen passing under the MR&FoDJR on its way to the Golden Valley Iron Mine, a concern which did not live up to its 'golden' name!

DRYBROOK

From Nailbridge the line climbed on gradients of 1 in 173, 44, 50 and 43. This view, looking south from the road between Drybrook and Morse Lane, shows the 'Forest Railmotor' approaching Drybrook Halt c.1908. *Collection A. K. Pope*

A similar view taken from track level, looking downhill towards Bilson, on 1st August 1949, showing the formation of Brain's Tramway which led under the bridge in the foreground to reach the Golden Valley iron mine. *L. E. Copeland*

Drybrook from Ruardean Hill.

A panoramic view over the village of Drybrook with the halt on the extreme left. The route of Brain's Tramway can be seen running across the field on a low embankment just above the wooden occupation crossing gates in the centre of the photograph. The back of Drybrook National Schools features on the right, whilst the low, corrugated-iron roofed building to its left housed a cinema. High Street can be seen climbing the hill out of the village towards the Stenders and Mitcheldean, whilst the isolated clump of trees on the skyline marks the summit of May Hill. *Collection N. Parkhouse*

After lying dormant for many years, the Mitcheldean Road and Forest of Dean Junction Railway was brought into use as far as Drybrook (7 miles 21 chains from Newnham) in 1907 with the introduction of the Forest railmotor service. The line terminated just beyond the platform, the track north of here eventually being taken up in 1917. This nicely-posed picture postcard shows '2101' class 0–6–0ST No. 2118 at the end of the line c.1908, but the station nameboard is a rather obvious faked addition to the plate. *Collection A. K. Pope*

DRYBROOK HALT 1907

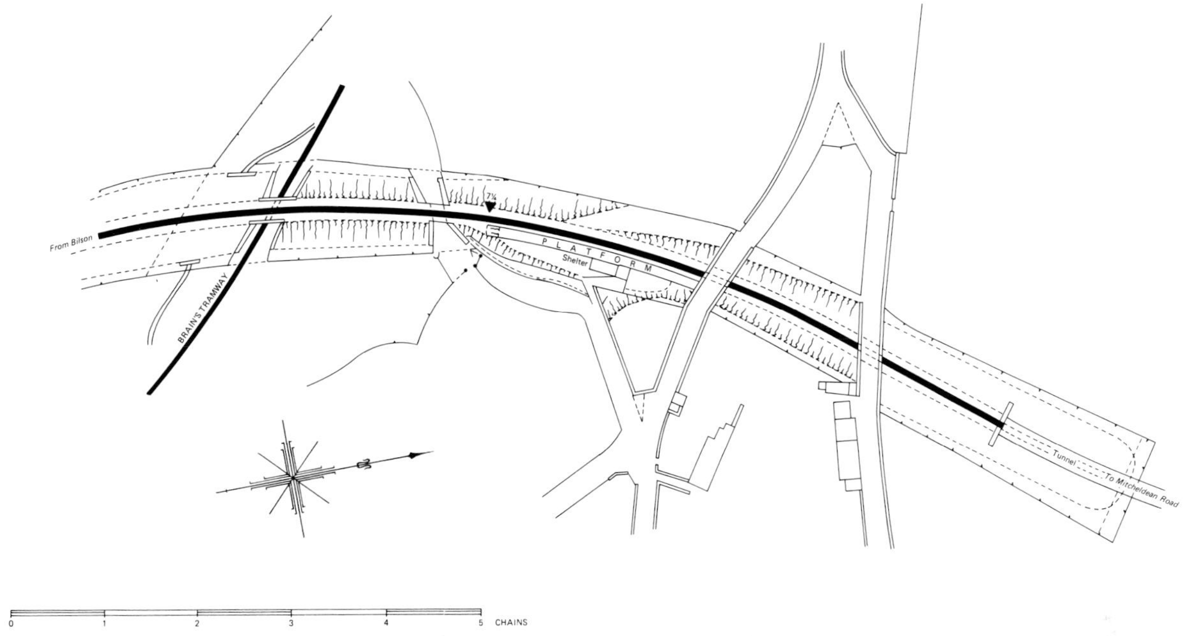

Another view of the halt, looking north from the occupation bridge with an unidentified auto-trailer alongside the platform.

Lens of Sutton

Even at this remote outpost there was a well-tended station garden to delight passengers after climbing the steep approach path. The strengthened train might have been a workmen's or a Saturday service.
Lens of Sutton

The halt features in the foreground of this postcard view showing Drybrook village with the Stenders beyond. *Collection I. A. Pope*

Fireman Jim Griffiths, the well-liked Bullo driver Harry Askew (see page 25), and an unidentified guard, pose for the camera at Drybrook Halt, probably around the time of the Great War. At about this time the beautifully proportioned tall chimneys of the '2021' class saddle tanks, and many other classes, gave way to shorter, less aesthetically pleasing types, like the example fitted to 2142. The railmotor train stayed here from about 3.00 to 4.00 p.m. during which time the fire was cleaned and the smokebox emptied. From 20th December 1923 a pit was provided here between the rails at the northern end of the platform so that the driver could go underneath to inspect the engine and oil round, and the fireman could empty the ashpan. The job of emptying the pit apparently fell to the platelayers. *Collection A. K. Pope*

Looking west towards Ruardean Hill, with the path leading towards the Morse Lane heading off across the field and the south end of the halt on the right of the picture. The left-hand underbridge had a segmental stone arch with a skew span of 15ft and stone abutments. The nearest bridge, like those at Nailbridge, was replaced with a steel trough floor in 1907 prior to the commencement of the passenger service.

Collection N. Parkhouse

The Motor Halt, Drybrook. 1241.

This late 1920s view shows the location of the halt in relation to the village, the two-road overbridges beyond the halt and the tunnel.

Lens of Sutton

The halt remained in place after closure until at least 1942 when an excursion train used the platform. However, it had gone by the time this panorama was taken, probably c.1950. *Collection A. K. Pope*

The view northwards from Drybrook Halt, showing the second of the two road overbridges before the tunnel. This stone fly arch is rather intriguing in view of the close proximity of the tunnel beyond. The trap point protected the running line from wagons which might 'stray' from Drybrook Quarry at the opposite end of the tunnel. It was worked by a 'slotted joint' – trains proceeding towards the tunnel could push through the sprung-loaded points, but, coming down, the points had to be closed using a one-lever ground frame (released by a key on the train staff). *L. E. Copeland*

A similar, but pre-1917 postcard view of the Hawthorns showing the unused track of the Mitcheldean & Forest of Dean Junction Railway disappearing towards Hawthorns Tunnel. *Collection N. Parkhouse*

DRYBROOK QUARRY

Quarrying on this site was being carried out prior to 1914 when in November of that year 'Drybrook Quarry' was advertised for sale. It was being worked by Thomas Roberts, who was working the Lower Dolomite which was used mainly for road stone. He appears to have had a contract to supply road stone to the Ross Rural Council who bought the quarry, retaining Roberts to work it for them.

The next reference comes in 1926 when the quarry was taken over by the Drybrook Quarries Ltd., a Sheffield-based concern whose registered address was Albion Works. As one of the directors was Joseph Ward, the company may have had some connection with T. W. Ward Ltd. According to the records of ARC Limited, the present owners of the quarry, a Thomas Roberts still had some connection, perhaps holding the lease on the quarry.

The Sheffield-based company took out a private siding agreement with the GWR on 30th April 1928 for provision of facilities for a quarry 'about to be opened'. Since the line beyond Drybrook Halt had been taken up in February 1917 as part of the war effort, the GWR had to re-lay the track at its own expense from Drybrook Halt as far as the site of the quarry, a distance of a quarter of a mile, on the trackbed of the old Mitcheldean Road & Forest of Dean Junction Railway. Just short of the quarry, a gate and stop board were erected whilst within the quarry area two loop sidings were provided off the running line. Both of these were fitted with catchpoints at the Drybrook end as the whole layout was on a gradient of 1 in 46, falling towards Cinderford. The estimated cost to Drybrook Quarries Ltd. was £794 plus an easement of £10 per annum for a crushing plant and weighbridge to be built on railway land.

The line was brought into use on 18th October 1928 but, although local railwaymen had been told it was 'to be a big job', traffic never materialised.

Most of the quarry traffic went out by road, and in June 1946 it was reported that in the last six months there had only been six inwards wagons and no outward loaded traffic. In 1949 the inward traffic to the quarry consisted of about 33 tons per year of oil in tank wagons from Avonmouth Docks and about 30 tons of coke from Aberbargoed. This level of traffic obviously made the retention of this stretch of line uneconomic and in April 1950 a proposal was put forward to close the line between

For a number of years the abandoned trackbed north of Drybrook Halt languished as a grassy byway after the unused track was recovered in 1917, the eeriness of the abandoned Drybrook and Hawthorns tunnels here doubtless proving an irresistible lure for local children. This view was taken looking north from the hill above Drybrook Tunnel.

Collection A. K. Pope

This third picture of the view from above Drybrook Tunnel was taken during the 1930s and shows the track reinstated in 1928 to serve Drybrook Quarries. Trains serving the quarry were brought to a stand at the gated entrance to the quarry and waited while the guard opened the gate and signalled the train in on the running line (on the right in this picture) as far as the accommodation level crossing opposite the crusher. Because of limited clearance, locomotives and brake vans were not allowed to enter the north end of the siding straddled by the crushing plant (seen on the left), and the hand points at that end of the loop were normally set for the middle road and padlocked. Incidentally, both the siding and the middle road were fitted with catch points at their lower (Drybrook) end. When the loco had run round its train and finished shunting, the train drew forward to the stop board on the Bilson side of the gate where wagon brakes were pinned down before continuing down the 1 in 46 gradient to the catchpoint above Drybrook Halt. Loco crews remember that it was an 'awkward job' bringing loaded wagons out of the quarry; if the rails were greasy great care had to be taken to stop short of the catchpoint. Euroclydon House on top of the hill, beyond the crusher, had been built by the Brain family, owners of Trafalgar Colliery. *Collection A. K. Pope*

The northern entrance to Drybrook Tunnel on 12th June 1955 after the abandonment of the line to the quarry which was lifted soon after this view was taken. *John Marshall*

Whimsey, i.e. Cinderford Goods, and the quarry. The coke traffic was to be collected by quarry company lorry from Whimsey whilst it was believed that the oil would go direct to the quarry from Avonmouth by road tanker. The loss of receipts to the railway totalled £50 whilst the annual reduction in expenditure was calculated at £939. No decision had been reached by September when the matter was forced slightly by the impending need to replace the level crossing gates at Steam Mills at an estimated cost of £1,375 in connection with a road-widening scheme.

It was not, however, until 18th August 1952 that three months notice was given to Messrs. Drybrook Quarries Ltd. over the termination of the private siding agreement which was to end on 30th November. The quarry company were also informed that they had to remove their crushing and loading plant and their weighbridge from railway-owned land. In the event, a separate lease for the land was taken out. The line to Drybrook Quarry was officially closed on 1st December 1952 from a point 250 yards north of the point at the north end of the yard at Cinderford Goods.

Drybrook Quarry on 29th June 1948. The trap points show more clearly here, but even by this time the track was little used; indeed, the crusher siding looks virtually derelict. The trap points within the sidings were worked by adjacent levers and were additional to the trap point in the single line at the south end of the tunnel shown on page 367. Crews remember usually taking only a couple of empty wagons from Whimsey to the quarry and certainly not every day. After running round quickly, they often only left with two or three ordinary opens loaded with road stone. *Chapman*

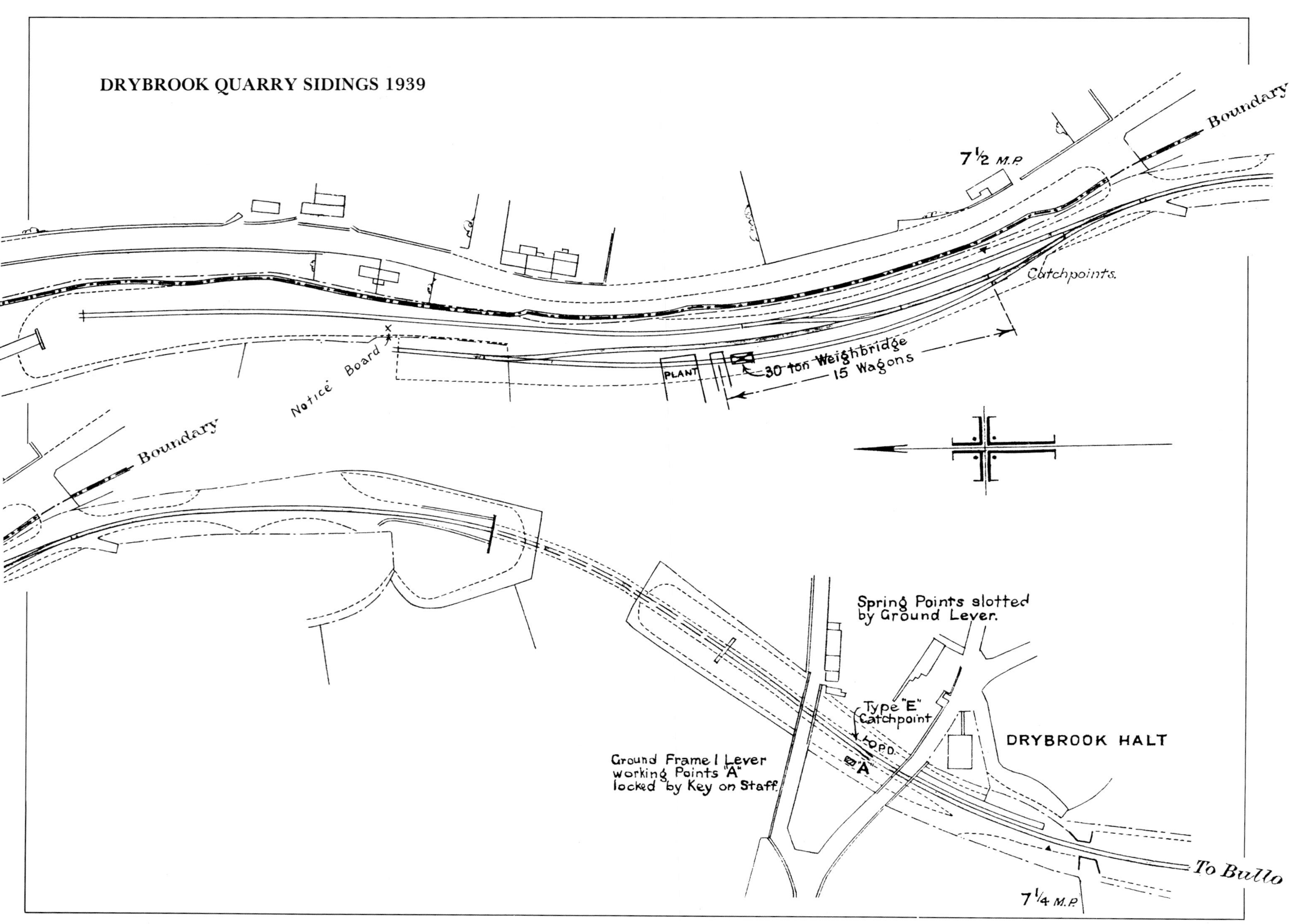

DRYBROOK QUARRY SIDINGS 1939
Boundary
7 1/2 M.P.
Catchpoints.
30 ton Weighbridge
15 Wagons
PLANT
Notice Board
Boundary
Spring Points slotted by Ground Lever.
Type "E" Catchpoint
F.P.D.
"A"
Ground Frame 1 Lever working Points "A" locked by Key on Staff.
DRYBROOK HALT
To Bullo
7 1/4 M.P.

DRYBROOK QUARRIES. 29.6.48.

Two views of the quarry, both again taken on 29th June 1948. The upper view was taken looking eastwards from within the quarry behind the crushing plant. The lower photo gives a closer view of the loading and crushing plant with a road vehicle beneath. The building to the left housed the machinery for a 30-ton weighbridge on the railway siding. *Chapman*

This more distant view of the quarry shows the revised track layout left from the work carried out in connection with the Admiralty use of Hawthorns Tunnel during the war. The crossover, which was put in between the running line and the middle road, can just be discerned in front of the crusher. *Chapman*

Another view of the plant, looking south-east from the top of the quarry, with the village of Drybrook visible beyond. *Chapman*

Looking southwards through the sidings. *Chapman*

HAWTHORNS TUNNEL

Following the removal of the track on the Mitcheldean Road and Forest of Dean Junction Railway, some local entrepreneur took the opportunity to work the stone in the cutting leading to Hawthorns Tunnel. An agreement signed on 8th May 1920 gave Simeon Harris permission to quarry the cutting itself, and another the following year granted him an extra 100 cubic yards. On 6th August 1925 another agreement was taken out with Henry Batt of Drybrook for an area of land to the west of the cutting. In both cases, it was stipulated that no blasting should be carried out without the authority of the railway engineer and that in no circumstances should the work go below the existing formation level.

The requisition of Hawthorns Tunnel by the Admiralty during the Second World War has already been mentioned as part of the general history of the line on page 40. The re-laying of track along the formation of the Mitcheldean Road and Forest of Dean Junction Railway from Drybrook Halt as far as the quarry had left the line 11 chains short of the tunnel mouth. At first it was envisaged that wagons of ammunition would simply be stabled inside the 634 yard tunnel but before the track was re-laid the bore was in need of examination as water had percolated through for years. There was also a defective culvert not far from the tunnel mouth and in bad storms water overflowed and ran into the tunnel.

In the event, the track was only re-laid a short distance just up to the tunnel mouth (7 miles 44½ chains) and, instead of continuing inside, the bed of the bore was concreted and a narrow gauge Decauville track was laid to take the explosives from a standard gauge transfer shed to wherever they were required inside the tunnel. Two 1-ton hand cranes were provided inside the shed to lift the shells and three grounded coach bodies were also provided for accommodation. As the whole project was kept very quiet, it is now difficult to establish exactly what was provided. In January 1941 the rock face in the approach cutting to the tunnel was cleaned down at a cost of £817, and at the same time extra land was purchased for the sum of £50. The site was enclosed with unclimbable railings and plans show a guardroom adjacent to the entrance gates. Certainly a brick-built cabin with a reinforced concrete roof and protected windows survives today just inside the gate.

In providing access to Hawthorns Tunnel, an alteration was made to the layout of the quarry sidings to enable the engine to run round its train with minimal interference with the quarry. This modification was covered by a new private

Shrouded in even more mystery since being requisitioned for the Admiralty's use, pictures of Hawthorns Tunnel have not yet come to light. This postwar view of the abandoned transfer shed and the narrow gauge line used to transfer ammunition from standard gauge box vans into the depths of the tunnel, seems to add to the intrigue. Even today the cutting approaching the converted tunnel is surrounded by unclimbable fencing and unchecked vegetation. *L. E. Copeland*

siding agreement with the quarry company dated 22nd May 1940 which also prohibited the quarry from doing any blastings without permission of the station master at Cinderford and certainly not while wagons full of explosives were stood on or passing by the line alongside the quarry sidings.

The arrangements with the Admiralty were covered by a private siding agreement of 7th August 1943 dated to take effect from 24th June 1939.

Traffic for Hawthorns Tunnel was sorted at Bilson and worked there in special trains only, under similar arrangements to those already described for trains serving the quarry. Crews remember only a limited number of wagons could be handled at the tunnel. They worked there several times a week, running round the train in the quarry loop and propelling box vans of ammunition, depth charges, etc., into the siding. They also remember the military guard at the gate.

After the war it took until 27th May 1949 for the Admiralty to take all the ammunition away, and the line to the tunnel was formally regarded as closed.

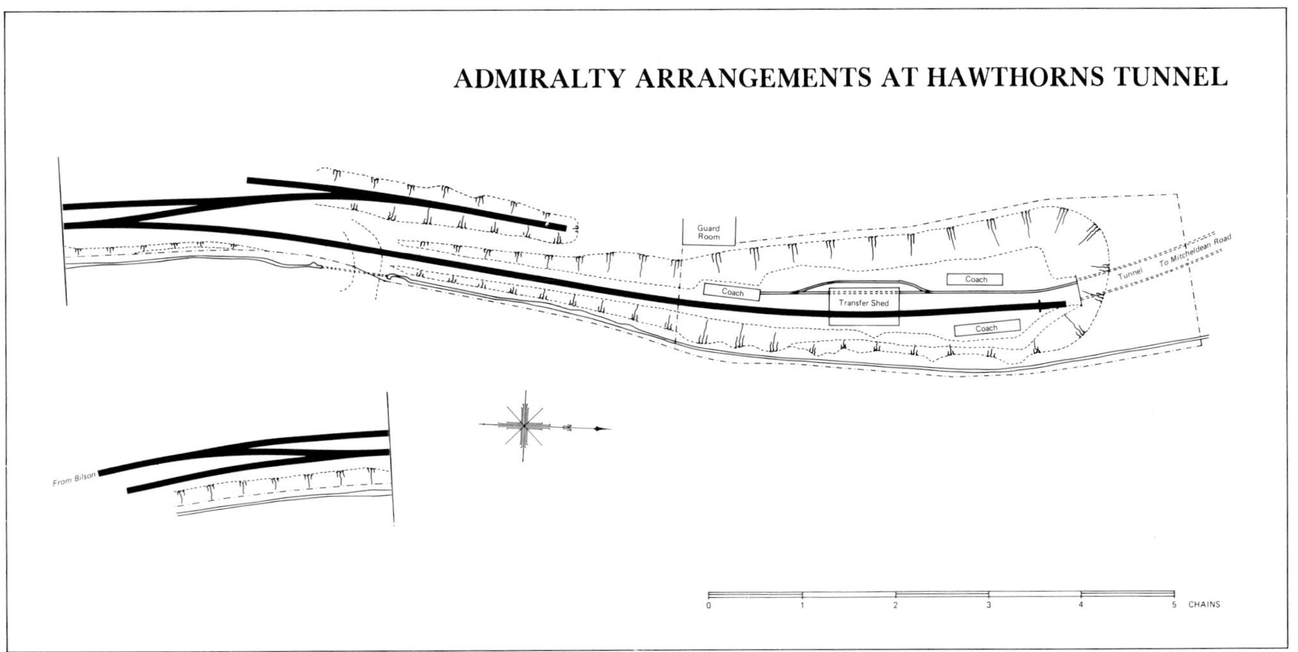

THE COLLIERS ARMS
WILLS'S
STAR
CIGARETTES

THE POSTWAR YEARS

ALTHOUGH the concluding paragraph of the outline history in Volume 1 took us briefly beyond the Second World War, we will now consider the lean postwar years in a little more detail. As if the fuel and food shortages were not enough to contend with, the severe winter of 1947 brought more hardship. Footplate crews recall that snow started to fall at about 3.30 p.m. on Tuesday, 3rd March, when an up train had just left Northern United Colliery and halted at the stop board to pin down brakes. Snowflakes were soon driving in through one cab opening and sticking to the inside of the other.

Conditions were such that the coal train and a mixed goods were combined in Bilson Yard and worked to Bullo together. On the way down the gradients, conditions deteriorated and drifting snow was encountered in the cutting south of Haie Hill tunnel. On reaching Bullo, this information was passed to the yard foreman with the suggestion that the 5.30 p.m. empties to Eastern United be cancelled. The train was nevertheless despatched, albeit with a reduced load, and on reaching the cutting, the vibration of the train dislodged a drift, which came down and trapped the engine.

There was nothing for it but to send the fireman back to Bullo on foot with the token. Another engine was sent to try and pull the train out, but, after detaching the wagons from the trapped engine, the act of pulling them back over the compacted snow resulted in fetching them off the rails. Consequently, the fire on the trapped engine was dropped and all concerned rode back to Bullo on the rescue engine.

The snow continued throughout Wednesday and it was not until the Thursday that a breakdown train was sent to re-rail the wagons, together with a party of German prisoners of war awaiting repatriation, to dig out the engine.

Later, when a spare crew was sent to light up the engine, it was discovered that the digging party had removed a mud-hole door from the firebox in order to obtain water for tea-making purposes! The engine was consequently towed back dead.

On the Friday, a snowplough was sent over the branch and, after its return to Bullo, Bob and Harry Trigg worked a freight to Cinderford which conveyed vital supplies of flour. The town had been cut off and local bakers had completely run out, so the crew were received as heroes by a sizeable gathering of residents who carried them shoulder high across to the Railway Inn for a celebratory drink!

After the nationalisation of the railways in 1948, the future of the Drybrook branch came under scrutiny,

These two views give some idea of the snow which fell in Cinderford in March 1947. *Collection A. K. Pope*

A 54XX 0–6–0PT-hauled FoD branch auto-train at Cinderford in June 1951. *Derek Clayton*

particularly following the eventual clearance of ammunition from Hawthorns tunnel.

Stone despatched by rail from Drybrook quarry declined and in 1949 the number of loaded wagons collected from the quarry each month were: January – 10; February – 11; March – 10; April – 5; May – 6; June – 8; July – 2; August – 3; September – 2; October – 2; November – 3; December – 3. The figures from January to June were higher as they included wagons of ammunition which was still being cleared from the tunnel at that time.

The Admiralty depot was closed in 1950, after which the line above Whimsey was only used for occasional traffic to and from Drybrook Quarry with small quantities of coke from Aberbargoed, about 30 tons per annum, and about 4 oil tanks a year from Avonmouth.

Traffic figures for the Drybrook branch for the year ending 31st July 1949 were as follows:

	Outwards	*Inwards*
General merchandise	977	33
Coal	–	33
Other minerals	10	–
Totals	987	66

Receipts	*Outwards*	*Inwards*	*Total*
General merchandise	2,443	31	2,474
Coal	–	19	19
Other minerals	9	–	9
Totals	2,452	50	2,502

Consideration was given to the closure of the whole of the Drybrook branch, but in 1949 the demand for tarred roadstone led bitumen manufacturers Berry Wiggins & Co. Ltd., whose head office was in Stratford, East London, and later Fetter Lane, to establish a tar distribution depot at Whimsey (Cinderford Goods) to serve various quarries in the area. They also established a depot at Hereford for quarries at Knighton. As it was anticipated that the depot would receive some 5,000 tons of bitumen per annum, it was obviously 'beneficial' to retain the line as far as Whimsey, and thereafter rakes of bitumen tank wagons were regularly conveyed in mixed goods trains over the Forest of Dean branch, much to the benefit of the line's revenue. Indeed, the traffic made sufficient impact on the line for some footplate crews to refer to it as 'the Tank invasion'. The bitumen was brought from Berry Wiggins' production plant at Sharnel Street on the Isle of Grain, Kent.

Since nationalisation had brought an end to the sharing of income between the GWR and LMS at Cinderford Joint station, traffic now tended to be concentrated at the new station. Even so, according to official correspondence, in 1950, traffic still being dealt with at Whimsey included 'coal, cattle food, explosives and sundry general traffic', including supplies for A. A. & H. Hawkins, sawyers, J. Joiner & Sons Ltd., timber merchants, who had recently moved from Soudley, and BRS coal haulage.

Berry Wiggins at Whimsey was not the only company to move into the area and bring traffic to the line. The Dursley-based engineering company, Messrs. R. A. Lister & Co. opened a new manufacturing plant at Cinderford in 1944. They produced a wide range of products, including wood-slatted waste bins used in parks, park benches, garden machinery, and diesel engines (Lister/Petter, etc.). Lister engines were fitted to things like narrow boats, lighting sets and pumping plant, much of which went to Third World countries. Cinderford just produced engines, some of which were handled by rail along with components such as crankshafts. During the early 1950s, Messrs. Meredith & Drew built a biscuit factory alongside the curve into Cinderford station and this brought regular supplies of flour from Cam flour mills (coincidentally also on the Dursley branch) which arrived by rail in two or three vans at a time. However, whilst some biscuits are believed to have been sent out by train, most were despatched by road.

Finally, during the same period, Messrs. Rosedale established a plastics factory on Treforest Trading Estate. The parts were moulded at Treforest and brought to Cinderford for assembly. Things like a wide range of buttons were put onto cards at Cinderford, and sufficient quantities of toys were despatched by rail to warrant two or three bogie parcels vans being conveyed as tail traffic on the 4.0 p.m. auto to Gloucester.

Sadly, even against this background, plans mooted in 1940 by the Forest of Dean Industrial Development Committee for a rail-served industrial estate at Cinderford did not come to fruition until the mid-1980s, long after the demise of the branch.

On weekdays in 1950, the branch was served by two return freights to Bilson, one of them serving Northern

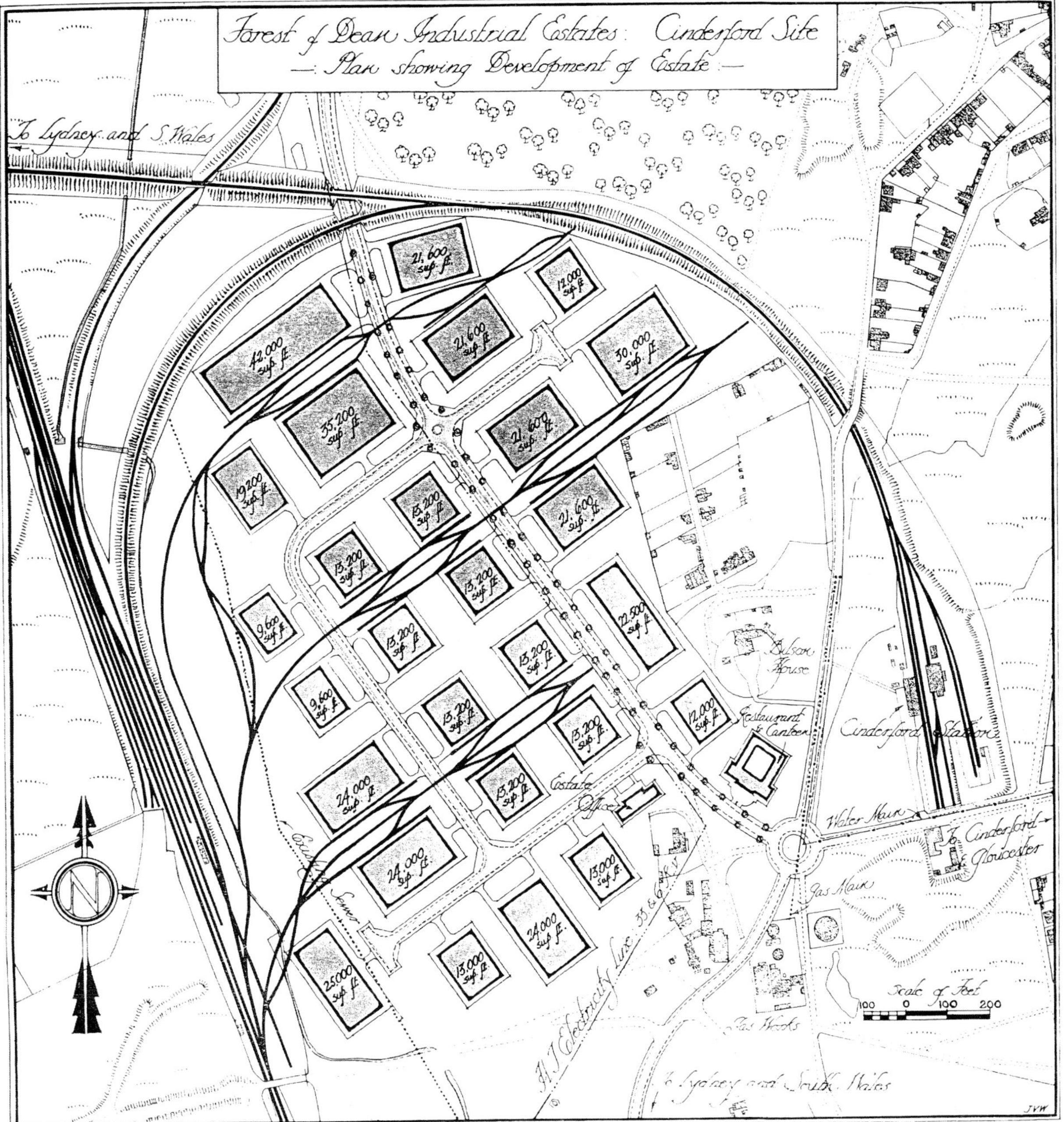

The plan produced by the Forest of Dean Industrial Development Committee in 1940, showing the extent of the trading estate proposed for Cinderford.

The guard's view from the rear of a branch goods train climbing through Soudley on its way to Bilson Junction in 1950. *Coll. Bob Brown*

United Colliery, and one Whimsey and beyond, three return trips to Eastern United Colliery, the last of which took empties up and returned light engine and brake, and three return auto trains between Gloucester and Cinderford.

The first train over the branch in the mornings, was the 7.20 a.m. freight from Bullo, which for many years was worked with Lydney '2021' class 0–6–0PTs and later the larger 77XX or 36XX 0–6–0PTs. Lydney men worked the engine light to Bullo where they shunted the yard to form a train which was usually made up of general traffic, tank wagons for Berry Wiggins and empties for Northern United Colliery. The tank wagons and empties were detached on arrival at Bilson, after which the remainder of the train was pushed back out of the yard and taken round to Cinderford. They were usually there between about 8.0 a.m. and 8.15, and, after placing the wagons in the yard, the loco returned to Bilson for the crew's breakfast. The usual routine was for the engine crew to cook eggs and bacon on the shovel, then take it into the guard's van to eat in comfort. The guard apparently prepared his own food on his van's stove or took sandwiches. An amusing aside to the breakfast arrangement was that one of the signalmen from Bilson box often used to go into the van to see the crew and occasionally literally snatched a piece of bacon! The loco crew got their own back one day when they got hold of a quantity of laxative chocolate out of a damaged carton from a box van at Cinderford. During the years of rationing, chocolate was one of the commodities which was not easy to come by, so when they returned to Bilson Yard, they made great play of having chocolate to eat during their tea-break. The signalman concerned ran true to form and, having come to see what he was missing out on, was given a generous quantity. Another engine crew also became involved in the prank and within a short space of time gave him some more. The signalman never did catch on but blamed his inevitable indisposition on the beer at a public house run by one of his relations!

However, to return to our story, the engine from the 7.20 a.m. was then used to trip out to Cinderford Goods, or Whimsey as it was often referred to, to deliver Berry Wiggins tanks and any other traffic, calling at Broadmoor brickworks if required and occasionally going out to Drybrook quarry.

Regardless of whether or not the trip to Drybrook was required, the freight did not set out from Bilson to Bullo until 11.5 a.m. At Eastern United it was held in the loop to

0–6–0PT No. 7723 approaching Bilson Junction with coal from Northern United Colliery on 27th June 1951. *J. E. Norris*

cross with the 11.10 Gloucester autocar due at Staple Edge Halt at 11.48.

After they reached Bullo at 12.29, the crew were relieved by another set of Lydney men who had booked on at 11.50, travelled to Newnham on the 12.05 p.m. passenger, and walked back to Bullo. The earlier crew then walked to Newnham to catch the 1.0 p.m. passenger from Gloucester back to Lydney.

The relief crew began their duty by working the 1.30 p.m. empties to Eastern United Colliery and returning with coal at 3.0 p.m. after being held in the loop there to cross with the 1.45 Gloucester auto which called at Staple Edge Halt at 2.46.

On return to Bullo at 3.34, the engine was used to form coal trains for Stoke Gifford, which included wagons for Castlemeads power station at Gloucester, and one for the opposite (down) direction which they would later work home to Lydney after working another load of empties to Eastern at 5.30 p.m. and returning engine and van at 6.15 p.m. When they reached Lydney, the down coal train was put into the sidings and the engine taken on shed for disposal.

The branch was also served by a Gloucester engine, which began its day's work on the 3.3 a.m. Docks Branch Sidings at Gloucester. The engine was always a 77XX or 36XX 0–6–0PT, the Lydney men at least finding the contractor-built 77XX more powerful than the nominally identical (except for cab) Swindon-built 36XX. After completing work at Docks Branch Sidings, they set out for Bullo at 5.0 a.m. and on arrival shunted the sidings to form trains including the 7.20 Bilson and the 8.40 a.m. to Eastern United Colliery, which the Gloucester men worked over the branch. The Eastern working was due at the colliery at 9.0 a.m. and was put in the loop out of the way of the 9.1 a.m. Cinderford to Gloucester auto-train which called at Staple Edge Halt at 9.8 a.m. The Gloucester engine worked back with a coal train at 10.0 a.m., arriving at Bullo at 10.33 a.m.

The Gloucester engine was taken over by Lydney men who booked on at 10.19 a.m. to catch the 10.34 to Newnham and walk to Bullo. They continued work in the sidings and worked the 1.5 p.m. empties to Northern United which was propelled from Bilson Junction to the colliery, as detailed on page 24. The Gloucester engine collected loaded coal wagons from the loaded sidings and set out on the 5-minute journey back to Bilson at 2.15 p.m. After just 15 minutes the loco set out for Northern again, if required, with more empties, arriving back at Bilson again at 3.7 with more coal.

Some crews recall running out to Whimsey for empty Berry Wiggins tank wagons, but, whatever the case, they were scheduled to set out from Bilson Junction to Bullo at 3.40 p.m. but recall 'we were always late'. They were supposed to be out of the way in the loop at Eastern where the 4.0 p.m. Cinderford to Gloucester auto was due to pass them but they often followed it instead. However, they usually managed to get back to Bullo in time to clear the single line for the 5.30 freight to Eastern.

When they arrived back at Bullo, Gloucester men took over, leaving the Lydney men free to walk back to Newnham to catch a passenger train for Lydney. However, in later years when Harry Trigg was driving the 5.30 auto-train from Gloucester, he would make an unofficial call at Bullo to pick up his Lydney colleagues.

Passenger services over the branch were push-pull worked with 14XX 0–4–2Ts or 54XX 0–6–0PTs from Lydney shed. The 54XXs allocated to Lydney, 5408, 5417, 5418 and 5421, are remembered as being rough riding in comparison to the 0–4–2Ts, particularly No. 5417 which had a bad reputation. They are also said to have not

FOREST OF DEAN BRANCH.

Single Line worked by Electric Train Token between Bullo Pill West Box, Eastern United and Bilson Junction, and by Train Staff only (one engine in steam or two or more coupled at a time) between Bilson and Churchway, and Bilson and Drybrook. The only intermediate Crossing place is Eastern United Colliery. The Cinderford Loop is worked on the Electric Train Tablet System between Bilson Jct. Box and Cinderford Junction Box **and Train Staff only between** Cinderford Junction Box and Cinderford Station.
Worked by Electric Train Token between Bullo Pill West and Bilson Junction **when** Eastern United Box **is** closed.
Two Passenger Trains conveying passengers must not cross at Eastern United Colliery unless specially arranged in case of accident.
Freight trains may be booked to pass at Bilson Jct. via Bilson Goods Yard.

Down Trains. Week Days Only.

Dis-t'nce M	C	Mile Post Mileage from F'rest of Dean B'nch Jct. M.	c.	STATIONS.	Gradient 1 in.	Point to Point Times	Allow for Stop.	Allow for Start	K Freight. arr.	K Freight. dep.	B Auto ex Grange Court. arr.	B Auto ex Grange Court. dep.	K Frght SO dep.	K Freight. SX arr.	K Freight. SX dep.	K Frght MX dep.	K Frgt RR SO dep.	B 11.10 a.m. Auto ex Glos. arr.	B 11.10 a.m. Auto ex Glos. dep.	K Freight. SX RRMO arr.	K Freight. SX RRMO dep.	K Frgt SX dep.	K Frght SX dep.	B 1.45 p.m. Auto ex Glos. SO arr.	B 1.45 p.m. Auto ex Glos. SO dep.	B 1.45 p.m. Auto ex Gloster SX dep.	B Auto SO dep.	K Frgt SX dep.	B 5.30 p.m. Auto ex Glos. SO dep.	B 7.40 p.m. Auto ex Glos. SO arr.	B 7.40 p.m. Auto ex Glos. SO dep.
						Mins.	Mins.	Mins.	a.m.	a.m.	a.m.	a.m.	a.m.	a.m.	a.m.	a.m.	a.m.	a.m.	a.m.	p.m.	p.m.	p.m.	p.m.	p.m.	p.m.	p.m.	p.m.	p.m.	p.m.	p.m.	p.m.
–	–	–	–	NEWNHAM	—	—	—	—	..	..	8 7	8 20	..	..	..	..	..	11 31	11 32	..	..	..	..	2 6	2 8	2‡35	3 15	..	5¶55	8 0	8 2
–	76	–	–	Bullo Pill	—	—	—	1	—	7 20	822½0	W825½	..	..	..	8 40	..	11	35	—	1 5	1 30	..	2	11	2 38	3 18	5 30	5 57	8	4
1	37	–	32	Bullo Cross Halt	54 R	—	—	—	—	—	—	8 27½	..	..	..	..	..	—	1137½	W	—	—	..	—	2 13	2 40	3 20	—	6 0	8 6	8 7
3	12	2	7	Soudley Sidings	48 R	13	1	1	—	—	—	—	..	..	..	—	..	—	—	—	—	W	..	—	—	—	—	—	—	—	—
3	22	2	17	Upper Soudley Halt	*48 R	—	—	—	—	—	—	8 34	..	..	..	—	..	—	11 44	—	—	—	..	—	2 19½	2 46½	3 26½	—	6 6½	8 13	8 14
4	6	3	1	Shakemantle	49 R	6	1	1	—	—	—	—	..	..	..	CR	..	—	—	—	—	—	..	—	—	—	—	—	—	—	—
4	31	3	26	Staple Edge Halt	49 R	—	—	—	—	—	—	8 38½	..	..	..	—	..	—	1148½	—	—	—	..	—	2 24	2 51	3 31	—	6 11	8 18	8 19
4	37	3	32	Eastern United Colliery	71 R	3	1	1	—	—	—	—	..	..	..	9 X 0	..	C	XS	1 25	1 30	1 50	..	—	—	CXS	—	5 50	—	—	—
5	10	4	5	Ruspidge Halt	58 R	2	1	1	—	—	—	8 42	..	..	..	..	..	—	11 52	—	—	..	..	—	2 27½	2 54½	3 34½	..	6 14½	8 21	8 23
5	79	4	74	Bilson Junction	99 R	—	—	—	C	S	C 8	44S	..	..	..	..	..	11 54	X1156	C	S	..	..	C2	29½ S	2 57	3 36½	..	6 16	C8	25S
*6	32	5	27	Cinderford Junction	—	—	—	—	C	S	C	S	..	..	..	..	..	C	S	—	—	..	..	C	S	CS	CS	..	CS	C	S
*6	62	5	57	CINDERFORD	—	—	—	—	8 0	—	8 46	—	..	..	..	..	..	11 58	—	—	—	..	..	2 32	—	3 0	3 39	..	6 20	8 28	—
–	–	–	–	Cinderford Junction	—	—	—	—	..	..	..	..	..	..	..	..	..	..	..	—	—	..	..	..	..	..	..	..	..	..	..
–	–	–	–	Bilson Junction	—	—	—	—	—	—	..	..	..	..	..	..	..	..	..	—	—	..	..	..	..	..	..	..	..	..	..
–	–	–	–	Bilson Goods Yard	—	3	1	1	7 48	7 55	..	..	9 3	8 22	X9 15	..	9 50	..	..	1 40	1 55	..	2 35	..	..	..	..	..	..	..	..
–	–	–	–	Brick Works Sidings	—	—	—	—	..	..	..	..	CR	..	..	..	..	..	..	C	R	..	CR	..	..	..	..	..	..	..	..
7	22	6	17	Churchway (N.U.Coll'y)	41 R	—	—	—	..	..	..	..	9 15	..	..	..	..	..	..	2 0	—	..	2 40	..	..	..	..	..	..	..	..
6	45	5	40	Duck Colliery	—	—	—	—	..	..	..	..	..	—	—	..	—	..	..	..	..	..	..	..	..	..	..	..	..	..	..
6	65	5	60	Cinderford Goods	82 R	4	1	—	..	..	..	..	..	9 21	9 34	..	10 6	..	..	..	..	..	..	..	..	..	..	..	..	..	..
–	–	–	–	Drybrook Quarries	42 R	—	—	—	..	..	..	..	..	9 46	—	..	1018	..	..	..	..	..	..	..	..	..	..	..	..	..	..
																	Cinderf'd Gds arr. 9.56 a.m.									‡—Newnham arr. 2.6 p.m.			¶—Newnham arr. 5.49 p.m.		

W—When the combined load of 1.5 p.m. and 1.30 p.m. ex Bullo Pill does not exceed 40 wagons may be run as coupled train.
*—Distance Bilson Junction to Cinderford Junction, 33 chains, and to Cinderford Station, 63 chains. The length of the Loop at Eastern United Colliery is 380 yards, capable of holding engine, 50 wagons, and van

Forest of Dean Branch—continued.

Up Trains. Week Days Only.

Dis-t'nce M	C	STATIONS.	Gradient 1 in	Point to Point Times	Allow for Stop	Allow for Start	K Fr'ght dep.	B Auto to Gloster. arr.	B Auto to Gloster. dep.	K Freight SO dep.	K Freight. MX arr.	K Freight. MX dep.	K Freight. arr.	K Freight. dep.	K Freight SO RR arr.	B Auto to Gloster. arr.	B Auto to Gloster. dep.	K Frgt SX dep.	B A'to SO dep.	K Freight. SX arr.	K Freight. SX dep.	K Freight. SX RRMO arr.	K Freight. SX RRMO dep.	K Freight. SX arr.	K Freight. SX dep.	B Auto to Gloucester arr.	B Auto to Gloucester dep.	K Engine and Br'ke SX dep.	B Auto to Gloster SO arr.	B Auto to Gloster SO dep.	C Empty Auto to Lydney. SO arr.	C Empty Auto to Lydney. SO dep.
				Mins	Mins	Mins	a.m.	a.m.	a.m.	a.m.	a.m.	a.m.	a.m.	a.m.	a.m.	p.m.	p.m.	p.m.	p.m.	p.m.	p.m.	p.m.	p.m.	p.m.	p.m.	p.m.	p.m.	p.m.	p.m.	p.m.	p.m.	p.m.
—	—	Drybrook Qur.	—	—	—	—	..	—	—	..	..	..	—	10¶20	1028	..	..	..	..	..	..	..	..	Worked by Auto Engine and Trailer.		Starts from Cinderford on Saturdays		..	..	..	..	..
1	44	Cinderford Goods	42 F	—	—	—	..	—	—	..	..	..	C	R	CR	—	—	..	..	..	..	..	..					..	..	..	..	..
1	64	Duck Colliery	—	—	—	1	..	—	—	..	..	..	—	—	—	—	—	..	..	..	..	..	..					..	..	..	..	..
—	—	Ch'way N.U.Colly	—	—	—	—	..	..	..	9 40	..	..	..	..	..	..	..	2 15	..	..	..	—	3 0					..	..	..	..	..
—	—	Brick Wrks. Sid.	41 F	—	—	—	..	..	..	CR	..	..	..	..	..	..	..	CR	..	..	..	C	R					..	..	..	..	..
—	—	Stop Board	—	—	—	—	..	..	..	P	..	..	..	..	..	..	..	P	..	..	..	—	P—					..	..	..	..	..
—	—	Bilson Goods Yard	52 F	3	2	1	..	—	—	9 45	..	..	10¶40	11 5	1048	—	—	2 20	..	..	..	3 7	3 40			—	—	..	..	..	..	..
2	30	Bilson Jct.	76 F	—	—	—	..	—	—	..	..	..	—	—	..	—	—	..	..	..	..	—	—			—	3†45	..	..	..	..	..
—	—	Cinderford Jct.	—	—	—	—	..	—	—	..	..	..	—	—	..	—	—	..	..	..	..	M				C	S	..	..	..	..	..
—	—	CINDERFORD	—	—	—	—	8 15	—	9 1	..	..	..	—	—	..	—	12 40	..	2 40	..	..	—	—	—	3 20	3†50	4 0	..	—	6 30	—	8†35
—	—	Cinderford Jct.	—	—	—	—	CS	C	S	..	..	..	—	—	..	C	S	..	CS	..	..	—	—	C	S	C	S	..	C	S	C	S
—	—	Stop Board	51 F	—	—	—	P	—	—	..	..	..	—	—	..	—	—	..	..	..	..	—	—	—	—	—	—	..	—	—	—	—
2	30	Bilson Jct.	76 F	—	—	—	8‡22	C9	4S	..	Z		C	S	..	C 12	42 S	..	2 42	..	..	C	S	3‡25	—	C4	2S	..	C6	32S	C8	37S
3	18	Stop Board	178 F	4	1	1	‡Bilson Goods Yard.	—	—	..	..	..	11P10	11 15	..	—	—	..	—	..	..	3 44	P3..	‡Bilson Goods Yard.		—	—	..	—	—	—	—
3	19	Ruspidge Halt	99 F	—	—	—		—	9 6	..	..	..	—	—	..	—	12 44	..	2 44	..	..	—	—			—	4 4	..	—	6 34	—	—
3	72	Eastern U. Coll.	58 F	4	1	1		C	S	..	—	10 0	11 20	11X55	..	C	S	..	CS	—	X3 0	3 53	X4			C	S	6†15	—	—	—	—
3	78	Staple Edge Halt	71 F	—	—	—		—	9 8½	..	—	—	—	—	..	—	1246½	..	246½	—	—	—	—			—	4 6½	—	—	6 36½	—	—
4	29	Shakemantle	49 F	—	—	—		—	—	..	C	R	—	—	..	—	—	..	—	—	—	—	—			—	—	..	—	—	—	—
5	5	Stop Board	49 F	6	1	1		—	—	..	10P8	10 12	12 3	P12 7	..	—	—	..	—	3 8	P312	428P	4 32			—	—	6 21	—	—	—	—
5	7	Upper Soudley H.	49 F	—	—	—		—	9 12	..	—	—	—	—	..	—	12 50	..	2 50	—	—	—	—			—	4 10	—	—	6 40	—	—
5	7	Soudley Sidings	48 F	—	—	—		—	—	..	—	—	—	—	..	—	—	..	—	—	—	—	—			—	—	..	—	—	—	—
6	72	Bullo Cross Halt	50 F	—	—	—		—	9 16½	..	—	—	—	—	..	—	1254½	..	254½	—	—	—	—			—	4 14½	..	—	6 44½	—	—
7	33	Bullo Pill	54 F	§16	1	1	..	9	18	..	10 33	—	12 29	—	..	O 12	59W	..	2 59	3 34	—	4 54	—	..	..	O 4	19W	6 30	O 6	49W	8†52	9†5
8	29	NEWNHAM	—	—	—	—		920½	9 23	..					..	1 2	1 4	..	3 2					..	..	4 22	4 23		6 52	6 53		

M—On Saturdays Eastern United depart 4.20, Stop Board 4.28,—4P33, Bullo Pill arrive 4.53 p.m. **Z**—Train worked by one guard—load not to exceed 25 loaded wagons. ¶—Saturdays excepted.
§—To Bullo Pill Home Signal—3 minutes allowed thence to Bullo Pill Yard, including 1 minute to stop. Trains conveying less than equal 25 " 10 Ton " loaded wagons allowed 1 minute less Eastern United Colliery to Bullo Pill Home Signal.

Taken from the 1950 Service Timetable.

steamed so well. The 14XXs were preferred and, compared with Nos. 1401 and 1409, No. 1456 is said to have seen the most service over the line.

The early-turn Lydney men on 'the car' booked on at 6.15 a.m., came off shed at 7.0 a.m. and ran to the sidings at Otterspool to collect the auto-trailer to work the 7.20 Lydney to Grange Court. This train, which regularly delivered churns of drinking water to Naas Crossing, called at Awre and Newnham on the way to Grange Court. Here it reversed its direction and returned to Cinderford. It mainly carried schoolchildren for East Dean Grammar School, four or five joined the train at Grange Court and another dozen boarded the car when the train called at Newnham again, in the down direction, between 8.7 and 8.20. Although mainly used by schoolchildren, there were a few regular adults, including a sadler who worked at Eastern United Colliery. The working timetable allowed for a three-minute stop at Bullo for the engine to take water before venturing onto the branch. Some drivers would make this last the journey into Cinderford and then to Gloucester, but, with limited tank capacity, others would call at Bullo again to top up on their way back off the branch. There were children waiting to join the train at every halt, usually 5 at Bullo Cross, 15-20 at Soudley, 1 at Staple Edge and 6 at Ruspidge.

The 'car' arrived at Cinderford at 8.46 and left again at 9.1 a.m. with about a dozen passengers for Gloucester. On Saturdays this train was popular enough to require two trailers. Timing was more important on this run because, on the main line from Bullo to Gloucester, the car ran ahead of the Cardiff to Newcastle express.

After the passengers had got off at Gloucester, the car was shunted into the Hereford bay to await return at 11.10, and, when it reached Newnham at 11.31, the crew were relieved by Lydney men who had booked on at 10.19 and travelled down to Newnham with the crew for the 1.05 empties to northern. The early-turn men had to wait at Newnham for the 1.0 p.m. to take them home, so some spent time in the nearby 'cider house'.

The 10.19 relief men worked the car up to Cinderford, arriving at 11.58 and departing again for Gloucester at 12.40, stopping for water at Bullo on the way back. They returned from Gloucester at 1.45 but this time, on arrival at Newnham at 2.6, the car was backed into the bay platform to leave the down main clear for the 2.10 p.m. Gloucester to Cardiff. The car departed again at 2.35, and, after calling for water at Bullo, arrived at Cinderford at 3.0 p.m. The engine, usually with the car still attached, then made a trip out to Bilson with wagons for the 3.40 p.m. goods. After returning to Cinderford, it frequently collected two or three bogie parcels vans loaded with Rosedale's traffic for conveyance to Gloucester as a tail load on the back of the 4.0 p.m. auto-train which took all the schoolchildren home. At Gloucester the vans were put off in the 'next road from the Chalford Cars'.

During the week the 4.0 p.m. was the last train for Cinderford, the car returning from Gloucester at 5.30 and running to Lydney. However, on Saturdays, the engine and trailer worked another three trips in the afternoon/evening, the 1.45 from Gloucester arriving at Cinderford at 2.32, departing again at 2.40 but terminating at Newnham at 3.2 and returning to Cinderford at 3.15, arriving at 3.39. The 4.0 p.m. train ran through to Gloucester to form the 5.55 p.m. back to Cinderford, arriving at 6.20. The final departure of the day was the 6.30 to Gloucester, which returned from there at 7.40, arriving at Cinderford at 8.28 and returning empty stock to Lydney at 8.35. As these extra trips were beyond the bunker capacity of the auto-engines, some had to go on shed at Gloucester to be topped up with coal in order to complete the day's services.

The matter of closing the branch above Whimsey had been allowed to rest until September 1950 when a road widening scheme between Cinderford and Nailbridge called for expenditure of £1,375 on the provision of new gates at the level crossing at Steam Mills. This prompted action to close the line and, following the British Transport Commission's approval for the abandonment of the line, notice was given to Drybrook Quarries for the termination

Steam Mills Crossing in July 1952. *C. L. Mowat*

of their private siding agreement from 30th November 1942.

Official closure of the line took place from 1st December 1952, a 250 yard shunting spur being left in place north of Whimsey, and a rail being taken out beyond to physically break the line.

The Signal and Telegraph Department recovered the Steam Mills up and down distant signals, the ground frame, most of the pole route between Steam Mills and Nailbridge (except for six poles carrying GPO wires), and the ground frame at Drybrook, but recovery of the track did not commence until 1956.

The work was carried out by private contractors who employed their own diesel locomotive which was delivered to Whimsey by road. They started work on Monday, 8th October, working recovered materials into Whimsey Yard under special working instructions. In order to protect such movements in the yard and also to protect the dead line when the locomotive was working on it, wheel stops were provided 150ft below the points at the Bilson end of Whimsey Yard (normally secured away from the rail) and another 150ft on the Cinderford side of the fencing on the west side of the roadway at Steam Mills Crossing (normally secured across the road).

At the commencement of each day's work, the contractor's engine was required to enter Whimsey Yard to deliver loaded wagons and collect empties and return immediately to the dead line.

The wheel stops were padlocked by keys attached to the single-line train staff, so to enable this operation to be carried out, a responsible member of the Engineering Department stationed at Cinderford, gang No. 116, was deputed to collect the wooden train staff for the Drybrook branch, now relabelled Bilson Junction–Whimsey. On his way from Bilson, he locked the wheel stop south of Whimsey across the line and then walked through to Steam Mills to open the one across the rails to allow the contractor's train into Whimsey Yard. There he operated the Cinderford Crossing and Cinderford Goods Siding ground frames which were locked by the key incorporated in the wooden train staff. After the contractor's train had returned to the dead section, the wheel stops were locked in their normal positions and the single-line staff returned to Bilson signal box.

When the work was completed, the *Gloucester Journal* for 13th October 1956 reported that the gates at Steam Mills had been removed at last – 'Those few bumpy yards past where the gates stood are a thing of the past, and the road has been made up to ensure a safe and smooth crossing. All that remains to tell of the past are the two lengths of line which end abruptly at either side of the road.' The level crossing had obviously been a bone of contention for some time.

Following closure of the Severn & Wye Joint Committee's line between Serridge Junction and Cinderford Junction in 1951, all goods traffic for Cinderford had to be routed via

0–6–0PT No. 8729 exchanging loaded and empty tank wagons from Berry Wiggins' depot at Whimsey. *R. Dagley Morris*

An up goods held in the loop waiting for a passage to Bullo on 12th July 1956. *H. C. Casserley*

the Forest of Dean branch. It is difficult to establish what difference this made to the tonnage subsequently conveyed between Bullo and Cinderford, but it is doubtful whether it significantly enhanced the line's receipts.

After the Whimsey branch had been lifted, the contractors were due to recover the track and materials from the S&W's Cinderford Extension, but when it was realised that the contractor's mobile crane was too high to clear the bridges which crossed the Drybrook and Churchway branches, it was decided that both structures should be demolished.

In March 1957 instructions were issued for a 16XX 0–6–0PT to act as pilot for the removal of the contractor's diesel crane and diesel locomotive, under their own power, from the Whimsey branch over to the Churchway branch, but, despite the newspaper announcement about the demise of the level crossing at Steam Mills in October 1956, it was not until April 1958 that work on the Drybrook branch was officially reported as complete and that the contractor's crane and locomotive were still in the yard at Whimsey. The date at which the two bridges were removed has not been ascertained but photographic evidence shows them removed by January 1959. The diesel locomotive and crane were reported as waiting in Whimsey Yard for removal to Churchway.

Competition from motor buses had already resulted in the withdrawal of passenger services between Cinderford and Drybrook in 1930. In common with most of the rest of the country, local people continued to be lured away by the more convenient bus services in the Forest and, of course, the growth in popularity of the private motor car. The railway timetable did not exactly help the situation when, for example, the first train did not leave Cinderford for Gloucester until 9.0 a.m. This was not of much use to men now working in Gloucester following the decline of the Forest's mining industry.

The inevitable decision to close the line was met with understandable opposition, the *Dean Forest Mercury* for 27th June 1958 reporting:

> Because the service is unremunerative it is proposed to close the railway line between Cinderford and Gloucester to passenger traffic. A saving of £9,900 a year is estimated . . .

When this picture was taken on 7th June 1954 the fireman of this Cinderford to Gloucester auto-train had just surrendered the Bilson Junction to Cinderford train staff and collected the Electric Key token for the section to Bullo from the Bilson Junction signalman.

Geoffrey Oates

Facilities for the collection and delivery of parcels and goods "smalls" traffic in the areas at present served by the stations on this section of the line would continue to be provided.

Arrangements for the handing in and collection of parcels and goods traffic (including full truck load traffic) would also be maintained at all stations concerned with the exception of Ruspidge Halt and alternative facilities for dealing with freight and parcels traffic handled at this point could be made available at Cinderford Town approximately 1½ miles distant.

Daily average number of passenger journeys to and from each station (based on a count taken during a test week in 1958) were as follows.

	Joining	Alighting
Gloucester (Central)	40	48
Oakle Street	3	1
Grange Court	13	8
Westbury on Severn Halt	3	3
Newnham	25	22
Bullo Cross Halt	6	4
Upper Soudley Halt	14	14
Staple Edge Halt	9	9
Ruspidge Halt	10	11
Cinderford	35	39

In addition ten journeys were made daily by the Commission's employees.

British Railways say that careful consideration has been given to the possibility of making the passenger services concerned remunerative by the introduction of lightweight diesel units, coupled with simplified working methods, in place of the existing steam trains. It is clear, however, in the light of the minimum cost which would be involved in providing a service of this nature that the trains would still prove uneconomic to operate.

It is considered that the road facilities would provide a reasonable alternative to the existing rail service.

"There is no knowledge of any developments in the area which would lead to an appreciable increase in traffic at present conveyed by the train services in question", British Railways say in their circular to the local authorities.

The estimated minimum annual savings are given as follows:

a)	Minimum gross estimated savings per annum	£13,976
b)	Estimated annual loss of traffic receipts	£1,958
c)	Estimated cartage costs and other expenses	£2,098
d)	Minimum net annual economy	£9,920

"The withdrawal of the passenger train service will also enable certain adjustments to be made to the freight train working in the area resulting in further economies of approximately £2,700 per annum", the statement says.

"The road services already operating in the area would, subject to some duplication at certain periods, provide reasonable alternative facilities for the majority of passengers now using the rail services".

"Oakle Street, Grange Court, Westbury-on-Severn Halt and Newnham-on-Severn will continue to be served by trains operating between Gloucester and Newport, and, in the case of the first two stations, by Gloucester/Hereford services."

East Dean Rural District Council decided to send a strongly-worded protest against the proposed closing of the Cinderford line.

No strongly-worded protest could have had any real effect; people simply were not using the line in sufficient numbers. The service was withdrawn from Monday, 3rd November 1958, but in practice, the last train ran on the evening of Saturday, 1st November, an event marked by a handful of enthusiasts. The halts were removed shortly afterwards.

The last day of passenger services over the FoD branch on 1st November 1958. The views above show the 4-coach 2.52 p.m. Newnham to Cinderford hauled by 7750 approaching and calling at Ruspidge Halt. The right-hand picture shows the same train after arrival at Cinderford, whilst the one below shows the engine in the yard collecting a bogie siphon of Rosedales traffic for attachment to the 4.08 p.m. *Colin Green*

A loaded coal train passing Eastern United on its way to Bullo in December 1963. *R. H. Marrows*

An unidentified 45XX class 2–6–2T at Bilson Junction awaiting departure with a train of empties for Bullo, possibly on 26th August 1964. *D. A. Tipper*

For just two months goods and mineral traffic remained buoyant, that is until the sudden and unexpected closure of Eastern United Colliery in January 1959. This was a bitter blow so soon after the loss of the passenger service and a foretaste of things to come, for the whole of the Forest of Dean coalfield was to close within six years.

However, in the meantime, goods and mineral traffic remained relatively constant and it was not until Friday, 2nd October 1964 that further misfortune quite literally struck the branch when the bridge over the A48 at Bullo was damaged by a mechanical excavator being carried on a lorry. Despite the wonderful opportunity this incident presented for the closure of the branch (some locals suggested that Dr. Beeching might have been driving the lorry himself!), the bridge was repaired promptly and the branch re-opened within the week.

By this time, steam was being withdrawn throughout the Western Region and dieselisation was inevitable.

The remains of the bridge carrying the branch over the A48 at Bullo, seen on 3rd October 1964, the day after it had been struck by a lorry. These views were taken towards Cinderford and Bullo respectively. *A. K. Pope*

Lydney shed had been closed on 29th February 1964, after which locos for the branch were provided from Gloucester. The last steam working over the Forest of Dean branch was on 31st December 1965, just seven days after Northern United Colliery was closed on the 24th, and consequently so, too, was the Churchway branch from Bilson to Northern United on the 28th.

New D9500 Type 1 0–6–0 diesel hydraulics were now provided for branch services. A 350bhp 0–6–0 diesel shunter, D3991, had been used on the branch on 8th March 1962 when there was no water supply at Bilson due to a leak in the tank, but the diesel was not satisfactory.

The D9500s, nicknamed 'Teddy Bears' but known in the Forest as 'Yogi Bears', were not a great success, gearbox problems, among the faults recalled, often leaving them crawling along at shunting speed, even when on the main line. They entered service in 1964 and by 1966 were quietly decommissioned and stored at Worcester Works.

The tanks of 0–6–0PT No. 4614 being filled at Bilson c.1965. *A. K. Pope*

A signalman's view of a train of empty Berry Wiggins tank wagons passing through Bilson Junction headed by No. 3759 on 20th April 1965.

D9527 passing the Bilson Junction up distant on its way to Whimsey with a train of loaded tank wagons for Berry Wiggins on 23rd August 1966. *R. H. Marrows*

Another view of the same train heading towards Whimsey. Both these views were taken from the S & W Cinderford Extension embankment. *R. H. Marrows*

D9527 at Whimsey shortly after arrival with the same loaded tankers on 23rd August 1966. *R. H. Marrows*

D9527 collecting a couple of empty mineral wagons from Bilson Junction on the return journey with empty tank wagons from Berry Wiggins' depot. The picture opposite shows the same train just south of Eastern United on its way to Bullo. *R. H. Marrows*

BERRY WIGGINS
& Co LTD
FIELD HOUSE
FETTER LANE
LONDON E.C.4

. . . and a final view of D9527 and its train of empties passing through Soudley on the descent to Bullo. *R. H. Marrows*

They were followed on the branch by North British D63XX 'Baby Warships' which again were not found to be greatly successful.

At the start of 1966, Cinderford was closed to goods and parcels traffic, although some domestic coal was still delivered there. This left Berry Wiggins depot at Whimsey providing the main traffic on the branch. When Messrs. Painters, who built electricity pylons, moved into a new industrial unit alongside the branch at Whimsey, they intended to move their materials by rail. However, as Berry Wiggins were building a new depot at Lydney Junction, there was little reason to keep the branch open and, following excuses about insufficient wagons being found for Painters' traffic, the company turned to road transport, and left the district soon afterwards.

Berry Wiggins' Lydney depot was opened early in 1967 and the Forest of Dean branch was closed throughout on 1st August that year.

Cinderford station was demolished early in 1968, the fixtures, fittings and roof being removed by the simple expedient of deliberately setting fire to the buildings. The gutted shells were then knocked down. The entire line was lifted by the end of 1969 and so ended 160 years of railway and tramroad history in the area.

Today, the portion of line between Cinderford Bridge (Ruspidge) and Churchway has been converted into a linear park walkway. The embankment of the Bilson Loop has been removed entirely and the cutting beyond Cinderford Junction filled in and built over. The site of Cinderford station has been redeveloped as a housing estate, named 'The Keelings' in memory of the father and son who were engineers to the Severn & Wye Railway & Canal Co.

Large stretches of the Whimsey branch have also disappeared under industrial estate and roadways. The route can still be traced beyond Steam Mills as far as Nailbridge, but here a builder's yard has removed all traces of the embankment. The line can still be seen from the site of Speedwell Siding to Drybrook, and the position of Drybrook Halt only lacks the platform and rails.

South of Cinderford Bridge, the trackbed has been sold off as far as Staple Edge, but from there to Soudley the route can still be walked, although a deviation has to be made onto the original tramroad route around Blue Rock tunnel, which is bricked up. The crossing keeper's house at Soudley still stands, and just beyond is the bricked-up entrance to Bradley Hill tunnel. Little remains between the tunnels at Soudley Ironworks apart from some stone walling, and all is on private ground. South of Haie Hill tunnel, the ground is also private, but at Bullo Dock the basin is still in much the same condition as it was in the 1930s.

D6329 leaving Bilson Junction with empty coal wagons for Bullo on 11th July 1967. *A. K. Pope*

Empty tank wagons being collected from Berry Wiggins' depot at Whimsey by D9501 on 16th February 1967. *A. K. Pope*

Bullo Pill East Box, looking east towards Newnham. A solid brick structure, it had lasted for nearly a hundred years. February 1968. *A. K. Pope*

The interior of Bullo East, with relief signalman Grosvenor at the frame, on 2nd April 1968. Though the structure of the box was old, the frame was not, and by 1968 the box was on its third lever frame. The first was replaced in 1898, and the frame shown here was the vertical tappet frame for 34 levers at 4in centres, installed in 1930. A timeless scene which, but for the modern Bardic handlamp beside the teapot, could have been taken at any time in the preceding twenty years.
A. K. Pope

APPENDIX 1

Signalling on the Forest of Dean Branch

by Mike Christensen

THE opening of the Forest of Dean line as a branch of the broad gauge South Wales Railway (in place of a former tramroad) on 24th July 1854, is recounted in Volume 1, pages 2-4. At that time, and for a decade to come, the signalling was confined to local operation of points from hand levers with no interlocking between the points and the disc and crossbar signals. The form of the crossbar indicated the direction of travel to which it applied. Upward extensions at either end of the crossbar indicated that the signal applied to trains travelling in the up direction. Downward extensions showed that the signal applied to down trains. In the plan of East Slade Colliery on page 259, the signal protected the siding layout at Churchway from down trains (i.e. those travelling uphill from Bilson to Churchway) at a location where visibility from a distance was poor because of the curvature of the line. Evidence of the existence of isolated signals appears on the OS maps of the 1870s (see pages 178, 245/6 and 307). The detail of a typical installation appears on the plan of the proposed new siding for Hawkwell Colliery in 1878 on page 250.

By a quirk of history, one of the GWR pattern disc and crossbar signals on the FoD branch was to become one of the last survivors – if not *the* last survivor – of the type to remain in service. The signal was installed in 1878 to protect the crossing of the Churchway branch by Brain's Tramway. It remained in use long after the demise of the tramway, acting as an outer home signal worked from Bilson S&W Junction Ground Frame (page 239). The presence of an outer home was necessary because it was permitted to shunt without the train staff outside the home signal. The working of the end of Bilson Yard was unusual, because there was no distant signal for trains approaching from Churchway, and trains arriving from that direction effectively ran straight into a yard, under the control of signals worked only from a ground frame, not a signal box.

Bullo was an important location on the South Wales Railway (SWR) main line, and was the site of a policeman's post by 1855, if not from the opening of the line (see page 49). 'Locking gear' was added to the signalling in 1867, and by the date of the 1878 OS map there were three signal boxes – Bullo East, Middle and West. Bullo East was destined to have a long working life, surviving until 2nd June 1969. The other two boxes lasted for a much shorter time, being replaced – under work authorised on 27th October 1897 and ready for Board of Trade (BoT) inspection by 20th December 1898 – by a single new box. Known as Bullo Pill West, this box had a frame for 34 levers. The lever frame in Bullo Pill East box was replaced at the same time. The layout at Bullo West was not to remain the same for long, and was remodelled again in 1907, in connection with the opening of the FoD branch to passenger trains.

The 1872 working timetable gives an insight into the number of siding locations in operation at that time, listing:

Bullo
Soudley Furnaces
Coopers Siding
Silly Point
Blue Rock
Shakemantle
Quidchurch
Stapledge
Meerbrook

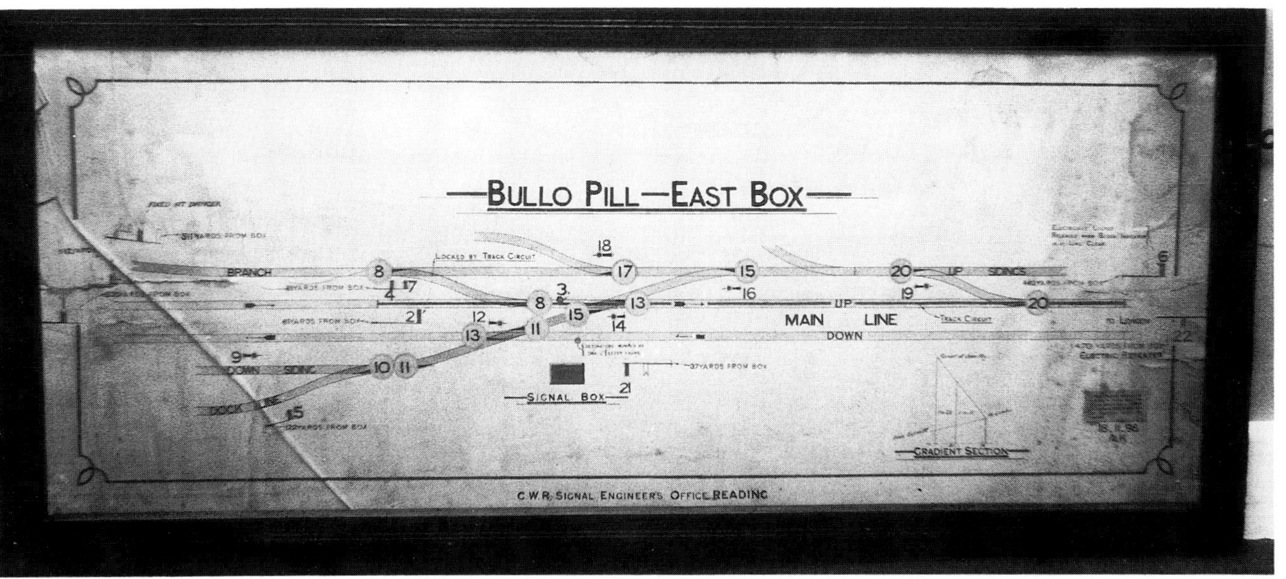

The diagram in Bullo East box, showing the Forest of Dean branch joining from the top left, and the Dock Line at the bottom. The gradient profile at the bottom right of the diagram indicated, if in exaggerated form, the steep nature of the FoD branch. *M. Christensen*

Cinderford (i.e. the location later known as Ruspidge)
Bilson
Whimsey
Churchway

As to the working of the line, the 1872 WTT stated "The Forest Branch is worked by train staff, and no engine may leave in either direction without the Staff or Ticket, to be carried by the engine driver, who will be held responsible accordingly. All trains from Bilson must stop at Cinderford to pin down Breaks, and drivers must be prepared to stop at the semaphore signal near to the Engine House if it shows 'Danger'."

At this time three engines allocated to the engine shed at Bullo Pill were rostered to work Bullo Yard, as the Branch

Bullo Pill West Signal Box, built in 1898. This view was taken on 2nd April 1968, shortly after the box had been taken out of use (on 16th March).

Bullo Pill West Signal Box, with the Bullo Dock branch formation passing close behind it. Because this branch had the status of a running line (latterly worked by train staff), the signal box had a nameboard on the rear (located as was proper at the centre of the box, even if this meant fitting it to the chimney). On the other side of the main lines, the Forest of Dean branch can be seen climbing steeply towards Soudley.

A. K. Pope

engine and as the Forest engine. The Branch and Forest engines worked the first train into the Forest each day, 6.30 a.m. off Bullo. Thereafter the Branch engine worked up and down the branch, with a short working from Bilson to Quidchurch, taking empties up and bringing ore back to Bilson. The WTT does not show a time for the Forest engine to return to Bullo, but this was evidently the last working of the day, for the footnote simply reads 'Forest Engine returns with the staff as soon as work at Bilson is done'.

It is unclear what signal boxes existed on the FoD branch prior to the introduction of signalling to passenger traffic standards in 1907. There was a structure at Soudley which was very much in the style of the GWR's signal cabins of the 1869-75 era (see the photos on pages 88 and 90 in Volume 1) but it has not been possible to establish for certain that this functioned as a signal box. The 1879 OS map shows the structure but does not refer to it as an SB, as was by then customary. The building was, however, in precisely the location which would be appropriate to work the points in the single line. Facing away from the ironworks and towards the railway, it may well have been a points cabin and as such (working no signals) not considered worth calling an SB on the OS map.

The junction yard at Bilson, where the Speedwell (Whimsey) branch joined the line up to Churchway, was a busy location as early as the 1870s. The OS maps of 1878 on pages 190, 200 and 202 show signal boxes at Lightmoor Crossing (at the southern end of the layout) and S&W Junction (at the northern end), and a signal beside the station at the centre of the layout. Reference in contemporary papers to the 'centre signalman' as having primary responsibility for the working of the station suggests that the north and south boxes were simply ground frames worked by pointsmen/porter signalmen, with the centre signalman controlling working from the station (see page 204). Unfortunately, the signalling of goods-only branches in this era is scantily recorded!

The 1883 WTT shows the branch still worked as a single staff section, but by July 1889 the working was as follows:

Bullo to Ruspedge [sic] – train staff and ticket, staff square in section, coloured blue
Ruspedge to Bilson – train staff and ticket, staff round, coloured white
Bilson to Churchway – train staff, staff square, coloured blue
The Dock Branch at Bullo was 'worked by target only'.

These new arrangements allowed the Forest engine to work north and south of Bilson instead of being confined to the yard. The WTT noted 'When the Forest Engine is at Churchway or Cinderford, the Engine and Guards of the Branch Train on arrival must commence to form the train for Bullo and continue forming it until the Forest Engine returns, or as long as is practicable, under the direction of the Centre Signalman'.

The October 1891 WTT stated that on the branch, Bilson was the only crossing place. The working was by Ordinary Train Staff and Ticket (i.e. not by the Electric Train Staff which was then coming into use) from Bullo Pill to Bilson and by Ordinary Train Staff from Bilson to Churchway and Bilson to Speedwell Siding. The sections were:

Bullo to Ruspedge – staff square, blue
Ruspedge to Bilson – staff round, red
Bilson to Churchway – staff square, blue
Bilson to Speedwell – staff round, red

No train was to stop to work at sidings between Bullo Pill and Ruspedge [sic] unless the train staff was in the possession of the driver, which implies that a siding *could* be worked by a train running on a paper ticket, suggesting that the siding points were not locked by the train staff at this time.

The July 1907 WTT records the train working arrangements which existed immediately before the alterations in connection with the start of passenger train services on the FoD branch. The single line was worked by train staff and ticket, with trains signalled by telephone, between Bullo Pill and Ruspidge (name now spelt correctly). Train staff and ticket was used from Ruspidge to Bilson, and train staff only from Bilson to Churchway and Bilson to Speedwell Siding. Bilson remained the only crossing place.

A delightful photograph showing the detail of the interior of Soudley No. 1 Crossing ground frame with lever 2 normal, bolting the gates in place across the roadway. Levers 1 and 3 (not in view) were pulled over, clearing the up and down distant signals. This crossing was (unusually for the FoD branch) equipped with an indicator (the centre instrument) repeating the state of the token instrument circuit, and a bell which repeated the bell signals exchanged between the signalmen on either side. The disc in the centre of the instrument shows 'Line Clear' – no trains about. The instruments on either side of the block repeater were the 'ALRs', the arm and lamp repeaters. Since the crossing keeper could not see either of his signals, their working was repeated to him in his cabin. The discs in the upper windows show 'Signal Off'. The lower apertures show the state of the signal lamps – in each case the indication is 'Lamp Out'. When one of the indicators showed a failure reading, an alarm bell sounded. The bell could be silenced by turning upright a small switch at the foot of the instrument. All four are upright in this view. April 1965.
B. J. Ashworth

The signalling arrangements provided for opening of the line from Bullo to Steam Mills to passenger traffic as from 3rd August 1907 are described in the BoT Inspector's report reproduced in Volume 1, but are set out again here for ease of reference.

Bullo Pill West, an old box, fitted with a replacement lever frame, now with 44 working and 5 spare levers
Soudley No. 1 Crossing GF, 2 distant signals and 1 gate lock, total 3 levers
Soudley No. 2 Crossing GF, 2 distant signals, 2 levers for points (locked by key on staff), 1 spare, total 5 levers
South Shakemantle GF, 2 levers locked by key on staff, 1 for FPL and 1 for points
North Shakemantle GF, 2 levers locked by key on staff
Ruspidge Crossing GF, 2 distant signals and 1 gate lock, total 3 levers
Ruspidge Goods GF, 2 levers locked by key on staff
Bilson signal box, 18 working and 5 spare levers. Not a passing place for two passenger trains
Bilson Yard GF, 2 levers locked by key on staff
Duck Siding GF, 2 levers locked by key on staff
Cinderford Crossing GF, 2 distant signals, 1 gate bolt, 1 FPL (locked by key on staff), 2 points traps, total 6 levers
Cinderford Goods North GF, 1 FPL, 2 points, total 3 levers
Steam Mills Crossing GF, 2 distant signals, 1 gate lock, total 3 levers
Name not given, temporary GF at Steam Mills until line opened to Drybrook, 1 lever for trap points north of Steam Mills platform.

The line was worked from Bullo West to Bilson by Electric Train Staff, and from Bilson to Drybrook by Ordinary Train Staff (i.e. a single wooden staff with key attached at one end). The points connecting sidings to the running line were now fitted with facing point locks, released by a key on each train staff. The electric train staff was the standard GWR equipment of this era wherever greater flexibility was required than that afforded by the wooden train staff (with or without paper tickets). Unusually, many of the ground frames were provided with shelter cabins to protect the levers but providing scant protection from the weather for the man working the frame (see photos on pages 127, 223 and 353).

The opening of the 'loop' line curving eastwards from Bilson up to the Severn & Wye line into Cinderford station as from Monday, 6th April 1908, required some alterations at Bilson. The BoT inspector noted that the lever frame (previously 18 working levers and 5 spare) was now 23 and 3 spare (sic, in fact the 3 spare levers were included in the total of 23). A new signal box to GWR design was opened at Cinderford Junction, containing 8 working and 3 spare levers (see photos on pages 224/5 in Volume 1). The new loop line was worked by the Electric Train Tablet system, which was then the standard on the S&W line and was placed under the care of S&W Section Signal and Telegraphic linemen based at Lydney.

The FoD branch was worked thus, with signal boxes at the junctions only, and a multitude of ground frames at intermediate locations, from 1907 until 1913. The expansion of Eastern United Colliery led to the installation of sidings and of a ground frame (inspected for the Board of Trade on 6th December 1909) immediately south of Staple Edge Platform (see page 137). In 1913, the extension of the sidings provided to serve Eastern United Colliery, and the volume of traffic handled there, led to the opening (14th December 1913) of a new goods loop and a new signal box to work the layout. The box had a 'stud' locking lever frame of 17 working and 4 spare levers, totalling 21 levers. The Electric Train Staff (ETS) sections were altered to become Bullo Pill West to Eastern United Colliery, and Eastern United Colliery to Bilson. Eastern United became a passing place, but the loop line was not available to passenger trains, and two passenger trains could not be crossed here 'unless specially instructed in case of accident', since Facing Point Locks were not provided on the trap points at the ends of the goods loop. The loop was lengthened to 380 yards during World War Two, and could then accommodate 50 wagons plus engine and brake. All freight trains having work to do at the sidings at Eastern United had first to be drawn into the Goods Loop clear of the main line, before shunting commenced. It was not permitted to leave any part of the train on the running line during shunting.

A view of Eastern United Colliery dated 19th October 1909, taken from Staple Edge Platform, looking towards Bullo and showing on the left the cover for the ground frame newly installed to work the points into the colliery siding. If the photo was taken on 19th October, then the frame had been in situ for quite a long time before it was formally inspected for the Board of Trade on 6th December 1909. Such lengthy delays were not unknown, especially where the installation was uncomplicated and the BoT inspector had faith in the stature of the railway company concerned and its ability to do the work to a satisfactory standard. But there is clearly a danger in accepting the date of inspection as the date when the equipment was brought into use. Note the luxury of a point disc working with the switch blades of the trap point. *Cty. Pam Powell*

It was not economic to staff Eastern United box for all the hours when the line was open for traffic, just to handle the colliery traffic. This issue came into focus during the Great War, when shortages of manpower became acute, and in 1915 equipment was installed to allow the signal box to be switched out of use when not required for traffic to the colliery (see p. 169, Vol. 1). Lever 8 was made the switching-out lever. The distant signals, which until now had been fixed at danger (as was the GWR practice at locations on single lines where all trains had to slow down to 10 mph to exchange the train staff), were made workable when applying to the through line while the signal box was switched out. The requirement to make the distant signals workable created a problem with the locking,

RUSPIDGE, SHOWING RAIL M

One that nearly got away! This postcard view of Ruspidge Halt, probably dating from soon after the commencement of the passenger service, turned up after the publication of Volume 1. It is included here because it shows the absence of stop signals to protect the level crossing, and the up distant signal is just visible in the background. However, there are several other points of interest. Notice the pristine condition of the fencing and gates, suggesting that they had either recently been erected or had been repainted for the start of passenger services. Comparison with the view on page 176 of Volume 1 reveals a building on the back of the goods shed which shows up in no other photograph. Its purpose and date of removal are unknown. This view also shows baulk road still in place in the siding serving the goods shed. In the distance a ballast siding can just be discerned curving away to the old iron works cinder tip site. *Cty. Dean Heritage Museum*

An early photo of Bilson Signal Box, with a large gang of PW Department staff posing for the photographer. The gang may have been augmented by men from gangs outside the Forest, but this photo serves as a reminder of the large numbers of men once employed on track maintenance, and why the adoption of 'economic' maintenance methods was seen as a priority worthy of capital investment in new signalling equipment (the Occupation Key system).

Collection Mike Rees

because the levers at the extreme ends of the frame (1 and 21) were already in use to work the home signals. There were enough levers in the frame to accommodate the two new signals (there were still three spares after allocating one to the switch lever), but to use them and still have the distant signal levers adjacent to the levers for the other running signals would have meant a wholesale relocking of the frame. The solution adopted was to add one lever at each end of the frame, making a frame of 23 levers in which the distant signal levers were 0 and 22.

The newly-created long section from Bullo Pill West to Bilson was worked by Electric Key Token (EKT) which had become the standard instrument on the GWR as from January 1914 (the instruments having been devised by GWR officers in 1912). The list of signalmen's duties (see page 208) includes the note '12/10/15 – (*second signalman*) Dispensed with, only one man at Eastern', so the work to allow the signal box to be switched out of circuit was clearly completed by this date. The 1927 WTT shows the box as open 8.40 a.m. until 5.25 p.m. or as required for specials. That remained the pattern, though during the busy times of World War Two the opening hours were 7.15 a.m. until the last train had cleared.

With the installation of the long section switching, the signalman at Bilson in 1915 had an unusually extensive collection of different signalling instruments to cope with:

Tablet instrument to Cinderford Junction
Electric Train Staff to Eastern United Colliery
Electric Key Token to Bullo West (long section)
Ordinary Train Staff (wooden) to Drybrook. (Note: the staff for the section Bilson Yard to Churchway was kept at Bilson S&W Junction GF and not at Bilson signal box)

The Forest of Dean branch had an unusually high proportion of working distant signals for a single line on the GWR, where fixed distant signals were normally to be seen. There were five level crossings, each of which had working distant signals, an acceptable practice since there was no need to slow down for staff exchange at any of them. Also remarkable was the fact that none of these level crossings had stop signals. At Ruspidge, Cinderford Crossing and Steam Mills Crossing, the red light on the crossing gate provided the indication of the need to stop, and the location of the stopping point. Since the roads at Ruspidge and Steam Mills crossed the line on the skew, arrangements had to be made to ensure that the light shone squarely down the road or railway when the gates were closed across them, because oil lamps give a feeble light unless viewed squarely to the flame. At Ruspidge this was achieved by a mechanism which rotated the lamp as the gates were moved (see the photo on pages 18 and 183), and at Steam Mills special arrangements were made in attaching the lamps to the gates (see pages 338/339). At the two crossings at Soudley, the gates did not open across the rails, and there was no fixed stop signal at all. Drivers finding the distant signal at 'on', then had to approach the crossing prepared to stop at any hand signal displayed or obstruction on the crossing.

Ground frames were installed as private sidings were opened. On 29th October 1924 a new frame was brought into use at Harrow Hill North. The existing Speedwell Sidings South GF working the connection at the Bilson end was to have become known as Harrow Hill South, and there was to have been a new Harrow Hill Middle GF. In the event, Speedwell South retained its name and Speedwell North became Speedwell Sidings Middle GF. All three ground frames were released by a key on the staff, and the sidings had to be worked with care, for the gradient was 1 in 46 falling towards Bilson.

The gradient down from Ruspidge to Bullo West always represented a challenge to the train crews, and inevitably some trains got out of control on the long and steep descent. The layout at Bullo West meant that runaways ran into the yard and not out on to the main line, but even this represented an unacceptable risk to the yard staff. In January 1930, a runaway sand drag (at 240 yards, quite a long one!) was provided in the Up Branch line at Bullo

Bilson Signal Box, looking north, with a coal train from Northern United Colliery easing off the Churchway branch, and the signalman waiting to hand up the token for the section to Bullo West. The sheds in the foreground housed the PW Department motor trolleys for gang 116 which was based at Bilson, the timbered areas around the rails assisting the task of turning the trolleys through 90° prior to pushing them into the sheds. The building beyond the PW huts housed the weighbridge. The two running lines to the right of the weigh hut were the Drybrook branch (cut back to Whimsey by the time this photo was taken) and to its right the line to Cinderford, curving away eastwards to climb to the level of the S & W line, which ran on the embankment in the background. The spur siding extending into the right foreground had been the motor car siding. The motor car from Bullo ran through to Cinderford, then came back to Bilson, and entered this siding to reverse, before proceeding on to the Drybrook branch. The same procedure was adopted in reverse for motor cars returning from Drybrook. This all ceased after the passenger service to Drybrook was withdrawn as from 7th July 1930, and the signals to and from the siding were replaced by a disc signal (compare the signalling diagram on page 408 with that on page 217) but the siding was called the 'Motor Car Siding' up until closure. *J. White*

Signalman Len Roberts at the frame in Bilson box on 17th February 1967 with, behind him, the key token instrument for the section to Bullo West and the wooden train staffs for each of the three branches. The one hanging on the door post is not so obviously visible as the other two. The curious trumpet-like device on the wall was an annunciator/buzzer commonly used by the GWR as part of the occupation key system, the key release instrument for which can be seen behind Len's back. The bell working with the token instrument is visible above Len's head, on a small shelf in the background.

A. K. Pope

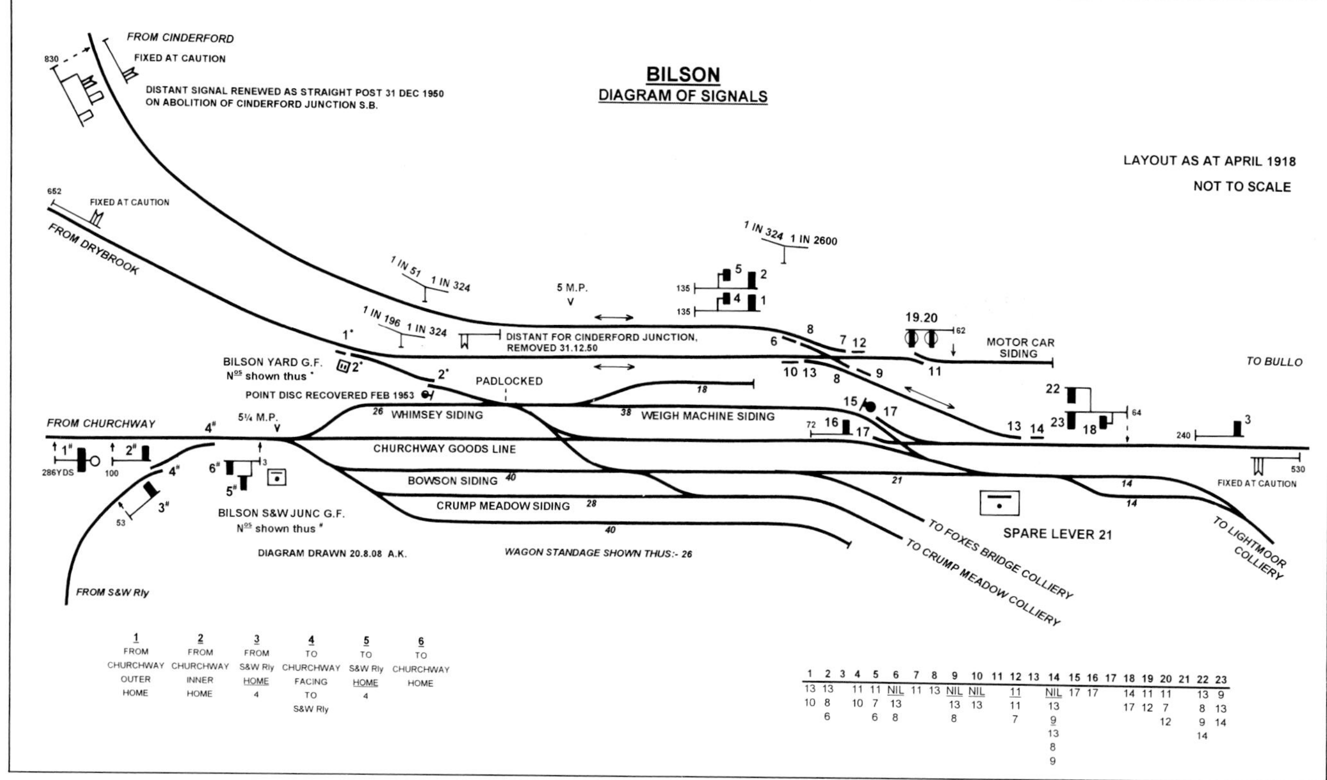

West, just in advance of the Up Branch Home signal (see pages 80/81).

The very difficult economic climate of the late 1920s and early 1930s demanded that the GWR look closely at the number of staff employed and make reductions wherever possible. The signal box at Cinderford station was closed over the period 17th-19th May 1927, its work being taken over by two 2-lever ground frames. The tablet instruments for the section Cinderford Junction to Cinderford Station were taken out of use, and replaced by a single wooden staff fitted with a key to unlock the ground frames. Reading Signal Works recorded the issue of the new train staff on 19th May, a round staff, coloured black, fitted with a point key, and showing the section 'Cinderford Junction–Cinderford Town'. This staff was replaced in 1932, the records containing a note of the issue on 20th April of a new staff (round, coloured red) 'fitted for exchange' and with the nameplate showing the more correct description 'Cinderford Junction–Cinderford Station'.

The maintenance of the permanent way was another area where economies had to be made. 'Economic maintenance' was achieved by providing motor trolleys (see page 218) for the men, allowing much longer lengths to be patrolled and maintained than could be covered by men on foot. Motor economic maintenance was brought into use on the FoD branch as from 10th April 1933. Trolley run-off points were provided at appropriate locations, allowing the ganger to remove his motor trolley from the line 'in section' between signal boxes. The trolley entered the section under the authority of an occupation key rather than the staff or key token, which was electrically locked up while the occupation key was out of its instrument. When the ganger had removed his trolley from the line, the occupation key could be restored to an instrument at the adjacent 'occupation box', thus releasing the train staff/key token for use until the ganger again used the occupation key to put his trolley on the line. The locations of some of the occupation boxes are shown on the signalling plans. In summary, the arrangements were:

Gang 22 was responsible for 0m 0ch to 1m 0ch.
Gang 116 (based at Bilson) dealt with the remainder of the Forest of Dean Branch.
The Group A occupation key covered the section Bullo West to Eastern United.
Occupation Key instruments and phones were at
Box 1 0m 30ch
Box 2 0m 79ch
Box 3 1m 57¾ch
Box 4 2m 43ch
The Group B occupation key covered the section Eastern United to Bilson, with one intermediate box
Box 5 4m 2ch

When Eastern United box was open, the signalman dealt with the request from the ganger to use the Group A occupation key. Bilson dealt with the use of the Group B key, and also Group A when Eastern United signal box was closed. When the line was closed to traffic during the night, the ganger had the use of the line. Before closing the signal box at night, the signalman at Bilson withdrew the token for the section Bilson to Bullo West, and placed it in a box so that the ganger could use it if required. The following day the token was restored to the instrument when Bilson signal box opened.

Occupation boxes were also provided in the FoD on lines which were worked by wooden train staff. These did not have an occupation key instrument. The signalman agreed with the ganger (all three branches north of Bilson were maintained by Gang 116 stationed at Bilson) what occupation would be taken, the ganger using one of the phones in lineside boxes as required. Permission was simply not given if the train staff for the section concerned had already been given to a driver (or in the case of the Churchway branch, where the staff was kept at Bilson S&W Junction GF, permission had been given to the porter signalman there for the staff to be handed to a driver).

In the search for further economies, representatives of the Signal, Traffic and Loco Departments met at Bilson on 9th December 1936, to consider the future of Bilson S&W ground frame. They noted that the connecting curve up to the S&W line had not been used for traffic for some years, and recommended that the ground frame and all signals (including the disc and crossbar) be abolished, the points to be put on hand levers, and the custody of the train staff transferred from the porter signalman to the signalman in Bilson box. The District Inspector based in Hereford, whilst agreeing that the disc and crossbar signal could be dispensed with (he had recommended in June 1929 that it should be removed), objected to the remainder of the proposal. Without signals there would be nothing to protect the personnel shunting in the yard from trains arriving from the Churchway direction. The ground frame cabin was an essential shelter at the north end of the yard, and the telephone which it housed was important to operations. Any saving on the porter/signalman post would be outweighed by the need to employ at least one extra shunter to work at the north end of the yard. The proposal to close the ground frame was not pursued, and the disc and crossbar signal was not removed until 1949.

The large Electric Train Staff on the short sections from Bullo West to Eastern United and Eastern United to Bilson were replaced by Key Token instruments as from 22nd March 1937.

A report on the recovery of the old Cinderford S&W Sidings at Bilson in March 1939 gives details of the Bilson signalmen's duties. Two Class 5 signalmen were employed on two shifts: 7.15 a.m. to 3.15 p.m. and 12.0 noon to 8.0 p.m. On the early shift the signalman worked in the box whilst the late-shift man commenced his duty in Bilson Yard, taking stock of the vehicles and preparing wagon returns. He also collected sheets and ropes and acquired signatures for traffic from Northern United Colliery and the Coleford Brick & Tile Co. When the 1.0 p.m. freight from Bullo arrived in the yard at about 1.30 p.m. he assisted with the shunting and the points. When that work was complete, he operated the signals for the Churchway branch (from the Bilson S&W Ground Frame) and handed the enginemen the staff. On the return of the train, he collected the staff and then took the wagon numbers before going to the signal box to relieve the early-turn signalman. If extra trips had to be made to clear Northern United, then he was delayed in completing his yard duties and the early-turn signalman remained on duty clocking up overtime. Half of the expenses of the duty were borne by the Severn & Wye Joint Committee, but, as by this date very little traffic passed over the S&W connection, they were not getting value for money!

The post of porter/signalman was regraded to Class 5 on 16th November 1936.

In connection with the installation of additional sidings to serve Eastern United Colliery – the Cast House Sidings – in World War Two (see pages 159 and 172), a ground frame was installed at the uphill end of the sidings. As is customary, the points were clipped and wedged until the day that the sidings were to be commissioned, but Eastern United Colliery Ground Frame was never brought into use.

The run-down of the signalling on the FoD lines continued gradually after 1950. The first major change came when Cinderford Junction signal box was closed as from 31st December 1950, at which date the Severn and Wye line into Cinderford was broken. A new fixed distant signal for Bilson Junction was erected at the site of Cinderford Junction to replace the arm on the junction bracket signal which was removed, and the wooden staff for the

The disc and crossbar signal, worked from Bilson S & W Ground Frame, originally provided to protect Brain's Tramway where it crossed the GWR's branch to Churchway. The post was made of a length of old Barlow rail. The operating rod on which the disc and crossbar were rotated was on the far side of the post, the lamp being attached to the rotating rod at a lower level. Two ladders were provided, one to allow access to the lamp, and the other to allow the lineman to attend to the top bearing together with the crossbar and disc. 1930. *L. E. Copeland*

SIGNALLING INSTALLATIONS ON THE FOREST OF DEAN BRANCH: 1905 TO CLOSURE

Location	*Date into use*	*Date out of use*	*Mileage M. ch.*	*How points locked*
GROUND FRAMES				
Forest Branch				
Soudley No. 1 Crossing	7/07	[a]	1.65	No points
Soudley No. 2 Crossing	7/07	[a]	2.07	Key on ET staff [m]
Shakemantle South	7/07	13/6/50 [b]	2.61	Key on ET staff [m]
Shakemantle North	7/07	13/6/50 [c]	3.10	Key on ET staff [m]
Staple Edge	6/12/09 [d]	14/12/13 [e]	3.21	Key on ET staff [m]
Eastern United Colliery	Not used [f]			
Ruspidge Crossing	7/07	17/2/60	4.03	No points
Ruspidge Goods	7/07	25/2/62		Key on ET staff [m]
Bilson Yard	7/07	2/7/64	5.13	Key attached to staff
Duck Colliery	7/07	2/9/51	5.40	Key attached to staff
Cinderford Crossing	7/07	[a]	5.54	Key attached to staff
Cinderford Goods	7/07	[a]	5.65	Key attached to staff
Steam Mills Crossing	7/07	2/5/53 [g]	6.02	No points
Speedwell Sidings South	11/07	1938?	6.60	Key attached to staff
Speedwell Sidings Middle (North)	11/07	1938?	6.65	Key attached to staff
Harrow Hill North	29/10/24	1938?	6.75	Key attached to staff
Drybrook [n]	18/10/28	2/5/53 [g]	7.26	Key attached to staff
Churchway Branch				
Bilson S&W Junction	By 1903	25/7/62	5.20	Locking frame
Bilson (north end of S&W triangle)	No GF			Point clipped and padlocked
Brickworks	12/37	29/6/65	5.67	Key attached to staff
Bowson Colliery South	1925	4/9/35 [h]	5.69	Key attached to staff
Bowson Colliery North	1/4/25	4/9/35 [k]	5.76	Key attached to staff
Northern United Colliery South	4/9/35	28/12/65 [g]	5.69	Key attached to staff
Northern United Colliery North	4/9/35	28/12/65 [g]	6.03	Key attached to staff
Cinderford Branch				
Cinderford North	17/5/27	[a]	5.45	Key attached to staff
Cinderford South	17/5/27	[a]	5.55	Key attached to staff
SIGNAL BOXES				
Eastern United Colliery	14/12/13	20/6/64	3.31	
Bilson	7/07	[a]	4.70	
Cinderford Junction	6/4/08	31/12/50	5.27	
Cinderford	2/7/00	17/5/27 [l]	5.50	

Distance in miles and chains from junction datum at Bullo Pill

Opening dates

3/8/07, Bullo to Steam Mills opened to passengers (open beyond Steam Mills to Speedwell for goods)
4/11/07, Steam Mills to Drybrook opened for passengers
6/4/08, Bilson to Cinderford Junction, opened to all traffic
18/10/28, Drybrook to Drybrook Quarry opened for goods

Closure dates

7/7/30, Bilson to Drybrook passenger services withdrawn
1/12/52, Line to Drybrook closed beyond Whimsey at 5.78, (a location midway between Cinderford Goods and Steam Mills)
3/11/58, Passenger services withdrawn Cinderford to Bullo, now no passenger services on branch
28/12/65, Northern United Colliery to Bilson closed to all traffic
2/5/67, Whimsey to Bilson closed to all traffic
1/8/67, Cinderford to Bullo closed officially to all traffic, last train 3/8/67

NOTES

[a] Line closed 1/8/67. Signalling formally taken out of use 9/11/67.
[b] Removed 9/6/53.
[c] Removed 27/5/62.
[d] Date of BoT inspection. Name uncertain.
[e] Replaced by Eastern United Colliery signal box.
[f] GF for north end of new sidings, work never completed, GF not commissioned.
[g] Line closed north of Whimsey 1/12/52. Signalling formally taken out of use 2/5/53.
[h] Replaced by or became Northern United Colliery South GF, same location.
Bowson Colliery North and South had been on same location (and may have been same frames) as earlier Brickworks Sidings West and East GFs, which had been in existence since c.1905.
[k] Abolished in connection with new work for Northern United Colliery.
[l] Replaced by two new GFs.
[m] Also released by Long Section Key Token from 1915.
[n] Name uncertain.

section Cinderford Junction to Cinderford Station now became the staff for Bilson to Cinderford.

Shakemantle North and South ground frames were taken out of use and the points spiked in the normal position on 13th June 1950. The decision to remove the connections was made in June 1953 and the south points were taken out soon after, but the connection which had been worked by the North ground frame remained in situ until 1962.

Following the withdrawal of passenger services on 3rd November 1958, the Crossing Ground Frame at Ruspidge was taken out of use on 17th February 1960, and the distant signals removed. The signals were replaced by stop boards, the task of opening the gates being transferred to the trainmen. Up trains requiring to pin down brakes did this work before opening the gates. Once across the road, the train stopped again to allow the guard to close the gates. A marker post 40 wagon lengths from the crossing was provided to allow drivers to judge where to stop. The keys to the gates were normally kept by the signalman at Bullo West box, and were passed out to the trainmen when the token was handed over.

Similarly, the signals worked from the frame at Cinderford Crossing were removed. The up direction signal was taken away in August 1955 following the abandonment

The ground frame working the connections at Duck Colliery, showing the small nameplate which was standard on the GWR for small frames such as this. This is an enlargement of the picture on page 312. Such ground frames were comonly laid out with the levers at right-angles to the track, but this required some depth of formation, and the frame would be placed parallel to the rails where space was at a premium, as at Speedwell South (see page 352). The rodding would be connected up in whatever fashion was most convenient, so that at some of these two-lever ground frames, lever 1 worked the facing point lock and lever 2 the points (as here), but elsewhere the numbering was reversed. 26th June 1933.
L. E. Copeland

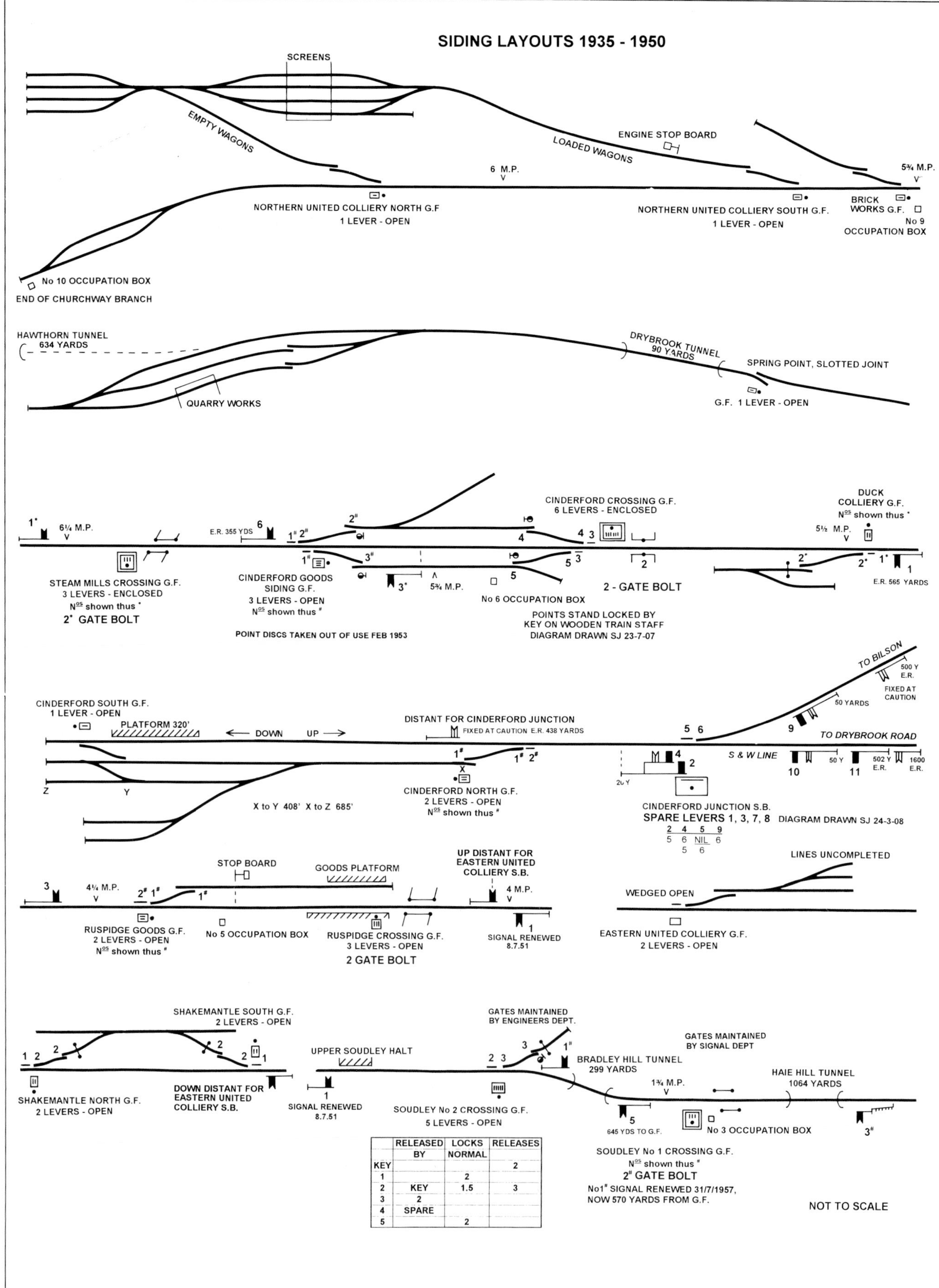

	RELEASED BY	LOCKS NORMAL	RELEASES
KEY			2
1		2	
2	KEY	1.5	3
3	2		
4	SPARE		
5		2	

of the line beyond Whimsey, and in 1958 the down distant signal — which served no useful purpose other than as a landmark — was recovered and replaced by a stop board adjacent to the crossing gates. The ground frame remained to work the siding points, still released by the key on the train staff.

On 25th July 1962 Bilson S&W Junction ground frame was abolished, some 25 years after the first proposal for its closure. The points at the north end of Bilson yard were converted to working by ground lever, and the limits of the yard (beyond which a train could not proceed without the Churchway branch train staff) were denoted by a double-sided board 'Start of single line/End of single line', seen in the photograph on page 241.

Eastern United Colliery signal box was closed over the period of 18th-20th June 1964, the former long section key tokens from Bilson to Bullo West being retained.

The remaining parts of the Forest of Dean branch were closed after the last train on 3rd August 1967 and the signalling department formally noted 9th November 1967 as the 'taken out of use' date for the following:

Cinderford Station North and South GFs
Cinderford Goods GF
Cinderford Crossing GF
Bilson Yard GF
Bilson SB
Soudley No. 2 Crossing GF
Soudley No. 1 Crossing GF

Bullo West signal box was closed on 18th March 1968, leaving Bullo East, the oldest of all, retained as block post on the South Wales main line until 2nd June 1969, when it was abolished as part of a multiple aspect colour light signalling scheme.

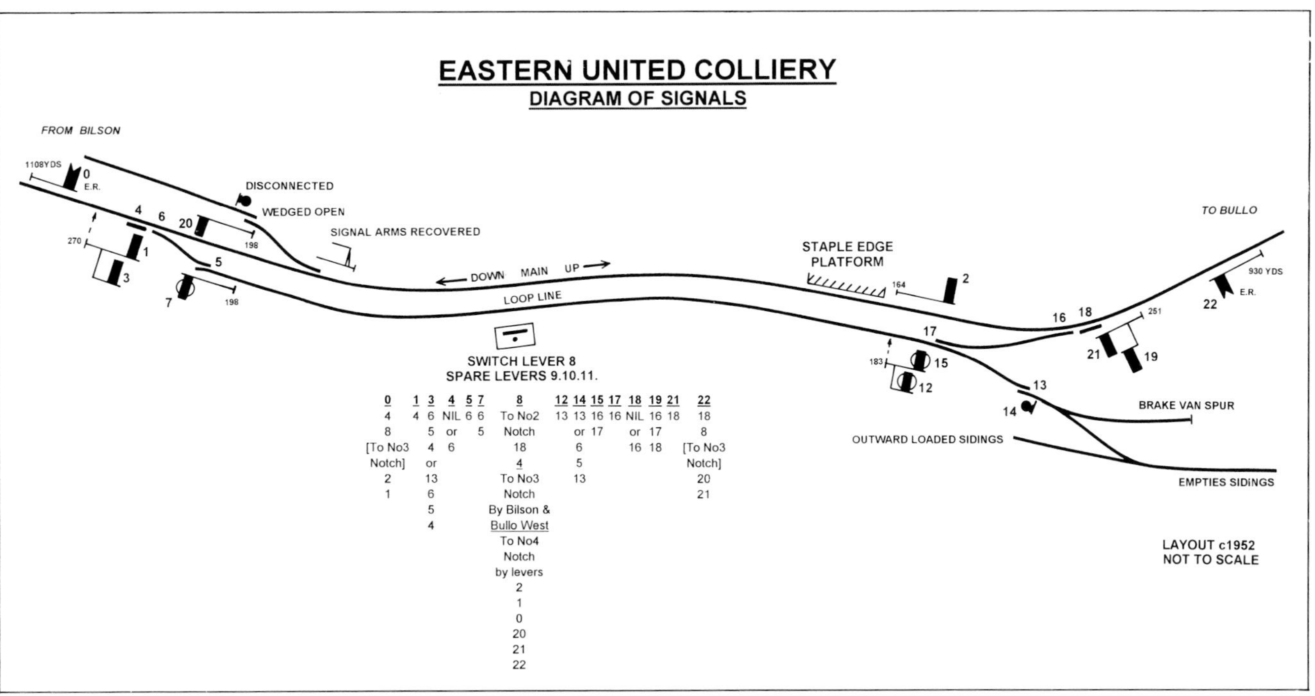

OMNIBUS TELEPHONE CIRCUIT - BULLO EAST BOX AND CINDERFORD GOODS	1906	1907	1916	c1930
Bullo East Box	5	5	5	1 - 5
Bullo Office	1 -3	1 - 3	1 - 3	2
Bullo West Box	4	4	4	3
Bullo Engine Shed	-	2 - 1	2 - 1	-
Soudley Furnace	2	2	2	1 - 3
Eastern United Colly	-	-	2 - 3	2 - 3
Ruspidge	3	3	3	4
Bilson Box	1 - 2	1 - 2	1 - 2	1 - 2
Bilson Office	4 - 1	4 - 1	4 - 1	-
Cinderford Office	1	1	1	1
S&W Junc (Bilson)	3 - 1	3 - 1	3 - 1	2 - 1
Cinderford S&W Goods Office	-	-	-	1 - 4
Cinderford S&W Station	-	-	-	3 - 1
Cinderford Station Master's Office	-	-	-	5

OMNIBUS TELEPHONE CIRCUIT - CHURCHWAY BRANCH
August 1953

Bilson Box	1 - 2
Churchway Branch Hut No 9	No call

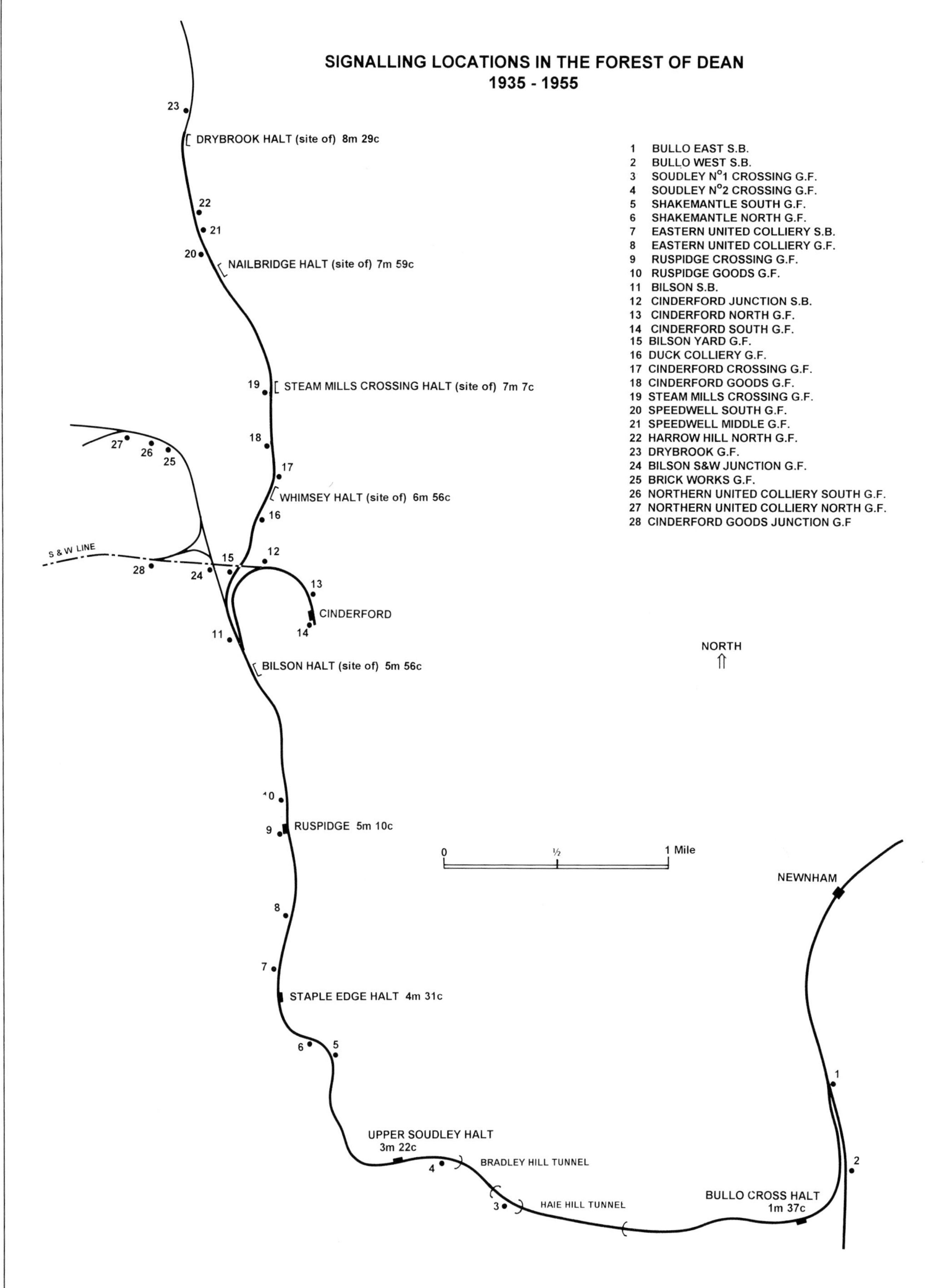
SIGNALLING LOCATIONS IN THE FOREST OF DEAN
1935 - 1955
1 BULLO EAST S.B.
2 BULLO WEST S.B.
3 SOUDLEY N°1 CROSSING G.F.
4 SOUDLEY N°2 CROSSING G.F.
5 SHAKEMANTLE SOUTH G.F.
6 SHAKEMANTLE NORTH G.F.
7 EASTERN UNITED COLLIERY S.B.
8 EASTERN UNITED COLLIERY G.F.
9 RUSPIDGE CROSSING G.F.
10 RUSPIDGE GOODS G.F.
11 BILSON S.B.
12 CINDERFORD JUNCTION S.B.
13 CINDERFORD NORTH G.F.
14 CINDERFORD SOUTH G.F.
15 BILSON YARD G.F.
16 DUCK COLLIERY G.F.
17 CINDERFORD CROSSING G.F.
18 CINDERFORD GOODS G.F.
19 STEAM MILLS CROSSING G.F.
20 SPEEDWELL SOUTH G.F.
21 SPEEDWELL MIDDLE G.F.
22 HARROW HILL NORTH G.F.
23 DRYBROOK G.F.
24 BILSON S&W JUNCTION G.F.
25 BRICK WORKS G.F.
26 NORTHERN UNITED COLLIERY SOUTH G.F.
27 NORTHERN UNITED COLLIERY NORTH G.F.
28 CINDERFORD GOODS JUNCTION G.F
DRYBROOK HALT (site of) 8m 29c
NAILBRIDGE HALT (site of) 7m 59c
STEAM MILLS CROSSING HALT (site of) 7m 7c
WHIMSEY HALT (site of) 6m 56c
S & W LINE
CINDERFORD
BILSON HALT (site of) 5m 56c
NORTH
RUSPIDGE 5m 10c
0 ½ 1 Mile
NEWNHAM
STAPLE EDGE HALT 4m 31c
UPPER SOUDLEY HALT
3m 22c
BRADLEY HILL TUNNEL
HAIE HILL TUNNEL
BULLO CROSS HALT
1m 37c

The train staffs for the three single-line sections north of Bilson. From top to bottom they are: Bilson Jcn–Cinderford (the body of the staff is round, coloured red); Bilson Jcn–Whimsey (the body of the staff is triangular, but rounded at both ends, coloured green); Bilson Jcn–Churchway branch (the body of the staff is square, coloured black). Normally train staffs show the names of the locations at either end of the section of single line controlled. Since the northern end of the line was at Northern United Colliery North G.F., the staff was unusually allocated the name of the whole branch covered.

The train staff to Whimsey had originally served for the longer section from Bilson Junction–Drybrook. A new staff was provided when the line was cut beyond Whimsey as from 2nd May 1953. This is the nameplate which was removed from the old staff.

The convention on the GWR was for train staffs working ground frames to include an integral key. The keys for adjacent sections were normally made different, so that one staff could not unlock the ground frames on an adjacent section, by the addition of locking pins. These were not fitted to the FoD line train staffs, and this close-up of the keys shows how similar all three were.

The top electric key token for the long section Bullo Pill West to Bilson, was brought into use in 1915, and is ferrous with a cast brass name plate. The lower token is a one-piece forging in high-duty aluminium alloy, with the lettering engraved into the token on one side only. Tokens of this sort came into use on the GWR as from 23rd October 1935 for sections containing ground frames to be unlocked by the token. This one dates from the replacement of staffs by key tokens on the short sections to Eastern United Colliery as from 22nd March 1937. The box at Bilson was by now referred to on train staffs and keys as Bilson *Junction*, but for consistency we have throughout the text used the earlier name, without the 'Junction' suffix.

APPENDIX 2

No views to date have come to light of Westbury Brook Iron Mine in an active state. This view looks east over the pond towards the roofless and empty engine house.
Collection N. Parkhouse

THE WESTBURY BROOK TRAMROAD

The tramroad which brought the majority of traffic to Whimsey was that laid by Sir Josiah John Guest and the Dowlais Iron Co. c.1842 to the Westbury Brook Iron Mine. Guest, who lived at Dowlais House, Glamorgan, was behind the Dowlais Iron Co. which had iron works and furnaces at Dowlais. It probably used part of the formation of the Bishops' tramroad, which served Newbridge Engine Colliery at Nailbridge and which had just been removed. The Westbury Brook tramroad left this route at the north-western corner of the Haywood Enclosure beyond Steam Mills. (The full history of Bishops's Tramroad is detailed on page 346.

The gale of Westbury Brook was originally applied for by Thomas and Moses Teague and James Mountjoy in the mid-1830s. However, as no grants were made after April 1832 while the division of Forest gales was being sorted out, no formal grant was made. This did not deter Guest, on whose behalf the application had been made. He commenced work on the shaft at Westbury Brook which was sunk to a depth of about 680ft circa 1837. The first ore appears to have been won in 1843, in anticipation of which the tramroad had already been constructed. Between 1843 and 1893 about 958,000 tons of ore were taken down the tramroad and, until the opening of the Forest of Dean branch as a broad gauge line in 1854, the ore went directly to Bullo Pill, from whence it was taken round the coast to

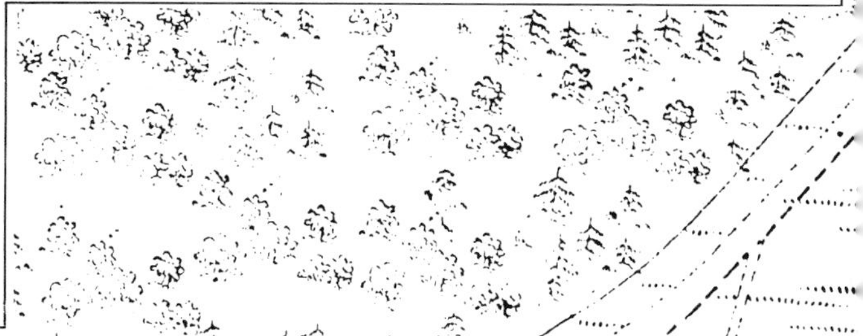

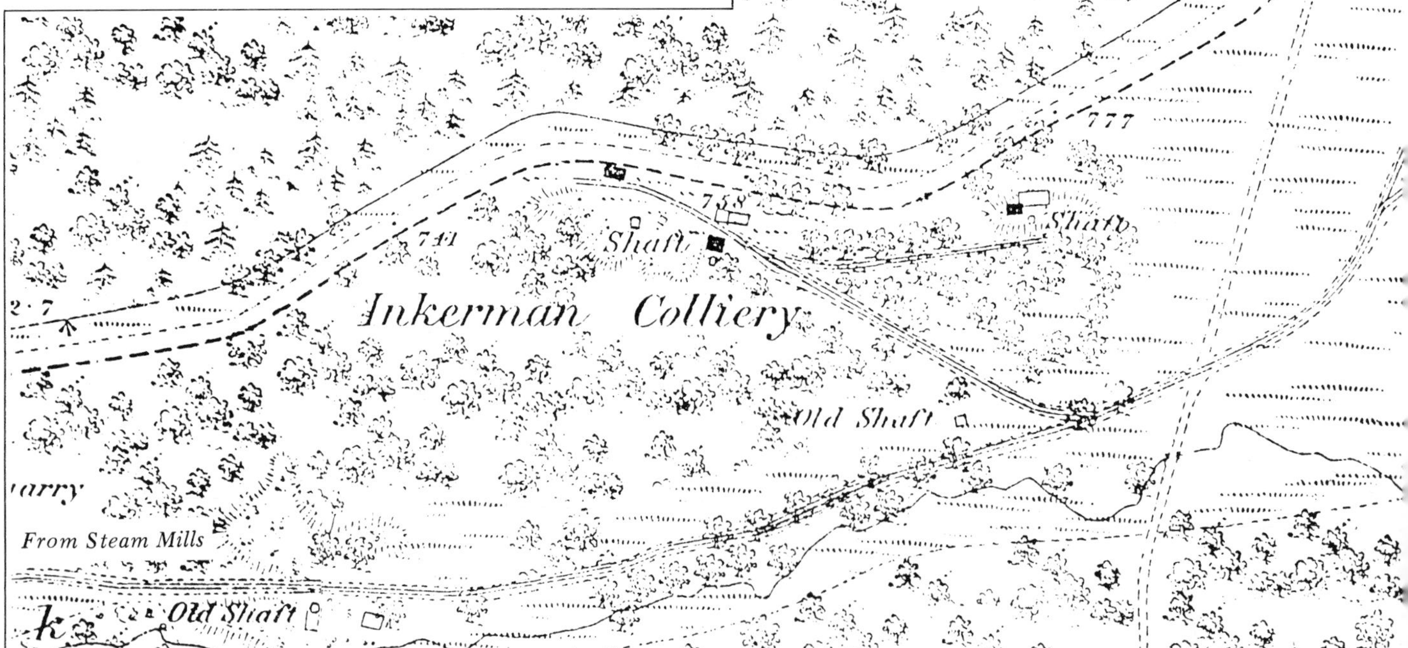

777
758
741
Shaft
Shaft
Inkerman Colliery
Old Shaft
From Steam Mills
Old Shaft

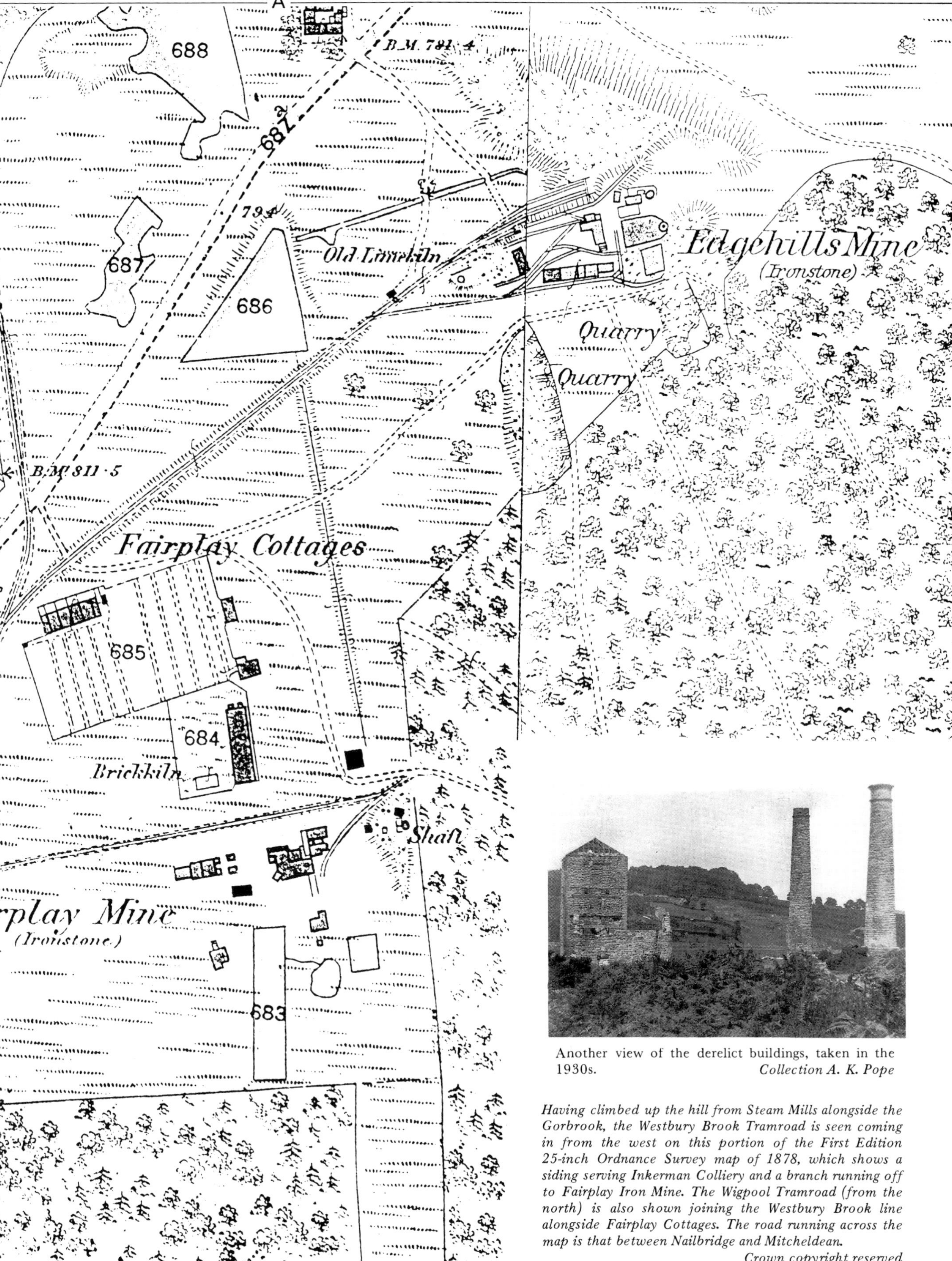

Another view of the derelict buildings, taken in the 1930s. *Collection A. K. Pope*

Having climbed up the hill from Steam Mills alongside the Gorbrook, the Westbury Brook Tramroad is seen coming in from the west on this portion of the First Edition 25-inch Ordnance Survey map of 1878, which shows a siding serving Inkerman Colliery and a branch running off to Fairplay Iron Mine. The Wigpool Tramroad (from the north) is also shown joining the Westbury Brook line alongside Fairplay Cottages. The road running across the map is that between Nailbridge and Mitcheldean.

Cardiff and then up to Dowlais. After 1854 the tramroad from Westbury Brook terminated upon a transshipment wharf at Whimsey. The broad gauge siding serving it became known as 'Dowlais', a name which lasted well after the closure of the iron mine.

Westbury Brook, which was also known as Edge Hill Iron Mine, worked an area about two miles in length from south to north and included the Deans Meend gale. Westbury Brook shaft was virtually in the centre of the property and from this two cross-cuts, or stone-lined headings, were driven eastwards into the Crease Limestone. They were at 550 and 666 feet below the top of the shaft and from each headings were driven both north and southwards. The deep level, No. 4, ran about two-thirds of a mile to the south and half a mile north whilst No. 2 level at 550 feet went virtually to both boundaries.

As at Shakemantle (page 120), water was a great problem and a Cornish rotary beam engine was erected at Westbury Brook. It had a 45 inch diameter cylinder with an 8ft stroke. At a rate of 10 strokes per minute, a total of 326 gallons were lifted 225 yards. The water was pumped into a long heading which virtually followed the Gorbrook and which had its outfall into the brook between Nailbridge and Steam Mills.

The mine closed in 1893, probably due to the cheapness of imported ores. By 1899 the buildings were said to be in a dilapidated state and arrangements were made in April to clear off all the machinery. The gale was surrendered to the Crown on 24th June 1902 but as late as February 1906 it was said that there was still a large stock of ore on the ground. The tramroad to Whimsey may have remained in use for the Fairplay Iron Mine until 1907 when the effects of the Chaston Syndicate, who were working Fairplay, were sold at auction. This included 4,090 yards of wrought iron tram rails on 'main tramway from Edgehills Mine to tramway belonging to the Crown near the corner of Haywood Enclosure' to which the line to Fairplay was connected. The tramroad was lifted by March 1908.

The remains of the Fairplay Iron Mine. *Cty. Harry Taylor*

WIGPOOL IRON MINE AND TRAMROAD

Wigpool Iron Mine comprised the Wigpool, Wigpool Belt, Injunction Belt, Belt, and Injunction iron mine gales, and was situated to the west of Mitcheldean in the area known as Wigpool Common. The first three gales were granted as follows:

The Wigpool Iron Mine gale was granted on 24th November 1846 to George Roberts of Edge Hill (one-eighth share); Thomas Hawkins, Lane, End, Coleford (one-eighth share); and a quarter share each to James Dubberly of Ruardean Hill; James Matthews of Drybrook; and Elisha Matthews of the Bailey. The grant was for a pit situated on Dean's Meend near Wigpool.

The Belt Iron Mine was granted on 3rd November 1846 to William Matthews, Nailbridge; Moses Harris of Nofold; John Harris, Drybrook; Nehemiah Marfell of Quarry Hill; Levi Harris of the Morse, and John Roberts, Drybrook. The grant was for a pit on Mitcheldean Meend at Pingary Tump.

Injunction Iron Mine was granted on 26th February 1850 to Nehemia Marfell and, like Wigpool, was situated on Deens Meend.

A report of the death of mining engineer Thomas Smith in April 1910 mentions that he came to the east side of the Forest from Ellwood in order to sink the Wigpool Iron Mine on behalf of Osman Barrett. Whether Barrett had an interest in Wigpool is uncertain, but by 1854 the gales were in the hands of Messrs Allaway, who held considerable interests in ironworks and tinplate works at Lydney, Lydbrook and Cinderford. Work was still progressing on developing the mine at this time and a Crown licence, dated 5th May 1854, was granted for a northwards extension of the Westbury Brook tramroad to serve the mine.

Insole and Bunning, writing in 1880, record that at Wigpool there was a horizontal rotary high pressure engine with a 30in cylinder and a 6ft stroke which both wound

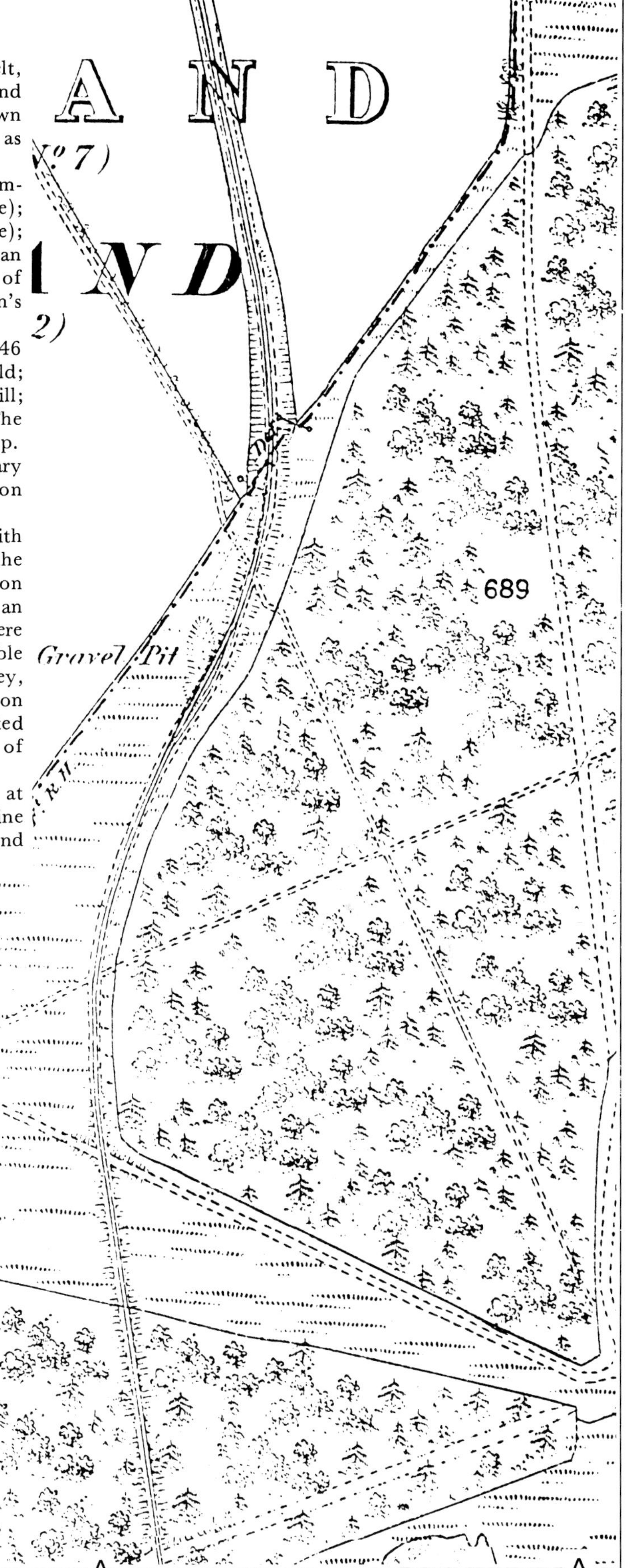

The Wigpool Tramroad with passing loop alongside the gravel pit.

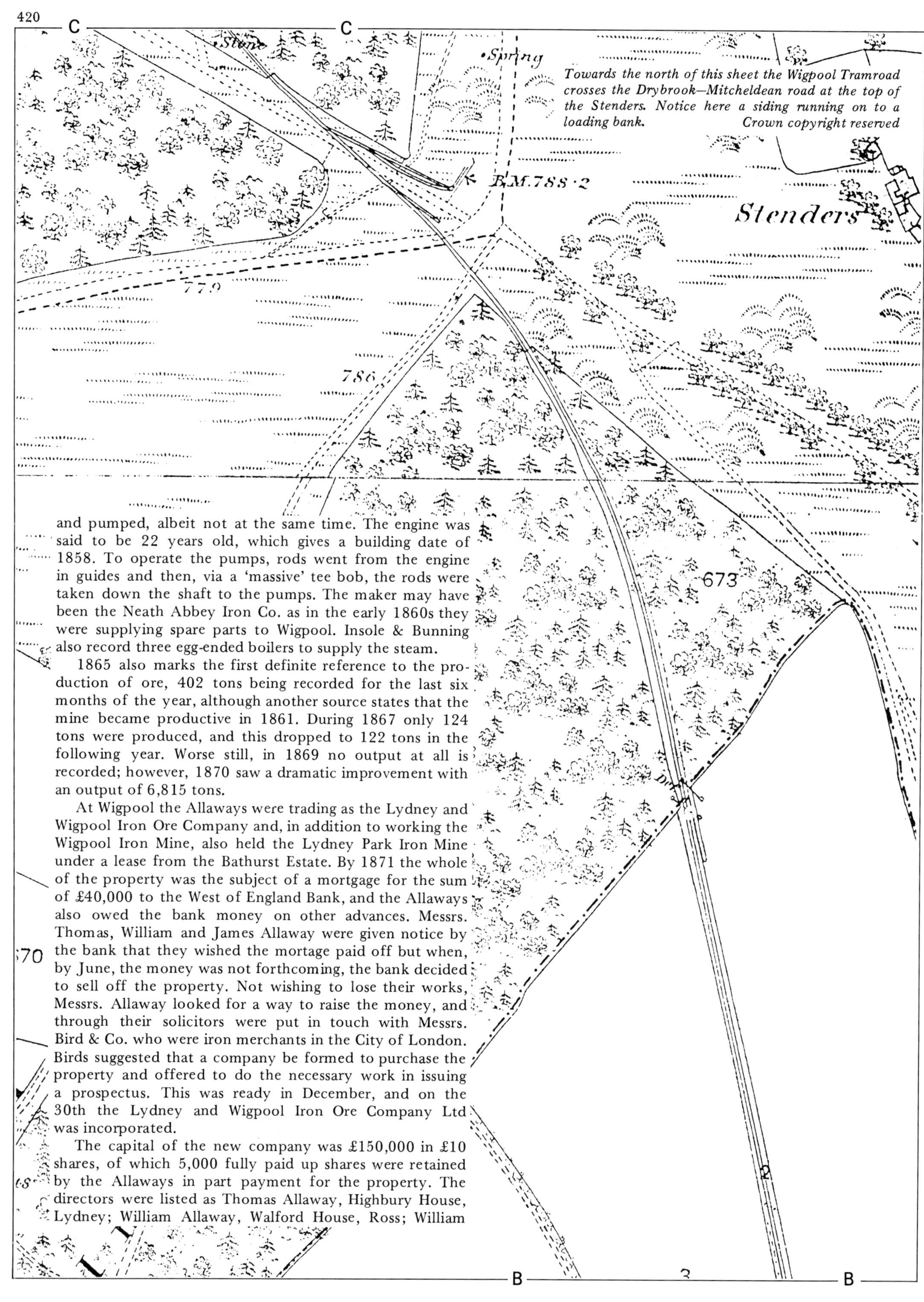

Towards the north of this sheet the Wigpool Tramroad crosses the Drybrook—Mitcheldean road at the top of the Stenders. Notice here a siding running on to a loading bank. *Crown copyright reserved*

and pumped, albeit not at the same time. The engine was said to be 22 years old, which gives a building date of 1858. To operate the pumps, rods went from the engine in guides and then, via a 'massive' tee bob, the rods were taken down the shaft to the pumps. The maker may have been the Neath Abbey Iron Co. as in the early 1860s they were supplying spare parts to Wigpool. Insole & Bunning also record three egg-ended boilers to supply the steam.

1865 also marks the first definite reference to the production of ore, 402 tons being recorded for the last six months of the year, although another source states that the mine became productive in 1861. During 1867 only 124 tons were produced, and this dropped to 122 tons in the following year. Worse still, in 1869 no output at all is recorded; however, 1870 saw a dramatic improvement with an output of 6,815 tons.

At Wigpool the Allaways were trading as the Lydney and Wigpool Iron Ore Company and, in addition to working the Wigpool Iron Mine, also held the Lydney Park Iron Mine under a lease from the Bathurst Estate. By 1871 the whole of the property was the subject of a mortgage for the sum of £40,000 to the West of England Bank, and the Allaways also owed the bank money on other advances. Messrs. Thomas, William and James Allaway were given notice by the bank that they wished the mortage paid off but when, by June, the money was not forthcoming, the bank decided to sell off the property. Not wishing to lose their works, Messrs. Allaway looked for a way to raise the money, and through their solicitors were put in touch with Messrs. Bird & Co. who were iron merchants in the City of London. Birds suggested that a company be formed to purchase the property and offered to do the necessary work in issuing a prospectus. This was ready in December, and on the 30th the Lydney and Wigpool Iron Ore Company Ltd was incorporated.

The capital of the new company was £150,000 in £10 shares, of which 5,000 fully paid up shares were retained by the Allaways in part payment for the property. The directors were listed as Thomas Allaway, Highbury House, Lydney; William Allaway, Walford House, Ross; William

MacDonald Bird, Gloucester Crescent, London; and Thomas Spencer, Brewood, Staffordshire. In addition to the Wigpool and Lydney Park mines, the company also held 14 acres of ground adjoining Lydney station on the South Wales Railway where it intended to erect blast furnaces. At Wigpool it was said that the surface works were laid out in a most substantial and satisfactory manner and of first class construction, with pumps in the No. 1, or deep, pit capable of draining the whole area. The iron ore occurred in three veins of brown haematite of high quality, yielding 57.85% of metallic iron. It was said that 720 tons per week were being raised at Wigpool, equivalent to 37,410 tons per year, whilst the whole property would yield an annual profit of £18,720.

Messrs. Bird, however, extracted a high price for their part in the formation of the company. They were to be paid £10,800 for forming the company and guaranteeing the purchase money, the business was to be run from their London address, and 2% commission was to be paid to them on sales despite the company's prospectus stating that 'No promotion money or other fees will be paid'. The £10,800 came out of the £100,000 purchase money paid to the Allaways. It was paid after the formation of the company, but was not made known to the company. This was to have serious repercussions later.

At this time the *Mining Journal* reported that £80,000 had been spent at Wigpool with no beneficial result whatever, but that the appointment of a new manager brought a change of fortune, with ore being found almost immediately within a few yards of the old workings. With the new company in place, expansion soon took place with the grant of the Wigpool Belt Iron Mine on 26th March 1873. This was united with the Wigpool and Injunction gales which had been surrendered to the Crown for the purpose of amalgamation. This period of growth is reflected in the output figures which were 19,972 tons in 1871, 11,729 tons in 1872 and 22,106 in 1873.

The deep pit was sunk on Wigpool Common and passed through the coal measures and the Drybrook sandstone before reaching the carboniferous limestone. The pit head was raised about 12ft off the ground and was at 850ft above ordnance datum. The shaft was sunk to a depth of 528ft into the lower dolomite but here a strong feeder of water was struck and the water began to rise in the shaft. A second pit was sunk about 500 yards north-north-east of the deep pit. It, too, reached the lower dolomite and two levels were driven in it at depths of 345ft and 378ft. The two shafts were connected underground.

From the deep pit, roadways were driven to the east and west. On the eastern side the workings were carried as far as possible to the north and also for 300 to 400 yards southwards. Ore was mainly won from the crease limestone but an important quantity of superior quality was obtained from the lower dolomite.

Between 1861 and 1883 the mine produced 150,000 tons, most of which would have been dispatched down the tramroad to Whimsey. The destination of the majority of the ore is not known but some went to the Parkfield Iron Works in Wolverhampton and some possibly to Stocksbridge, Sheffield, where an ironmaster held an interest in the company. However, 1883 saw the end of ore production at Wigpool with the company in obvious difficulties. An attempt to recover the £10,800 paid to Messrs. Bird, which the company (i.e. the shareholders) knew nothing about,

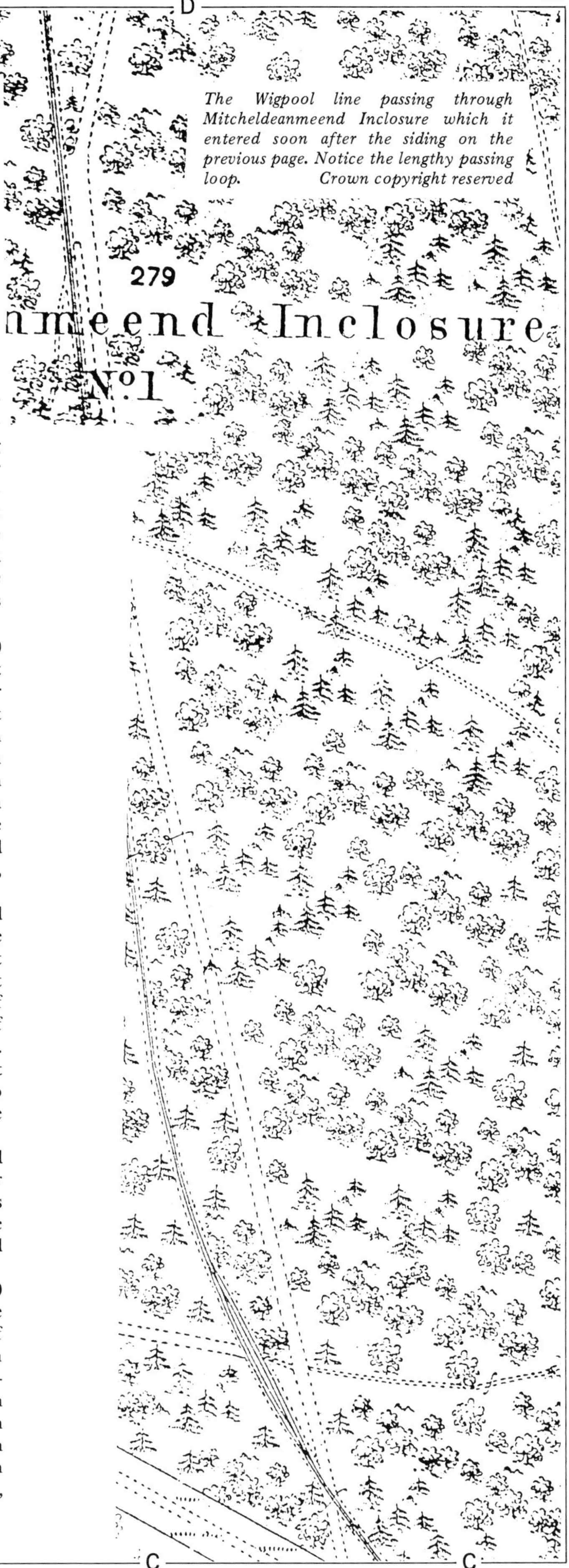

The Wigpool line passing through Mitcheldeanmeend Inclosure which it entered soon after the siding on the previous page. Notice the lengthy passing loop. *Crown copyright reserved*

After leaving the Inclosure, the line crossed over a rifle range, one of several in the Forest for local Volunteer units, before reaching Wigpool Iron Mine.

Crown copyright reserved

had commenced with an action in the Court of Chancery in July 1882. This was probably an attempt to obtain more working capital to keep the company going, but it also shows a rift with the Birds who were also acting as agents for the company. The court action was against William and James Bird, but the parlous state of the company's finances was demonstrated by the fact that James Bird took out a summons asking that the plaintiffs (the company) be ordered to give security for the costs of the action, and a sum of £200 was decided upon in April 1883. The judge, in deciding that a surety was advisable, stated that if the company had difficulty in finding the £200, then 'it is practically insolvent'. This debate may have delayed matters as the case was not again before the court until November 1885.

The action hinged around the role of Messrs. Bird in the formation of the company. Were they merely acting as agents for the Allaways or were they also promoters of the company? Although the £10,800 was nominally paid to the Birds by the Allaways, the latter claimed that the money in fact came from the company.

This did not end the matter as the Lydney & Wigpool Iron Ore Co. Ltd. went to appeal in May 1886 where they successfully managed to get the decision reversed, and it was decided that James Bird was liable to account for the £10,800 with a deduction of £600 legitimate expenses. Whether the money was ever repaid to the company is not known, but production at Wigpool did not start again. This was not, however, the case for the company's court appearances.

In early 1886 two petitions were heard in the Court of Chancery against the Lydney & Wigpool Iron Ore Co. Ltd. In the first a receiver was appointed to manage the affairs of the company. In the second case the petitioner was Samuel Fox, a Yorkshire ironmaster with a works at Stocksbridge, Sheffield. He held a second mortgage of £2,000 on the property, but there were insufficient assets to meet it and, as a result, the company went into liquidation. Under the instructions of the court, the plant at Wigpool was auctioned off on 31st March 1887.

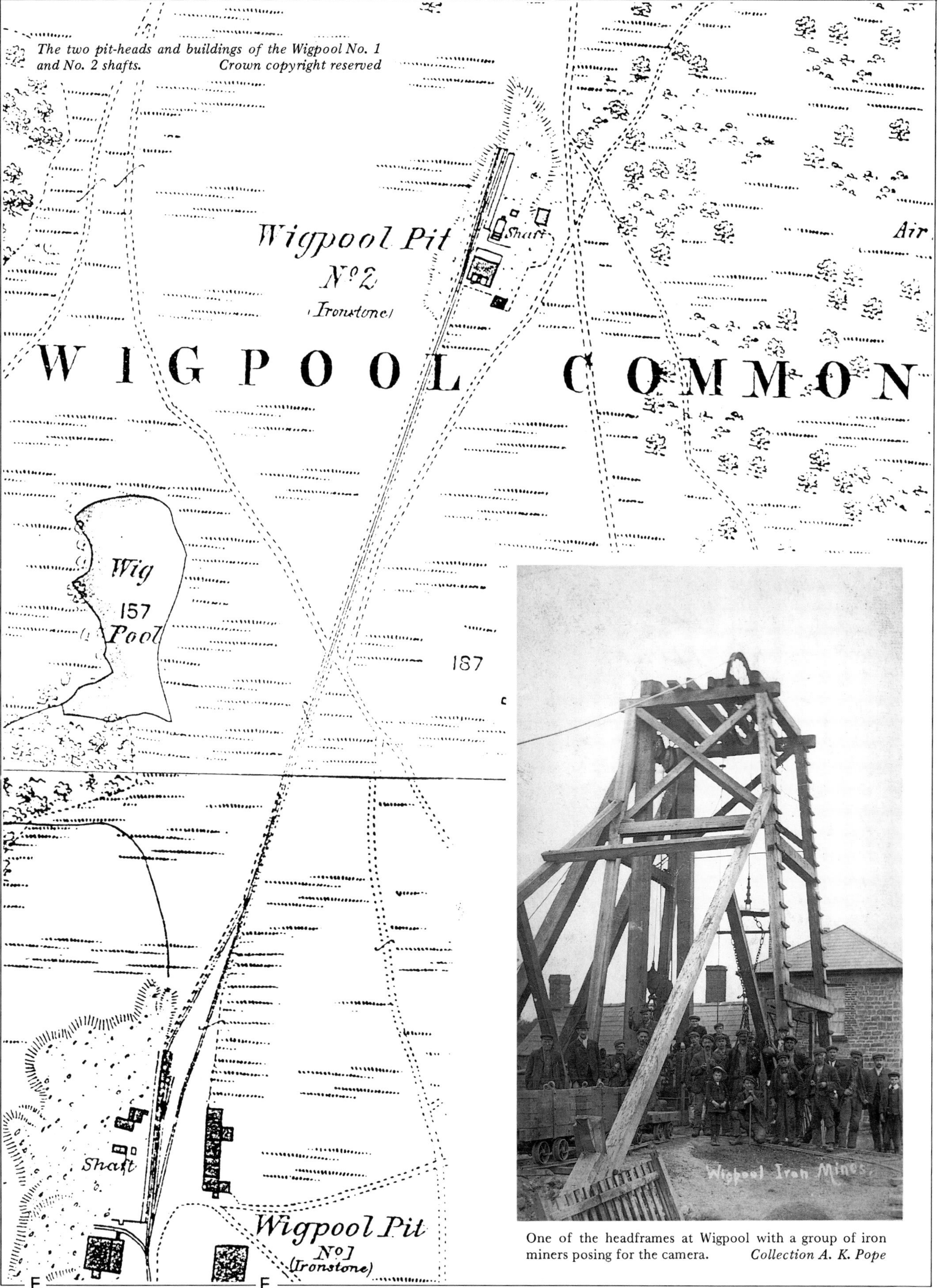

The two pit-heads and buildings of the Wigpool No. 1 and No. 2 shafts. *Crown copyright reserved*

One of the headframes at Wigpool with a group of iron miners posing for the camera. *Collection A. K. Pope*

Taken from Euroclydon House above the Hawthorns Tunnel, this view looks north-east and shows Wigpool Iron Mine in the distance. *Collection N. Parkhouse*

One of the Wigpool Iron Mine's chimneys being prepared for demolition, probably in the early 1930s. *Cty. Mrs. M. Wilkinson*

Interestingly, the auction was not held at the mine, possibly because of the remote nature of Wigpool, but in a field alongside Mitcheldean Road station on the Hereford, Ross & Gloucester line of the GWR. The Wigpool mine was connected to Mitcheldean Road station by a tramroad which ran north-north-east off Wigpool and descended the steep slope to Mitcheldean Road by means of an incline. Possibly the last traffic on the tramroad were all the fixtures and fittings heading for the sale. Not only were the small fittings transported to the field but so, apparently, was the main winding and pumping engine, a pair of 15in cylinder horizontal winding engines, the pumps, 140 wrought iron trams, 25 tons of rail and sundry other items. The mine, now devoid of all its machinery, was allowed to flood and it was not until 1911 that further attempts were made to work it.

Part of the gale became notorious in the district in 1908 with the formation of the Chastan Syndicate to work gold measures in the Bailey Level at Lea Bailey to the west of Wigpool Common. Things did not last long as only six grains of gold per ton of rock were extracted and many people lost money. The *Dean Forest Mercury*, in its edition of 26th February 1909, commented "The 'Chastened' Syndicate . . . their hopes had sunk a good deal lower than their shaft".

Several attempts were made between 1911 and 1918 to revive Wigpool, but they did not meet with any great success. This was attributed to inadequate methods being used, which probably translates to insufficient investment. Exploration and development were hampered by light pumping, since to really explore the potential heavy pumping was essential as the current workings extended little below the mean water level.

On 7th May 1915 the mine was offered for sale as a going concern at auction in London. The auction particulars stated that there were two shafts, one of which was stone lined, whilst the second was used as a ventilation shaft. The underground workings were said to be in first class order. On the surface there was a pair of good winding engines, two nearly new Lancashire boilers and a single winding pit-head gear. The largest portion of the mine area was said to have never been worked; the ore from it was said to be some of the finest in the country and with a small outlay it could be made into one of the largest iron-producing mines in the country – good sales brochure language! The sale was successfully completed, the purchaser being a Mr. Witfield who paid the sum of £4,000. How much work he did at Wigpool is unclear, but output figures for the years 1911 and 1917 show that 7,000 tons of ore were raised, and the mine was abandoned in 1918.

Some further work on the Wigpool Iron Mine gale was done by Captain Henry Arthur Pringle and Edward Smedley Tarlton, trading as the Wigpool Coal & Iron Syndicate. This work was concentrated at the Bailey Level, and a narrow gauge railway was laid along the trackbed of the Mitcheldean Road & Forest of Dean Junction Railway as far as Mitcheldean Road station.

In July 1923 it was reported that the development of the Wigpool Iron Ore Mines by Captain H. A. Pringle of Longhope Manor had culminated in the registration of the Wigpool Coal & Iron Co. Ltd. as a private company with a capital of £25,000 in £1 shares. The company was to take over the syndicate for the purpose of working coal and iron mines, limestone and other minerals, and soon set about acquiring property including Harrow Hill Colliery (see page 355). It appears, however, that the company went virtually straight into receivership! On 16th July 1927 it was reported that work at Wigpool Iron Mine had been suspended for some weeks owing to a dispute.

This picture was taken along the course of the Wigpool Tramroad on 20th July 1947.
L. E. Copeland

A wooden-bodied tramroad wagon used for the carriage of coal or iron ore.
National Railway Museum

APPENDIX 3

TIMBER TRESTLE BRIDGE AT HARROW HILL SIDINGS

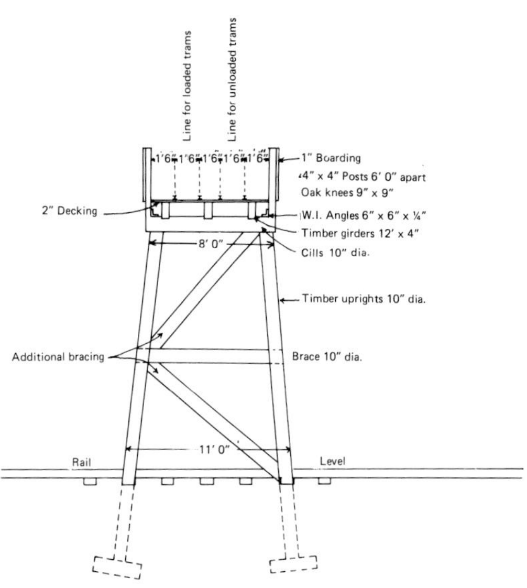

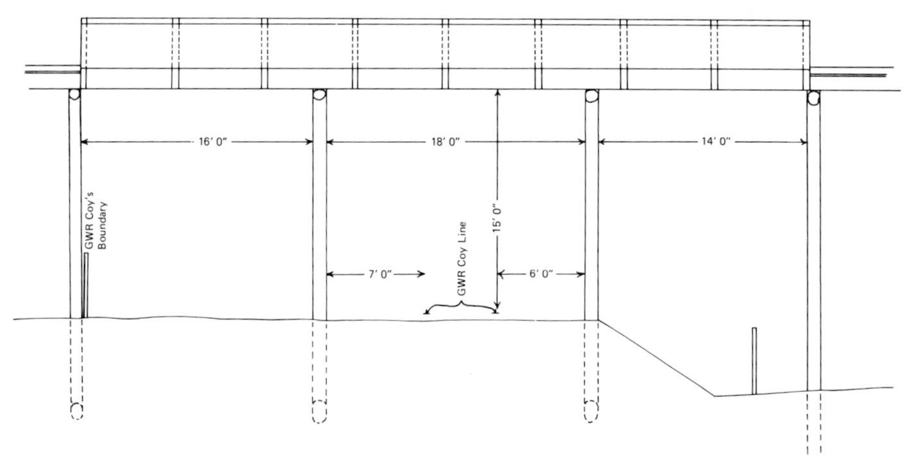

INDEX TO VOLUMES ONE & TWO

Volume One covers pages 1 - 234
Volume Two covers pages 235 - 426

BIBLIOGRAPHY

The Last Deep Mine of Dean. Maurice Bent. M.V. Bent Publishing. 1988.
The Great Western Railway in Dean. H. W. Paar. David & Charles. 1971.
The Severn & Wye Railway. H. W. Paar. David & Charles. 1973.
The Industrial History of Dean. Cyril Hart. David & Charles. 1971.
The Industrial Teagues. Ralph Anstis. Alan Sutton. 1990.
The Old Industries of Dean. David Bick. Pound House. 1908
The Laws of Dean Forest. James Wood. H. Sweet. 1878
Geology of the Forest of Dean Coal and Iron Ore Field. HMSO. 1942.
Iron Ores – Haematitites of the Forest of Dean and South Wales. HMSO. 1927
Track Layout Diagrams of the GWR, Section 37. R. A. Cooke. 1996

R. H. Marrows